D0257966

B
P

Bo
Boo
appl
D

06
8 6 9
18/1

[- '

Penguin Handbooks

A Parents' Guide to the Problems of Adolescence

Penny Treadwell was born in Cornwall in 1941. After leaving school at 17, she worked as a medical secretary, travelling to the United States, where she attended university. She returned to England and became a television announcer and journalist, eventually working both for independent television and the BBC. After her marriage she trained as a teacher and earned post-graduate degrees in English Literature and Art History from London University. She has two children and three stepchildren, all but one of them teenagers.

A *Parents'* Guide to the *Problems of* Adolescence

PENNY TREADWELL

PENGUIN BOOKS

PENGUIN BOOKS

Published by the Penguin Group
27 Wrights Lane, London w8 5tz, England
Viking Penguin Inc., 40 West 23rd Street, New York, New York 10010, USA
Penguin Books Australia Ltd, Ringwood, Victoria, Australia
Penguin Books Canada Ltd, 2801 John Street, Markham, Ontario, Canada l3r 1b4
Penguin Books (NZ) Ltd, 182–190 Wairau Road, Auckland 10, New Zealand

Penguin Books Ltd, Registered Offices: Harmondsworth, Middlesex, England

First published 1988
1 3 5 7 9 10 8 6 4 2

Filmset in 10/12 Monophoto Sabon

Made and printed in Great Britain by
Richard Clay Ltd, Bungay, Suffolk

*This book is dedicated
to Tom, Kati, Ross, John,
James and Matthew*

Contents

Preface

This book was originally the brain-child of Christopher Dolley, a father of three teenagers. He asked Sheila Moore, a writer friend, to produce a book that would help parents find ways of dealing with the problems of adolescents. Ms Moore's commitments at the time made it impossible for her to take on more work, so she invited me to do it. I owe a particular debt of gratitude to Christopher Dolley for his inspiration, and to Sheila Moore for offering me the opportunity to write the book.

This book could not have been written without the contributions of the many parents and teenagers who were willing to share their often painful experiences. While respecting their wish for anonymity, I should like to express my gratitude to them all. I should particularly like to thank my son, Ross, and my daughter, Kati, for allowing me on occasion to enter their very different teenage worlds. I am grateful for their trust and confidence; they taught me a great deal.

In the early stages of writing, adolescent-psychologist James Hemming was extraordinarily generous with his time, advice and encouragement. I was much influenced by his published works and by his kindness and his understanding of teenagers and their parents.

Chapter 4, Health and Sex, owes much to my collaboration with General Practitioner Dr Trevor Hudson. His assistance and encouragement are greatly appreciated.

I am especially grateful for the help and guidance of Dr Betty Jacobs and Peter Wilson at the London Youth Advisory Centre, to Dr Anton Obholzer of the Tavistock Clinic for reading and correcting some of the early manuscript, and to Dr Tony Jaffa of the Hill End Adolescent Unit, who read and commented upon the completed manuscript.

My thanks are also due to Marie Davies of Parents Anonymous, who supplied me with lists of names and addresses that have proved invaluable.

As a writer based in the London area, one of my main concerns was to obtain information nation-wide. This necessitated a fair amount of travelling as well as many hours on the telephone, but I was also helped by Caroline Burton's research in Scotland and I am very grateful for her assistance.

Since each chapter is the result of many interviews not only with parents and teenagers but also with professionals and organizations involved in coping with the problems of adolescents, there are so many people and organizations to whom I owe a debt of gratitude that it is impossible to name them all. Many, however, went a good deal out of their way to give help and advice, either personally or by letter or telephone. I should like to acknowledge in particular the following for their considerable contribution: The Advisory Centre for Education, Baroness Airy of Abingdon, Dr John Aspin, Liz Bailey, Steve Bamlett, Dr A. Banks, Gill Gorell Barnes, Dr Don Batten, Alan Billington, the Reverend Adele Blakebrough-Fairburn, the Brook Advisory Centre, Dr Brian Brown, Barbara Bullivant JP, Jan Bumstead, The Children's Legal Centre, Barbara Dale, Dr Christopher Dare, Carolyn Douglas, Roger Ellis, Dr Susan Issacs Elmhirst, Baroness Faithfull of Wolvercote, Gabbitas–Truman–Thring Educational Trust, Russ Hayton, Brian Heap, Dr Robin Higgins, Elizabeth Hodder, Independent Schools Information Service (ISIS), Hugh Jenkins, Dr Alan Kingdon, Geoff Martin, The Mental Health Foundation, Dr Emanuel Moran, MIND (National Association for Mental Health), The Northgate Clinic, Trevor Peacock, Dr Peter Reder, Kathryn Redway, Rose Robertson, Hilary Rogers, Professor Michael Rutter, Ruth Schmidt, Sergeant Bob Searle and fellow officers at the Juvenile Bureau in Feltham, Middlesex, Professor Marten Shipman, Dr Robin Skynner, the Social Services Department in Hounslow, Middlesex, The Standing Conference on Drug Abuse (SCODA), James Stephenson, Dr Ray Straton, The Terrence Higgins Trust, *The Times Educational Supplement*, Glenn Turner, Dr Julian Vahrman, Dr T. A. N. Waller, and I am especially grateful to Clare Toynbee whose professional advice and guidance has been invaluable.

I owe a particular debt of gratitude to my editors at Penguin, Barbara Horn and Marilyn Warwick, who have made a great contribution to the final appearance of the book.

Finally, I should like to thank my husband, Tom, for his support and encouragement over the three years it took to complete the project. Had it not been for his ability to tame and organize my word processor, the time spent writing the book would have been considerably longer.

Acknowledgements

The author and publishers are grateful to the following for permission to use extracts:

Advisory Centre for Education (ACE) for *Children with Special Needs* and *Sex Discrimination in Education*.

William Collins, Sons & Co. Ltd for *Sisters and Brothers* by Judy Dunn.

Simon & Schuster for *Crime and Human Nature* by Richard Herrnstein and James Wilson, New York, 1985.

MIND organization for *Understanding Mental Illness* (1987), *Understanding Schizophrenia* (1987) and *Factsheet 7*.

The *Independent* for the issue 26 June 1987, p. 3.

Her Majesty's Stationery Office for *Smoking Among Secondary School Children in 1984* by Jay Dobbs and Alan Marsh, London, 1985.

The *Practitioner* for 'Solvent Abuse and Adolescents', vol. 228, May 1984, by Dr Joyce Watson.

The Northgate Clinic for *Information Sheet for Patients*.

The Chest, Heart and Stroke Association for *Facts About Smoking for Young and Old* by Dr Howard Williams.

The *Guardian* for the issue 11 April 1984, p. 8, article by Ronit Lentin.

The Children's Legal Centre for *Working with Young People: Legal Responsibility and Liability* by Chris Davey, London, 1984.

Methuen & Co. Ltd for *Off the Hook: Coping with Addiction* by Helen Bethune, London, 1985.

Institute for the Study of Drug Dependence for *Drug Addiction and Polydrug Abuse* by A. Banks and T. A. N. Waller, 1983.

British Agencies for Adoption and Fostering for 'Adoption and Identity' by F. H. Stone and 'Factors Associated with Maladjustment in Adoptive Families' by Michael Humphrey, both taken from *Child Adoption*.

The *New Scientist* for 'How glue sniffers come unstuck' by Omar Sattaur, 1 March 1984.

The Times Educational Supplement for 'Doctor Defends Violent Television' by Mike Durham, 1982.

Faber and Faber for *Surviving Adolescence* by Peter Bruggen and Charles O'Brian, London, 1986.
London Gay Youth Movement for *I Know What I Am*, Joint Council for Gay Teenagers, London, 1980.
Comprehensive Education for issue no. 50, 1985.
University of London Institute of Education for *Girls and Mathematics: From Primary to Secondary Schooling* by Rosie Walden and Valerie Walkerdine, 1985.
British Journal of Medical Psychology for 'School Phobia: a Reappraisal' by A. C. Robin Skynner, no. 1, 1974.
The Times Educational Supplement for 'Alias Smith and Jones' by Keith Melton and Martin Long, 11 April 1986.
Open Books for *Fifteen Thousand Hours: Secondary Schools and their Effects on Children* by Michael Rutter et al., Shepton Mallet, 1979.
Harcourt Brace Jovanovich Ltd for *Journal of Adolescence*, vol. 2.

Every effort has been made to trace copyright holders, but in some cases this has proved impossible. The author and publishers apologize for these unwilling cases of copyright transgression and would like to hear from any copyright holders not acknowledged.

Introduction

My divorce and subsequent remarriage had a profoundly unsettling effect on one of my children. Serious behavioural difficulties, which began with the onset of adolescence, lurched from crisis to crisis for at least six years before she eventually caught up with happiness. Each crisis heralded a different set of circumstances, which in turn required different ways of responding. I had no idea what to do or where to turn for help. It was against this background that the book was written.

Once, at a social gathering, when the conversation came round to the progress of the company's various teenagers, I tentatively suggested that I had grounds to be seriously concerned. 'But how could you possibly allow your child to be involved with those sort of people and behave in that kind of way? My sons would never do that and if they did, I would stop them,' was one shocked parent's response. There are, of course, many parents – perhaps even the majority – for whom adolescence has meant no more than encouraging their maturing sons and daughters to have more baths, use a deodorant and lower the noise level. Others are less fortunate. When it comes to coping with the problems of adolescence, there are no rules; there is only instinct and, with luck, a firm belief in one's own child.

However hard parents struggle to do what is best for their troubled and troublesome teenager, there may come a point when their willingness to help and to understand gives way to despair and frustration. In order to help their child effectively, parents themselves need support and guidance. If a teenager is abusing drugs or alcohol, is in trouble at school or with the law or is causing havoc at home, the results of his or her behaviour tend to isolate the family. The feeling that they are alone with the problem adds to the burden of guilt and desperation. This book aims to reassure parents and others involved with adolescents whose paths have not been smooth that they are not alone, that serious problems can and do arise in the teenage years in every kind of family, whatever their material or emotional circumstances. These problems are not limited to a broken home or the single parent. The experiences of the many families who have so generously contributed to the book are proof that this is so.

From the moment I began my research, I was overwhelmed by the response from parents willing to share their troubles with me for the sake of helping others who might find themselves in a similar predicament. Their main concern was always that they did not know where they could turn for help and advice. The book attempts to overcome this need by combining their personal experience with practical advice from professionals and organizations involved in dealing with the problems of adolescents.

The names and addresses of organizations to turn to for help and advice are listed at the end of each chapter. These lists are not comprehensive, but provide parents with a starting point. They are a reminder that there is always someone to turn to for help and advice no matter how impossible a problem might seem.

Although every effort has been made to ensure that the names and addresses are accurate at the time of publication, changes do occur. If a particular organization does not respond to a telephone call, it may mean that they have a new number or perhaps (and less likely) no longer exist. Don't give up – try another.

The lists have been carefully compiled and include, where necessary, a brief description of the areas in which the organizations have a particular expertise. It must be emphasized, however, that although I have had experience of a few of them in my own quest for help and guidance as the text indicates, I am in no position to recommend them all generally. The choice of help is a personal matter and one that depends very much on the needs of the particular personalities involved.

Chapter 1

Other People's Problems

For the majority of families, problems encountered in the teenage years are generally short-lived, although at the time they may seem extremely painful. For others, not so lucky, the disturbing behaviour of their adolescent does not stand in isolation but forms part of a continuing pattern over the years, moving from crisis to crisis until the child becomes an adult. Fortunately, most of the problems of adolescence seem to work themselves through in one way or another, but in cases of drug addiction, for example, or anorexia, the pattern can remain impossibly hard to break and the self-destructive nature of the troubled teenager is carried as a continuing burden into adulthood. There are many situations in which parents can find a beginning to their child's particular difficulties but can see no end to them.

Family life is a dynamic process within a structure that may be ordered or chaotic, but which is always deeply personal and individual. Just as no two people are alike, neither are two family units, yet we may draw useful parallels from the experiences of others and derive a certain comfort from knowing that we are not alone – not the only parents to find that their life has been turned upside down by the actions of an adolescent. The family histories included in this chapter are unique accounts of problems familiar to many. As they recount their stories, parents are often aware that the problems began, perhaps early in childhood, during a period of family life that was especially difficult or unsettled. The stories offer no instant solutions, but each account demonstrates that despite the anxiety, stress and unhappiness involved, the parents' support for their teenagers is unassailable. They simply never give up.

Anna

Anna's life became unstable and insecure from the time she was 2 years old when her mother, Mrs B., was separated from the child's father. Mrs B. took Anna from her home in Manchester to London, where she found a job working as an au pair for an American couple. Their life-style changed when the couple decided to form a commune consisting of five adults and four children, the adults working a four-day week with one day off to look after the children. Mrs B. found the system unsatisfactory and Anna did not seem very happy. Mrs B. had no entitlement to council housing at the time and went to America for a year to stay with friends. She then returned to England to live with a girl-friend before moving into another commune, this time run by the housing association for whom she was working.

Although Mrs B. found that here the care of her child was more flexible and fell mainly into her own hands, the communal 'say' in the general discipline and organization of the children's lives was erratic and subject to the whims of the different parents involved, and there was considerable conflict between the individual styles of parenting that were thought suitable for the children of the commune. When the group took in three 16-year-old girls who had all been in care, Mrs B. became so concerned by their delinquent behaviour that she decided to move to north London with three other adults. She had a job in the area and Anna, then aged 8, attended the local primary school. Anna settled down well enough in class, but had problems with her peer group, not seeming to fit in. She was not a good mixer, and the school became aware of her difficulties when they noticed that she formed unusually strong attachments to certain teachers.

When Anna was 11 years old, Mrs B. had managed to earn enough money to buy her own property and put down roots in another borough of north London, where her daughter started secondary school. Anna found the transfer from primary to secondary school a traumatic experience. At first she did not show any outward signs of misery, but half-way through the first term she began to refuse to go to school, complaining of headaches, stomach-aches and generally feeling ill. Anna also started her periods, which were associated with increasingly moody and erratic behaviour. Mrs B. found that she was constantly nagging the child and their relationship was at 'a pretty low ebb'. Anna had uncontrollable outbursts of temper, to which her mother found that she could respond only on the same level, so there were screaming and 'slanging' matches and they swore and shouted at each other until they were both exhausted.

On one occasion Mrs B. went up to Anna's bedroom to find the child sitting on her bed waving a razor blade and slashing her arm. Very anxious, Mrs B. sought help from the local child guidance clinic. Anna, having refused to see the psychologist on her own and insisted that her mother be present, remained mute and uncooperative during the sessions, which Mrs B. felt were 'getting us nowhere'. Depressed and out of her depth, Mrs B. visited a consultant psychiatrist, who suggested that Anna was obviously miserable at the school and perhaps a transfer should be considered.

Mrs B. managed to find a private school in Hertfordshire, where for a while her daughter seemed quite happy and began to achieve good standards of work. At first Mrs B. was worried that Anna's background and London accent might be a disadvantage in a private school, but they did not seem to create any problems. Around this time, Anna's father reappeared after a gap of nine years and began to see his daughter at infrequent intervals.

Anna had close friends in London who had dropped out of school and she began spending more time in their company. They were encouraged by their parents to go to the local pub and Anna joined them. At that time she was 13 but looked older. Although relations between mother and daughter had worsened, at first Anna still worked well during the week, finishing her homework and keeping up her standards at school. At the weekends at home, however, late nights out with her friends led to bitter rows with her mother. Mrs B. then discovered that Anna had been playing truant. When Mrs B. lost her temper, the child shouted 'I don't want to live with you. I want to be taken into care. I don't want to go to school.' Her mother decided to allow Anna to stay with her friends in north London at the weekends in order to establish a 'cooling off' period. The 'foster' family proved to be unsuitable and the girl became even more difficult to control.

Mrs B. called upon her parents for support, in the hope that they might be able to exert some influence over their grandchild. This led to more serious rows, during which Anna attacked her grandfather. At this juncture Anna decided that she would prefer to live with her father, an arrangement to which Mrs B. agreed since she and her daughter could not seem to live together. Although Anna was still attending the boarding school in Hertfordshire as a weekly boarder, the staff found that they were unable to cope with her. After a few weeks spent with her father, Anna returned to her mother's house late one night; she had run away from school and told Mrs B. that she felt that she was 'cracking up'. As Mrs B. put her to bed, the child's crying alternated between 'Fuck off', and 'Come back, I love you'. The following morning Mrs B. took Anna to the family doctor, who made an appointment for her with a psychiatrist. This doctor, in turn, recommended that Anna be taken into care. Mrs B. was not prepared to let this happen although the girl still refused to return to school. The day after the visit to the psychiatrist, on her way to work, Mrs B. discovered that her daughter had stolen £50 from her purse. When she returned home in the evening, she found that Anna had left.

Mrs B. later received a call from the Department of Social Services informing her that Anna had asked to be taken into care. Although the social workers considered the problem 'temporary', they agreed to take the girl into voluntary care (p. 195). She was given free access to travel to see her father at his home in west London and it was arranged that Mrs B. could visit her and take her on outings from the children's home. On these occasions, which took place about once a week, mother and daughter found communication difficult and their relationship strained and painful. One day after spending a weekend with her father, Anna did not return to the home. Mrs B., unable to contact her ex-husband, was afraid that he had taken Anna out of the country. She consulted a local solicitor, who persuaded a judge to issue a court injunction against the father to prevent him abducting his daughter, and to make Anna a ward of court.

Anna remained out of sight for nearly a month. Then, one day Mrs B. was convinced that she saw her daughter near her home. She informed the police, who responded immediately, but Anna had disappeared by the time they arrived. Finally, one of Anna's friends confided to Mrs B. that the girl was staying with the mother of a friend in another area. The police located Anna and took her back to the local police station, where Mrs B. met her, but scarcely recognized her. The girl was emotionally distraught and physically debilitated. She returned to the home, this time in compulsory care, but it was decided that she should be moved to another children's home closer to her mother in north London, with a view to returning to the secondary school where she had originally been a pupil.

At the new home Anna was placed under the care of a key worker, who was directly responsible for her. Unfortunately, just before the start of the school term the key worker, upon whom Anna had come to rely for two months, left because of illness. Without her support, Anna's relationship with her mother broke down completely and they no longer communicated. Mrs B. would have glimpses of her daughter in the neighbourhood. Often, while she was out walking the dog at night, she would 'bump into the child', who was very defensive and refused all her mother's offers of lifts back to the home.

Shortly after the beginning of term Mrs B. heard that Anna, still living in the children's home, had been suspended from the school. She then received a message from the social services to say that Anna had been taken into hospital suffering from stomach cramps. The girl had referred herself after a violent outburst at the home, and was diagnosed as having a duodenal ulcer. It became apparent to Mrs B., that the social workers had given up on the child since they did not attempt to contact Anna or visit her during the two weeks that she remained in hospital. Mrs B. went to the hospital each day, and gradually found that she was beginning to build a new friendship with her daughter. Anna began to talk about 'wanting to come home', and filled her mother with renewed hope. However, no sooner had she been discharged from hospital and returned to the children's home than Anna again told her mother to 'fuck off'.

By this time Anna's mother felt herself to be near a complete breakdown. In retrospect, she realizes that she should have returned for advice to the solicitor who had arranged the court order. Instead, she did not see her daughter for a month or so, and then the social services called a case conference to decide the girl's future. Mrs B. was not consulted until the last minute when obligations at work prevented her from attending the meeting. She learned that while Anna would continue to live 'in care', she could go back to the special unit (see p. 173) within the school for three days a week and return to the home for tuition for two days. The home seemed unable to exert any control over the child. She was out all night, returned to the home for a bath and change of clothes, and walked out again. In the meantime, the court issued a seek-and-find order, which gave the police the power to pick up the child in the event of their finding her wandering on the streets and take her to an assessment unit (see pp. 195–6).

After disappearing from the home for three weeks, Anna turned up on her mother's doorstep in floods of tears. Her appearance was 'horrifying – she looked really ill and had mutilated herself by idly stabbing her hands and arm with a pin.' However, she refused to stay for the night. Instead, she insisted that Mrs B. telephone the police to take her to an assessment unit. During her years of despair Mrs B. has had nothing but praise for the police. At times 'they seemed the only sympathetic public body' she had had to deal with. On this occasion the police drove Anna to the unit, arriving at 4.00 a.m. but when the authorities there refused to let the girl telephone her mother, she walked out and went missing again.

This time, shortly after Anna's fifteenth birthday, Mrs B. applied to the juvenile court to put her daughter in secure accommodation. Anna then turned up at the Department of Social Services and told a social worker that she wanted to go home to her mother. She was allowed to leave the premises, despite the seek-and-find order that had been issued for her. She telephoned her mother in desperation, but Mrs B., although she wanted to have the child at home, was afraid to fall foul of the law. Nevertheless, Anna returned home 'in a terrible state'. Her mother put her to bed and she slept for fifteen hours, but the next day she left once more.

Knowing that she could find Anna, but not wanting 'to turn her in', Mrs B. phoned her own psychiatrist for help. Meanwhile, the police picked the girl up again and returned her to the assessment centre where she was placed in a secure unit for twenty-four hours. The social services felt that they could not cope with her and the court ordered Anna to be put into a secure home. Mrs B. found her daughter's new residence – a highly special-ized unit with a high ratio of staff to children – to be immensely successful in helping Anna. After one week's stay, the girl was transformed. She looked healthy, well dressed and happier. She wanted to return home and the authorities were willing to allow her to leave the unit two weeks earlier than had been previously arranged because her behaviour had improved dramatically. However, Mrs B. felt that the problem of Anna's education had not yet been resolved, and that she herself needed support in order to re-establish a sound relationship with her daughter, with whom she had not really been able to communicate for at least a year. At Mrs B.'s request, the court decided to keep Anna at the home during the week and encourage her to spend the weekends with her mother.

Now almost sixteen, Anna has a steady boy-friend and is at last beginning to talk to Mrs B. Despite the educational limitations of the unit, (see p. 173), she has resumed her schooling with enthusiasm and is working to-wards GCSE examinations.

Peter and Susan

Amelia and Nick live in the Bristol area. She is English and he is an Indian from South Africa. Amelia, a primary school teacher, does not believe that her 'mixed' marriage has had anything to do with her children's difficulties. 'They're more likely to have had something to do with my dominant per-sonality,' she laughs. There are two children in the family, Peter, aged 13, and Susan, 15.

As Peter was nearing his thirteenth birthday and due to move on to secondary school, his work suddenly deteriorated. Complaints from his teachers drew his parents' attention to unfinished homework, lack of concentration and poor performance in class. They contacted an educational psychologist privately (see pp. 161, 163). Peter's I Q and abilities were found to be 'well above average' but it was felt that the boy had 'stagnated'. Amelia and Nick were advised to 'either take him out of the system and find a school in the private sector or, on moving to secondary school, to ensure that he is kept busy with plenty of activities outside school hours'.

Peter was keen to go to a private school and his parents decided that they could find the money for the fees. Anxious not to provoke the already considerable rivalry between their children, Amelia and Nick asked their daughter, Susan, whether she would object to her brother having a private education. They said that if she too would like to sit the qualifying exam (see p. 153), they would try to find the money to pay for her schooling also. Susan, however, refused to contemplate a private school. She made it clear that she was pleased at the thought of Peter being away from home; 'It will give me a bit of peace,' she said.

Amelia and Nick took advice from Gabbitas-Thring (now Gabbitas-Truman-Thring, see p. 154) and made their choice of boys' public school. Peter settled down quickly and seemed very happy, although in the first term he received a black eye from a boy in his dormitory and, during another fight, managed to knock out another boy's front tooth.

In the middle of the second term Amelia received a phone call from the police to say that Peter and a friend had been caught shoplifting. He had taken three packs of blank cassette tapes and a book on fishing. 'Angry and ashamed and in floods of tears', she went to the police station – in this instance, the juvenile bureau (see p. 185) in the town near Peter's school – accompanied by her husband. The police, Amelia said, were 'extraordinarily kind and sympathetic. They made Peter feel thoroughly ashamed of himself and he was so sorry that I'm certain he'll never do such a thing again.'

After their interview with the police, Amelia and Nick took their son back to school, where his housemaster 'was none too pleased'. Peter was suspended for the rest of the week, and when he returned, he found that his punishment continued. Blamed by boys and staff alike for every petty theft in the school, he was even suspected of stealing his own belongings. When he entered the classroom with a new pen brought from home, he was asked by his form master, 'Where did you steal that?'

During the time that her brother was in trouble with the law and having to come to terms with the consequences at school, Susan took nine O levels. She passed only one. Despite the fact that she had received extra coaching in maths and French and was apparently coming home each day to complete her homework and revise for the exams, 'whatever else she was doing in her bedroom, it wasn't work,' said her mother. In a letter to Peter, Susan later confided: 'Mum thinks I'm working away every night, but I'm just fooling her. I'm not doing a single stroke!' Susan had been upset by the events in Peter's life. 'Look at him, with his private education, bringing shame on the family, even from a distance,' she had said to her parents.

At the time Amelia felt a 'terrible sense of betrayal. Susan had betrayed herself as well as me,' she said. The girl's defence was to taunt her mother: 'Imagine you as a teacher having to go back to school and tell your colleagues about my failure. No wonder you're so upset.'

Both Nick and Amelia were adamant that Susan should return to school to retake her O levels. She did so but with great reluctance, becoming so difficult to live with at home that on one occasion her father was provoked to beat her for the first time in her life. Immediately after the incident, Susan went to a friend's mother, who also was a teacher, to show her the marks of the beating. The woman took time off work and travelled several miles to report the incident to the headteacher in Amelia's school, at the same time taking Susan in to live with her family. Amelia, helpless and humiliated, felt that her daughter had 'deserved her punishment', and was being 'unreasonable and disloyal'. Her headteacher was very sympathetic, saying:

> My dear, brace yourself, because in my experience there's a lot more to come. But you know, Susan places great store by your opinion. She feels that you have to shoulder all the responsibilities and decisions in the household. She is also afraid of your health and thinks that perhaps your job is more important than your family.

Determined to show her daughter that this was not so, Amelia took the day off work and visited Susan, who had taken a part-time job near the home of her friend. She persuaded Susan to return to her own home, although did not insist upon it. 'Oh, well, I suppose I'd better come back. You can pick me up tomorrow morning; although, remember, you asked me. I don't specially want to. For one thing, they have a cleaning lady here and I don't have to do the hoovering twice a week,' Susan told her mother.

The rivalry between brother and sister began, Amelia thinks, when her daughter started to put on weight at about the age of 10; she soon was about a stone and a half overweight. Now 18 years old, she weighs 16 stone and is 5'5". Peter is tall and has always been slender despite tucking away huge amounts of food. 'I think Susan resents him for that,' Amelia said. And, despite all former assurances, Susan is now bitter about her brother's public school education. She is also jealous of the attention paid to him during the holidays and the amount of money that goes towards his school fees.

Although Susan was troubled by her obesity, she seemed unable to control her weight. Amelia said:

> At first she insisted that her weight didn't matter, but eventually she broke down and cried, begging for some help. Over the years I've tried everything. We went to the GP, who gave her tranquillizers, which she refused to take and decided to change her doctor. I've been on diets with her where I've lost weight but she's just continued to put it on. We've been to Weightwatchers together. Recently, I've put on a lot of weight myself and I'm sure it's because I'm so damned unhappy. I think Susan probably puts it on for the same reason. Perhaps psychotherapy might be the answer or a drastic change in her life, like a great romance.

At this time Amelia's mother died, which was a great blow to her. During a particularly difficult school holiday, when the children's quarrels seemed to dominate the family's existence, she felt 'threatened and un-wanted'. She told me: 'I retired to a room in the house which I made my own and I just let them all get on with it.'

One year after the original interview, I had the chance to talk to Amelia again. She told me that Susan had retaken her O levels and had triumphantly passed them all. She was now studying for three A levels, with a view to going to university. Peter, on the other hand, had refused to continue the A level courses at his public school and had decided to complete them at a college of further education, but left after one term without knowing what else he wanted to do. Amelia complained that his behaviour at home was so disruptive and difficult that she was forced to turn him out of the house 'just to keep the rest of us from going insane and to stop the family breaking up in chaos'. After three months, during which time she saw nothing of him, Peter returned home when his grandfather became seriously ill. 'It was wonderful to see him,' Amelia said. 'He looked well. He was sharing a flat with some friends and was busy trying to make his way as a disc jockey. The job doesn't bring him in much money, and I can't see much future for him in it, but never mind, at least he seems happy.'

Sarah

When Sarah L. was 10 years old, her parents' marriage broke up and her long history of problematic behaviour began. Her form teacher complained of her lack of concentration in class and pointed out the general deterioration in her work and behaviour. At the age of 11 she, along with her class-mates, moved up to the senior school. At first the move was perhaps sufficiently exciting to curb the decline in Sarah's general behaviour but after the onset of menstruation when she was 12, she displayed violent mood swings accompanied by disruptive and insupportable activity in the classroom. Her friends worried about her, and their parents reported their concern to Mrs L., who had recently remarried and was involved in setting up a new home. She was in regular communication with the headmistress, who thought that Sarah would gradually settle down despite the current difficulties at home and at school, and, with a little patience from the teachers, Sarah would again begin to achieve the high standard of work of which she was capable.

Around this time Mrs L. noticed that the word 'hate' had crept into her daughter's vocabulary and gradually seemed to take over the child as well as her language. She 'hated' the school; she 'hated' the teachers, she 'hated' her new home and most of all she 'hated' her stepfather. There were signs that she was also beginning to hate herself. She refused to have her hair cut or styled and was determined that her fringe should grow long enough to cover her face. She began to wear black clothes with exaggerated carelessness. Each item bought was cut up and mutilated before it was considered fit to wear. Sweaters had to be excessively large and the sleeves were worn low so as to cover the hands. Earrings in the shape of skulls dangled from holes pierced in her ear-lobes. At one time she had as many as five holes in one ear-lobe whereas from the other a single ring protruded, declaring A for anarchy. One hole had been pierced by a friend with what must have been a dirty needle because a truly frightful infection developed on the side of her face and neck. The condition necessitated a week off school, but it did not prevent her adding a further two holes as soon as the blisters, scabs and crusts had disappeared.

The extremely close relationship that Sarah had hitherto had with her mother began to deteriorate to the extent that she met any of Mrs L.'s attempts at conversation with sullen silence or outbursts of angry insults. Since Sarah's school was situated close to her father's home, in order to be near her friends and continue her very active social life, she spent most weekends with him. During the week Sarah's mother drove her to and from school, which was some way from the area in which they now lived and was difficult to reach by public transport. In the circumstances the arrangement seemed best for the child, although it was by no means ideal. Both her parents agreed that it would be wrong to take her away from the school and her friends at a time when her home life had undergone such severe disruption.

Although there were opportunities to make friends in the area in which she now lived with her mother and stepfather, Sarah could not bring herself to join the various clubs and activities that were available to her. She was 13 years old when she began to play truant from school and became friendly with a crowd of youngsters who lived in a 'squat'. From them she learned to smoke cigarettes and 'pot', and she learned about hard drugs and pushers. She also developed a strong social conscience. She understood the plight of the pushers, who were forced by their own addiction to peddle heroin, and she felt the injustice of her privileged education. 'Why should I be different?' she asked her mother. 'Why can't I be normal and go to a comprehensive?'

Troubled by her inability to communicate with her daughter, and concerned by the child's erratic behaviour, both in and out of school, Mrs L. decided to seek outside advice. By this time the school felt increasingly unable to cope with Sarah's outbursts of rage in the classroom and she was threatened with expulsion. Since it became apparent that the teachers themselves disliked Sarah as much as she hated them, the future looked uncertain. A friend who was a medical social worker suggested to Mrs L. that she try family therapy. At her wits' end and unable to see a way forward, she arranged for the family to attend a therapy clinic.

The experience, consisting of four sessions altogether, was by no means appreciated by all members of the family. Sarah remained monosyllabic and uncooperative throughout whereas her father and stepmother considered the time to be generally wasted and unhelpful. Her mother, however, took a different view. Already aware that much of Sarah's behaviour was the result of jealousy of her stepfather and extreme insecurity, it now became evident to Mrs L. that Sarah's presence in her father's house was not always welcomed and that Sarah's stepmother found the child extremely difficult to cope with. Despite an optimistic start to their relationship, it had deteriorated to a 'hate campaign'. At Christmas, for example, Sarah presented the entire family with gifts excluding her stepmother, and at a large lunch party she deliberately cleared all of the guests' plates from the table but left her stepmother to clear her own. Not surprisingly, the woman did not 'look forward to the weekends', when the presence (or usually absence, since

Sarah was seldom at home and arrived back at all hours generally refusing to declare where she had been or where she was going) of her stepdaughter caused argument and discord between herself and Sarah's father.

With the family feelings on display, Mrs L. concluded that Sarah's life near her school friends did not compensate for the security of a solid home base and that a radical change was needed. It seemed that Sarah's unpleasant and antisocial behaviour was forcing her into a more isolated position. Certainly unwanted at her private school, she must also have felt unwanted in either of her family homes. In consequence it was agreed that a firm base should be formed for her with her mother and stepfather, and a place was found for her at a coeducational comprehensive school a few minutes' walk from her mother's home. Sarah began as a pupil there in the autumn term of the fourth year, at the age of 14, intending to work towards eight subjects at O level.

Although Sarah was undeniably pleased and excited by the prospect of the move, she continued to go out of her way to create problems at home. She swore and shouted at her mother, but the more vile her language and the louder her voice, the quieter Mrs L. would be. Sarah was deliberately and unpleasantly rude to her stepfather, exaggerating this behaviour in the presence of her friends. He also adopted a policy of non-aggression, so that although tension in the household ran high, the arguments were one-sided and tended to be fairly brief. In order to help Sarah over the transition from her private school to the comprehensive, and protect her from the initial loneliness of the first few weeks as a 'new girl', a companion was found for her whose role was primarily that of an older sister. Maria was 17, attended the rival all-girls comprehensive and was studying for her A level exams. She was a serious and ambitious girl, an extremely hard worker, and proved a kind and good friend to the troubled Sarah. The pot went off the boil – at least for the time being.

Sarah settled down at her new school very quickly, bringing home two new friends within the first fortnight. She worked quietly and well in the classroom and gave her homework in on time. Although her behaviour at home continued to be vengeful and anarchic, it seemed to her mother that at least part of the child's life was happy and settled.

About a month after Sarah had begun the term at her new school, Mrs L. had to go into hospital for a week to have an operation. She returned home to learn from the school that Sarah's behaviour in class had deteriorated slightly, although in general her teachers were satisfied with her progress – but 'would she please tone down her mauve hair'! Gradually, as Sarah's social life developed and expanded, it became evident that she was doing very little homework and, according to her teachers, her school work was less well presented and carelessly produced. Now Sarah refused to stay at home in the evenings, and refused to tell her mother where she was going. Short of chaining her to her bed, it seemed to Mrs L. that there was little she could do to curb the girl's increasing rebelliousness. Afraid of the dangers that Sarah faced out alone at night, she could only offer to collect the girl 'any time, anywhere, day or night'. At this stage, she was frequently telephoned at two o'clock in the morning, and ended up collecting not only Sarah but one or two of her friends as well.

At the beginning of her second term at the comprehensive Sarah was sent home for three days as a punishment for rudeness and disruptive behaviour in the classroom. Mrs L. was devastated. She was summoned by the assistant head of the school for a discussion about the child and her future – which, if she didn't manage to conform to the system, looked bleak indeed. Sarah herself seemed affected by the 'talk' she received and by the punishment. She returned to school and became noticeably easier to deal with in class and, more particularly, at home, where she began to leave notes or to indicate verbally to her mother which friends she would be with and where she was going. She seldom returned later than 10.30 p.m. and was usually accompanied by a friend, who was also a close neighbour. If Sarah was going to be home later than anticipated, she began to telephone her mother and discuss her immediate plans. Although her behaviour and manner in the home were still trying, there was in general such a marked improvement that it seemed to Mrs L. that, at last, life with Sarah was beginning to look up; a sigh of relief that came too soon.

When Mrs L. and her husband went away for five days, leaving Maria (by this time 18 years old and more in control of Sarah than any older adult appeared to be) in charge, all went well – until the night they returned home: they opened their door to be met by a drunken daughter and a houseful of partying friends. Maria had evidently turned her back for an hour – enough time for the clans to gather.

Since Sarah had been expressly forbidden to hold a party in her parents' absence, Mrs L.'s distress at the chaos was accompanied by a sense of disappointment that she could not trust her daughter. The party broke up and it was not until the following day that the extent of the damage was discovered. Furniture had been broken, panes of glass cracked and a series of holes punched into the soft plaster of an old ceiling (see pp. 47–50).

After this episode, which Mrs L. gathered had been organized partly as an expression of anger that she had gone away for a few days, Sarah settled back into as orderly and routine a way of life as her teenage years would allow. About six weeks later, however, the relatively peaceful atmosphere was shattered once more. Sarah returned home from school with bleeding knuckles and a severely scratched face, and explained to her mother that she had been fighting another girl. As a result she had been suspended again. Following a suspension of two weeks, Mrs L. was summoned to appear before the headmaster with Sarah, and was then told that the girl was involved with a gang of school bullies and had become one of the ringleaders. The head made it clear that he did not want Sarah in the school, but Mrs L. eventually persuaded him to give the girl a last chance.

Over the next two years Sarah was suspended on two further occasions, but the second time Mrs L. considered the action unjustified. This time, when she was told by the headmaster that Sarah was no longer wanted in the school, Mrs L. insisted that he take her back, and refused to move her until she had passed her two O levels and three CSEs the following term. Sarah seemed impressed by this display of force, and as they were driving home, she turned to her mother and said, 'Thank you for making them take me back. I thought you would have given up on me by now.' 'Sarah,' said Mrs L., utterly exhausted, 'it's time you learned that I will never give up on you, no matter what you do or how far you go, but isn't it about time you gave me a break?' Sarah remained at school without further incident. After taking her exams in the summer, she applied for a job, was accepted and began working before the end of the school term.

Elizabeth

Elizabeth is the mother of five children who were all touched to some extent by serious problems in adolescence – drug addiction, delinquency, anorexia and bulimia. As they have now reached adulthood she traces their careers to the present time and, on reflection, sees how their difficulties became inextricably bound up in each other's; that as one child's problem took over the family, a crisis would develop with a second child and divert Elizabeth's attention.

Elizabeth's first husband, Michael, was a Church of England clergyman when she married him. The five children – George, Eric, Caroline, Emily and Rose – emerged at regular intervals of between eighteen months and two years. When George was 14 years old, Michael became a convert to Catholicism. He was a strict disciplinarian, and religion, which had inevitably informed the daily life of the family, now became the main focus, dictating the rules and codes of behaviour by which the children were expected to live.

Both George and Eric went to a local preparatory school, which subsequently moved to another area. When the school changed locations, Elizabeth was afraid that the standard of education would deteriorate, so a decision was made to send the boys to another school some distance away, where their father was offered a teaching job. The advantages were that the boys' fees were greatly reduced and Michael could drive his sons to and from school as a matter of course. From the outset, both George and Eric expressed their unhappiness with the change, but since the older boy quickly became involved with a circle of friends who regularly travelled some distance to see him, Elizabeth was not especially concerned. Just how adversely affected they were did not come to light until one day, half-way through their second term, Elizabeth went up to George's bedroom and found half a dozen bottles of aftershave lotion hidden in a drawer. A search revealed numerous other items, which Elizabeth dragged out and laid on the bed until it was completely covered. When her son returned home from school to find the loot exposed, he immediately admitted that it had been stolen. It appeared that George's friends had formed a gang – which, in his loneliness, he had willingly joined – with the express purpose of raiding the shops in a town sufficiently far away from their own homes to lessen their chances of exposure.

Michael suggested that his son put the stolen articles into groups, parcel them up and take them back to the various shops concerned. He accompanied George to every shop, where the boy was made to face the manager and explain the theft. On the whole, he was met with a stern and hostile reception, although one or two managers took a more lenient view of the crime and expressed their appreciation at his apparent repentance. The worst punishment was having to face his friends after he had been forced to name them. Although he continued to go to school, life there became unbearable. George found himself ostracized, not so much by the individual boys concerned but by their parents, who made it known that he was no longer welcome in their houses.

After this episode George developed a craze for motor bikes, borrowed one and crashed it, then drove another without L-plates or insurance. He came up before the Juvenile Court, which let him go with a caution. Next, he 'borrowed' a car and crashed it into a neighbour's wall. Luckily for him, the neighbour was reluctant to prosecute, and the car owner felt partly to blame because he had left his keys in the ignition. There were no further incidents and George left school at 16 with six O levels. He went to art college, where he did not work and left before his final exams, but he is in regular employment and has an absorbing hobby. Although his mother feels that the job is well below George's capabilities, he seems settled and happy.

Eric was a happy and gregarious all-rounder and gave his parents no reason for concern until he was 12 years old and beginning his new school. Although he begged to be allowed to stay on at his old school, he seemed to settle down and work well at the new one until one day he returned home with a toothache, which required some quite painful and prolonged treatment. Following this, Eric kept retiring to bed saying, 'I feel tired'. He became seriously depressed and refused to eat. Shortly afterwards, he had a manic fit, screaming and banging his head on the floor and walls. He was taken into a children's hospital, where his mother was told that he had a mental disorder. He was released from hospital and treated for two years by a psychiatrist, who came to the house at first, because there were times when Eric refused to leave his bed, often lying motionless upon it all day. After about six months, he was able to return to school, but he had developed a nervous habit of pulling out all the hairs on his head, until he was almost bald. When he was 14 years old, the psychiatrist suggested a local school and Eric was transferred to a boys' public day school in the vicinity. Now he began to frequent pubs and 'started experimenting with drugs', although he managed to keep this a secret from his mother for three years.

At this point, Elizabeth's fourth child, Emily, aged 12, had become seriously ill with anorexia and was hospitalized. The marriage was going through a period of considerable stress and, seemingly as a result, Michael told Eric that the boy was not his son. Eric was appalled. Although his mother reassured him that Michael was indeed his father, and that she should know, Eric could not decide whom to believe.

Eric remained at school until he was just 18, leaving with five O levels and an A level in music. Acting on his parents' suggestion, he moved into his brother's flat, but far from feeling liberated, he became increasingly introverted and depressed. One day Elizabeth received a phone call from a friend of his, who described a repeat of the first manic attack. Eric was taken to a psychiatric hospital and admitted for nine weeks, during which time he was diagnosed as schizophrenic. Eric later described the condition as like 'living in a comic strip, with voices coming at me from bubbles'. He lost all sense of reality and did not even know his own name. He was prescribed a drug upon which he became totally dependent, and lived in constant fear of the next attack. After leaving the hospital, he also began using heroin regularly.

In the meantime Elizabeth and Michael had decided to separate; a divorce followed. Elizabeth had been living with her new partner, Henry, for two years when she first discovered Eric's addiction. She learned of it from a close friend whose own son was a heroin addict. The friend knew about Eric's involvement only through hearsay, and Elizabeth was reluctant to believe her. She talked to George, however, and asked him to talk to Eric to find out whether there was any truth in the rumour. Although the brothers decided to cover up, Eric later confessed to his addiction. Now the boy was obviously ill and deeply in debt. He had been spending about £100 a week to support his heroin addiction, although Elizabeth has no idea how he managed to afford it. When he received an irate letter from his bank manager concerning the state of his overdraft, Elizabeth interceded on his behalf and he was allowed a reprieve.

Elizabeth was anxious that people should not learn of Eric's addiction because of the criminal implications and sought advice from her GP, but he refused to become involved. Eric went to his own GP, who said that he was unable to help beyond giving him a letter of introduction to a drug clinic. At the clinic Eric was put on methadone and was told firmly that his prescription for this drug would be cancelled if he had a 'fix'.

Henry suggested that Eric come back home to live in order to try to 'kick the habit'. This he did, but suffered terribly from withdrawal symptoms, which he described as being like 'the symptoms of bad flu which continues for weeks and months without respite'. For a while Elizabeth thought Eric was cured. He had an excellent relationship with his stepfather and remained at home for two months before returning to live with George. It was not long before he was taking heroin again. After a period of stability, he gave it up and returned to the clinic for the regular prescriptions of methadone.

Aged 30, Eric's lifeline seems to lie with his psychiatrist, whom he sees frequently. Unfortunately, the psychiatrists involved change at regular intervals and Eric sometimes finds it difficult to establish a relationship with a new doctor. He is still prone to attacks of schizophrenia but Elizabeth reports with great pride and admiration that he has managed to cut out methadone and has cured himself of his heroin addiction.

Caroline, Elizabeth's oldest daughter, is now 28. She was, her mother says, 'quite horrible as a teenager', but looking back, Elizabeth feels that the girl was under extraordinary pressure during her adolescence. At 15 Caroline was diagnosed as being 'borderline anorexic'. It seemed to Elizabeth that Caroline, by nature, self-confident and bossy, was attempting to carry the burdens of her mother's stressful marriage, her brother's addiction and her younger sister's severe anorexia on her own shoulders. She became jealous of Emily and decided at the time that she hated her. Emily also remembers hating her sister, but at the same time she feared her. In retrospect Elizabeth sees that not only had the family's attention been focused on Eric during his periods of crisis, but when at the age of 12 Emily became seriously anorexic and was finally hospitalized, Elizabeth visited her every night after returning from work, so the other children saw very little of their mother during that period. Even when Emily was able to return home after two months, she remained the centre of her mother's concern.

Despite her problems, Caroline continued to achieve good results at a large private girls' day school. She left after taking A levels, and went to university. She is now a very successful career woman.

When she was 11 years old, Emily had been told that she would be incapable of coping with the work in the senior department of her public day school. This came as a terrific blow to the child, at a time when her older, dominant sister was doing so well at the rival establishment and her younger sister, Rose, was having considerable success three forms below her in the junior school. Emily moved to a smaller, less academic school, where she became anorexic in her first year. She recalls that her decision to lose weight stemmed from the time when Caroline became diet-conscious and decided to shed some of her not inconsiderable puppy fat.

Emily weighed less than five stone when she was admitted to hospital. Treated on a reward/punishment basis, she was allowed to return home only when her weight had reached a safe level. Not long after she left hospital, however, she took a drug overdose (see p. 130) and was readmitted, although the hospital found her difficult to accommodate. At 13 she was not really suitable for the children's ward nor was she remotely eligible to be placed in the adult psychiatric wing. The resident psychiatrist also felt that he was unable to make much progress with her. After a while, Emily was able to return to school, still painfully emaciated. She then took a second overdose, swallowing the entire contents of an aspirin bottle. Elizabeth felt that the attempt was definitely a cry for help, and asked the child's psychiatrist if such an attempt should be taken seriously. He was unable to advise her and she received the impression that she should regard the event with some scepticism.

After the second suicide attempt, the hospital psychiatrist refused to treat Emily. He was, Elizabeth feels, particularly unhelpful in giving her advice as to where she might turn for help, and, after much difficulty, she finally managed to persuade a psychiatric hospital to accept Emily as a patient. Here she was seen in family therapy sessions (see pp. 209–11) by one of the hospital's senior psychiatrists.

In the general hospital where Emily had been an in-patient attempts at family therapy had failed partly because her father had been uncooperative, believing that the answer to the problem lay in the power of prayer, and partly because it had been difficult to mobilize the remainder of the family to attend the sessions. Hence, the psychiatric hospital accepted Emily for treatment only on condition that all members of the family attended every session. This proved extremely difficult because the children felt reluctant to co-operate. The times were often inconvenient, and Caroline and Rose had to be taken out of school for the sessions, which amounted to about twelve in all.

Elizabeth's experience of family therapy was not, in her opinion, a success; she feels that in some respects it was harmful. She did not like the therapist personally and felt that his methods were not appropriate. In the first instance, the family were 'not warned until the last moment' about the use of video cameras to record these sessions and they found this unnerving and inhibiting. The psychiatrist, Elizabeth relates, used the 'silent technique', saying nothing until a member of the family broke the silence. Elizabeth felt that the effect of the sessions was especially detrimental to Rose, who was 11 years old at the time and remembers being very frightened.

During this period Emily's condition seemed to stabilize for a while. Although her relationship with her father was not good, he took her to France, ostensibly for a holiday but in reality to Lourdes for a divine cure. Shortly after Emily returned home, Eric had his second breakdown. Elizabeth had always been very well supported by her family, and now her sister-in-law, May, a very dominant personality, suggested that Emily stay with her while Elizabeth was preoccupied with Eric's illness. May insisted, however, that if Emily agreed to stay with her, there would be no more visits to the psychiatric hospital (although she was later persuaded by the girl's psychiatrist there to allow him to visit Emily for 'follow-up'). All pleas to return home would be ignored. May felt that she understood Emily's problem, as she herself was always engaged in some form of diet. Emily stayed with her aunt for several weeks and returned to Elizabeth weighing about seven stone. At the end of the year she weighed ten stone, a gain of five stone in a year. She was then diagnosed as being bulimic, but was an unusual case because she was too squeamish to make herself vomit and seemed unwilling to take laxatives (the two methods most bulimics use to counteract the results of their eating binges, see p. 129).

When Elizabeth married Henry, Emily seemed happier and more tranquil. She was back to a relatively normal weight and at 18 acquired a boyfriend, Mark. Some time after the beginning of their friendship, Mark's digs burned down and Henry invited the young man to live with them, which he did for about eight weeks. Contrary to expectations, Emily hated the arrangement, feeling that 'it was all wrong'. She also didn't seem to like seeing quite so much of Mark, despite the fact that their relationship was serious and he wanted to marry her. They moved into a flat together, but within four months Emily had become anorexic again. It appeared to Elizabeth that Emily was unable to cope with a long-term relationship and the implications of leaving home and setting up on her own with Mark were too much for her to bear.

Now Emily shares a flat near the family home with two girl-friends and sleeps in one half of her double bed, while the other half remains permanently made up for her in her mother's house. She has a key and comes and goes as she pleases, but even this arrangement has not prevented her becoming bulimic again. 'It seems,' Elizabeth says, 'that she just can't break the umbilical cord.' Elizabeth has given up keeping the kitchen and store cupboard under lock and key. Signs of Emily's binges seem to her to be left lying about deliberately – large blobs of jam, mounds of biscuit crumbs, chocolate wrappers – in places where they are likely to attract attention. Often Elizabeth has returned home after work to an empty refrigerator.

Rose, Elizabeth's youngest child, had no idea that her parents were unhappy together and only learned that there were difficulties during one of the family therapy sessions. She was devastated and begged her parents to stay together. To please her, Elizabeth decided to stay with Michael, but the strain became too much and the marriage broke up shortly afterwards. Rose adored her father and initially hated her stepfather. Out of sympathy with her father, she began to attend church regularly. Eventually she followed him to Canada, where she lived with him for a year, but was unable to accept his religion and returned home to her mother. At 18, prior to going to university, Rose worked as an au pair. It proved to be an unhappy experience for her and she returned home extremely ill, suffering from anorexia. Once she began her university career Rose had no more problems and obtained a first class honours degree.

Epilogue

When reading about other people's problems, it often appears to us that we can point out the cause and even perhaps suggest a solution. Whereas we might not be able 'to see the wood for the trees' in our own situation, other people's 'woods' can seem perfectly clear; but of course, we are viewing their crises from a very great distance, unaffected by emotion or stress. Only those involved in a situation have the power to change it, and even then circumstance may militate against them. Thus Mrs B., a single parent, had no choice but to remain at work even though at times she desperately wanted to be at home for Anna's sake. Elizabeth felt that she had failed her family by not spending more time with them after work – but how could she have done so with a child seriously ill in hospital? Mrs L. realized that Sarah's behaviour problems were to a large extent exacerbated by the jealousy she felt at having to 'share' her mother with a stepfather, but also felt she could not remain single to accommodate her daughter. It seemed to Amelia's children that their mother's job as a teacher was more important to her than they were, but she felt that without her work she would have lost her sanity.

In order to help children over an emotional crisis a psychiatrist will look to the past to discover where, in the first place, things 'went wrong', but for the parents, the present is the only exhausting reality. If education is disrupted by suspensions, school refusals or expulsions; if brushes with the law and an appearance in the juvenile court become a part of a teenager's experience; or if a young life is destroyed by drug addiction, the future is difficult to plan. Along with the acute anxiety that parents experience when trying to cope with adolescent crises, troublesome and difficult teenagers can easily induce feelings of such anger and resentment that it may be difficult for parents to recognize their children's underlying confusion and vulnerability, which requires their sympathy, tolerance and understanding.

The letter below was written by a 17-year-old girl, Tina, who had almost lost a friend through an attempted suicide. Tina had been living for four months in a 'squat', and when she went home for a visit it was evident to her mother that she was very disturbed and unhappy. After many hours of patient but insistent probing in the face of prolonged verbal abuse and obstruction, Mrs M. learned that her daughter in part blamed herself for her friend's suicide attempt. Tina was also feeling lonely and isolated at the time so that she identified closely with the loneliness that had led her friend to take an overdose.

Dear Mum,

This is just a letter trying to explain about today. There's so much I need for you to know but sometimes I explode and it all comes out in the wrong way. I love you. I love you more than anything and I need you and all the time I try to explain but I hurt you and we argue but you're the only person I can take things out on but I don't want to hurt you but I need to but then it makes me feel worse and I get so confused. I am happy but the way I get my happiness is the life I'm living but I know you think the worst. I also know that you understand me more than I'll ever know but I also know there's a side of me you'll never understand but I so much need you to but my life just hurts you so. We're so close and that makes me happy but it also makes me sad coz I know you hurt. I know that coz although Mike is my brother and I hardly even know him any more I hurt when I know he's sad and I hate it, so that's how I know you must feel when you see me sad. I love you, Mum, and I know I'm alright. I just wish you could believe that too. I don't know what I'm really trying to say and I also know that you're sad but I need for you to live your own life and be happy coz that makes me happy, just seeing you happy, so much so that you'd never understand. I suppose it works both ways. I don't quite know what else to say but I'm gonna talk to you soon and I love you. Thank you for helping me today. You'll never know how much you did.

Luv,
Tina.

The letter movingly illustrates how lost and confused youngsters can become and how, even when they appear to want nothing whatsoever to do with their parents, they rely on them so much for comfort and support.

Chapter 2

Home Conflict

The seeds of serious rebellion are sown in the early years and in the home. Often those who depreciate their parents most and are most cruel to them, are the insecure ones who find the leaving of their parents the most difficult. It is as though only by denying how important their parents are to them can they bear to try to tear away.

J. R. Gallagher, MD and H. I. Harris, MD, *Emotional Problems of Adolescents*

In all families a certain amount of conflict is normal, natural and inevitable. Indeed, Anna Freud felt that passivity in a teenager was something to be slightly concerned about:

> We all know individual children who as late as the ages of 14, 15 or 16 show no outer evidence of inner unrest. They remain, as they have been during the latency period, 'good' children, wrapped up in their family relationships, considerate sons of their mothers, submissive to their fathers, in accord with the atmosphere, ideas and ideals of their childhood background. Convenient as this may be, it signifies a delay of normal development and is, as such, a sign to be taken seriously.[1]

A 'family row' can be a constructive and cathartic way of helping to clear the air and prevent prolonged tension. Research has shown that family conflict in the home during the teenage years centres primarily around the everyday concerns such as hairstyles, dress, staying out late at night and untidiness,[2] and that disagreement over major issues is much less common. Some of the universal battle zones can become problematic if they go beyond a parent's level of tolerance and understanding to become the cause of bitter, damaging arguments or if they are the external manifestation of serious underlying behavioural difficulties.

If avenues of communication can be kept open, conversation and laughter between the teenager and his parents make any conflict easier to resolve. The real problems occur when relationships are so strained that confidence is lost, talk is reduced to monosyllables and the child becomes a worrying enigma. At this stage it may well be time to consider calling for help.

Everyday problems

Freud left us in no doubt that we as parents are absolutely responsible for the way our children behave, but if we accept this theory too readily, we give them a licence to rebel in any way they like: after all, 'it's all our fault'. But it isn't!

Setting the family rules: discipline

Problems of rule-making form the main area of contention in the everyday life of a teenager. Psychiatrists and psychologists agree that some form of discipline in the home is vital for young children and adolescents alike, but we know that in the case of the latter, it is a great deal more difficult to apply. Children of all ages gain security from boundaries. Without them, they can feel lost and unprotected; there is no freedom for teenagers whose lives are uncontained. Even though they constantly attempt to climb the boundary fence, testing it for strength and consistency, they need to know that it is there. Children who say 'My parents let me do exactly what I like', are really saying 'My parents don't care what I do'. Professor Michael Rutter of the Institute of Psychiatry reckons that:

> The particular methods of discipline employed appear to be rather unimportant on the whole. Properly applied, a wide range of techniques seem to be reasonably effective. On the other hand, the consistency and efficiency of the discipline and the affectional context within which discipline takes place are relevant. Markedly inconsistent or haphazard discipline is associated with an increased likelihood of conduct disorder and delinquency. This is probably because it provides no clear guidance to the child as to what behaviour is expected of him and because inconsistency tends to be associated with parental tension and conflict.[3]

Dr Christopher Dare, also at the Institute of Psychiatry, and no stranger to teenage problems in his own family, is adamant that there is a need in all families for parents to set limits 'beyond which the children should not go'.

He feels that parents should go to any lengths to maintain those limits, including restricting their children to the house ('difficult', I objected!), and 'being prepared to throw the teenager out of the home if necessary'.

Gary May of the National Committee for the Prevention of Child Abuse in Chicago writes that:

> Parenting style has to be in harmony with the parent's personality, and what works for one parent may not work for another. Parents cannot be expected to behave in unnatural or uncomfortable ways. The style of discipline must flow naturally. It is also unrealistic to think that both parents are going to have the same style. Consistency does not mean that their methods are alike. It means that both parents act in keeping with their own personalities and that they use techniques they are comfortable with. For discipline to work smoothly, each parent accepts the parenting style of the other.[4]

Given then that discipline is necessary in adolescence and that without it the teenager will not develop a sense of moral responsibility, respect for the rights of others, or confidence in himself, how can it be maintained in the face of rebellion and defiance?

All those experienced in adolescent guidance advise parents not to be overstrict, not to threaten or attempt to dominate. Authoritarian control produces more hostility, greater rebelliousness and destroys communication.

One mother, exhausted by the torrents of verbal abuse from her 15-year-old daughter, asked the girl why she thought the two of them were always engaged in such serious conflict. 'Serious!' the girl exclaimed.

> No, no. Our fights may be upsetting, but they're not serious, because you don't shout back. If you shouted back at me, I'd be worse. If you started being bitchy to me like I am to you, the fight would be your fault. Then it really would be serious! Now, you see, it's just me, so it's my fault and therefore not so serious!

Curious logic, but one sees what she means.

'You can't expect discipline to work all the time; no discipline method works all of the time; but if it's not working, change it,' advises Gary May.[5]

Sibling rivalry

In Europe and America 80 per cent of children grow up with siblings. They spend more time with them than with their parents and the relationship is likely to last until the end of their lives, the ties between them providing an important buffer against the insecurity of aging and the loss of parents. Judy Dunn in her book *Sisters and Brothers* seeks to explain why it is that some siblings are great friends while others are hostile and often aggressive towards each other.

The traditional way of thinking about differences in how well siblings get along and of explaining differences between siblings within a family has been to stress the importance of the birth order, age gap and gender of the children. Yet the studies we've described show that these are notably *not* the most important variables in accounting for differences in the affection, co-operation, aggression, imitation, hostility or empathy shown by siblings in the pre-school period, in middle childhood, or in adolescence. Birth order is important (unsurprisingly) in the dominance and the power relations between siblings, and in the kind of care-giving children show towards their siblings; age gap too is important in these more 'parent-like' behaviours. And a first child's interest in and affection for his or her younger siblings has a powerful fostering effect on the relationship between them. But recent research strongly suggests that psychologists should 'think again' before assuming that what matters most in a child's relations with his siblings are the old favourites – birth order, age gap, and gender.

For parents the issue is of real practical importance. There is, as we have seen, evidence that the quality of the relationship between siblings is linked to each child's relationship with the parents. Although it would be unrealistic to try to draw practical rules-of-thumb from the finding that in families with an intense relationship between mother and first-born daughter the siblings are likely to be hostile, it is likely that certain types of parental behaviour towards siblings do encourage supportive affectionate behaviour. Talking to each child about the other, explaining feelings and actions, emphasizing in a consistent way the importance of not hurting the other all appear to be linked to the development of a more harmonious relationship . . . However, individual differences in how well siblings get along are linked to many other factors besides the parent-child relationship, and among the most important of these are two that a parent can hardly hope to influence – the children's gender and their temperaments. In the early years hostility is often more common between siblings of different gender. It is important for parents to know just how common this hostility is – and for them not to feel primarily responsible for the aggression between their children. The fact remains that most first-born children are at least ambivalent about their siblings, and quarrelling is frequent and uninhibited in most families. Siblings don't choose each other; we should not be surprised that some should find it profoundly difficult to live together, forced as they are to daily and intense intimacy.[6]

Physical abuse of a parent

If many parents learn to come to terms with the verbal abuse directed at them by their teenager, physical abuse is another matter. The frustrations of a boy, already perhaps taller and stronger than his mother, may lead to expressions of violence towards her. Newspapers tend to report cases of filial aggression and violence that have led to murder, but less sensational cases of assault tend to remain family secrets.

A widow, whose son was the head boy of his school, quarrelled with him and after a furious argument he struck her and she was hurled to the floor by the force of the blow. She immediately sought the help of a psychologist who she knew specialized in the problems of adolescence. He suggested to her that she was not allowing her son the kind of independence and consideration that his maturity required. As head boy, he was used to being looked up to by the other boys and respected by the staff. A considerable burden of responsibility went with his position. At school he was treated as an adult, while at home he was still treated very much as a child, and the only way he could make his mother come to terms with his maturity was by angry force.

If parents are physically abused by their teenager, it is a serious matter even if the blows are minor; it is the meaning behind the blows that requires investigation. Professional help should be sought to prevent a relatively minor incident from becoming a major tragedy.

Running away from home

Small children threaten to run away from home: teenagers actually do so, and, we are told, in ever increasing numbers. Whatever their reasons for running away, the authorities (the police and the social services) and the caring organizations are placed in an almost impossible situation, particularly when dealing with children under the age of 16, who by law must be returned to their parents, except in the most exceptional circumstances (see Chapter 6). Teenagers who run away from close and loving families leave behind devastated and terrified parents. Which of us would not be inclined to think the worst in such a situation? How would we set about trying to trace our missing person? Where would our more-or-less penniless teenager be likely to go for food and shelter?

Thousands of young people in Britain run away to London every year. They arrive with no money, no friends and nowhere to stay. Many are under the age of 16. It may be of some comfort to parents of such children to know that in the London area, where youngsters still seem to think the streets are paved with gold, there are many organizations that deal exclusively with apparently homeless teenagers. One such agency is Centrepoint in London's Soho. Here 16- to 19-year-olds are given shelter for two to five nights, during which time they are referred to various other agencies for advice concerning their future plans, given information about accommodation, employment and social security; advised on personal and legal problems; and offered long term support where appropriate. Parents are contacted only at the request of the runaway, and the only information that they can expect to receive from such an agency, whose main priority is to respect the wishes of the teenager, is that their child was 'seen here two or three nights ago'. There is a 'message home' telephone service, which allows wary runaways to send a message to their parents without direct contact with them or Centrepoint. This may seem somewhat cold comfort, but at least it gives parents the satisfaction of knowing that their youngster is still alive and well. Centrepoint publishes a *Survival Guide for Young Homeless People in London*, which parents may find worth obtaining to see the kind of help available to teenagers in the area.

There can be few actions in a parent's life that can be as despairing as having to report a child to the police as a missing person. Mrs P.B. described to me her miserable ordeal:

> My 17-year-old daughter, Lisa, was living in a squat in Brixton with a young man who was, I suppose, her first real boy-friend. The squat itself was pleasant enough, with heating and electricity and even a television, but the estate – and their block in particular – was known to the police for racial violence and drug dealing. When she didn't turn up one weekend for Sunday lunch as usual, I became alarmed and even more so when one of her friends telephoned to say that she had heard that Lisa had left the squat and her boy-friend and was sleeping under the arches at Waterloo Station. It was Monday night

when I received this call and I just got into the car, collected two of my daughter's loyal friends and we searched among the cardboard box community at Waterloo and Charing Cross. No one had seen her, so the next day I went to the police station and reported her missing. They felt that the case was grave enough to initiate a search and were very sympathetic, but when I returned home, she telephoned to say that she was alive and well and living in Hackney. I was immensely relieved, of course, but it was the worst twenty-four hours of my life.

Some time later I spoke to Lisa, who, apart from being rather grubby, seemed cheerful, in excellent health and well-nourished. 'I haven't run away from home,' she assured me, but for her mother, who had to live with the knowledge of her daughter's dangerously itinerant life and whose contacts with the girl were becoming increasingly irregular, it seemed as if she had indeed 'run away'. Although somewhat contrite at having made her mother anxious, Lisa was predictably angry that the police had been involved. Certainly she had spent a couple of nights under the arches at Waterloo before moving into another squat with friends and had rather enjoyed the experience. 'It was good fun,' she said. 'They're nice people and the Salvation Army come round and bring you food.' For parents who, like Mrs P.B., find themselves in this nightmarish predicament, perhaps Lisa's comments can offer a crumb of comfort.

Teenagers who find the natural process of breaking away from home especially difficult and painful will sometimes take an extreme course of action. Mr and Mrs M.O. came down to breakfast one morning on a day when their daughter, who was living in a squat at the time, had arranged to bring her friends home for a large meal. On the doormat lay a letter:

Dear Mum and Dad

I called round today (Sunday evening) but you weren't there. I really wanted to see you to say goodbye as I'm going to Birmingham to live for a while very early tomorrow morning. I'm really sorry about dinner tomorrow but it was a very last minute decision. As soon as I get there I'll write or phone to tell you that I'm safe! I'll be back to London to see you as soon as I can get the money together, but I'll keep in contact always. I'm going with Andy and a girl called Katie. I'll miss you very much but I waited as long as I could but you didn't turn up. I'm really sorry, I should of phoned earlier but everything has happened so fast. I can't think of anything left to say except that I love you very much. There's a lot of brilliant people in Birmingham – a lot nicer than most of the ones in London – so we all decided that we are going to Birmingham for a change. We are going to live with Andy's brother there. Give love to everyone.

Luv
Rachel.

P.S. Not to worry – it's not as drastic as it sounds! (I'll contact you as soon as poss!)

One of the most poignant stories was told to me by a couple in Coventry. Their son was away at university and their daughter, aged 17, had been living at home and training to be a secretary. They did not feel that their relationship with Patricia was either especially bad or especially good. In fact, they knew very little about her private life. She seldom brought friends home, yet she used to go out almost every evening to meet them. Usually she arrived home before her parents went to bed, but one night she did not return until the early hours of the morning. Her parents were frantic with worry and very angry. When they confronted her the following day, she was unwilling to give them an explanation as to why she was late but sat impassively as they chastized her. That night she left the house to visit her friends as usual and never returned. When I talked to her parents, Patricia had been missing for two years. There have been no letters home and no telephone calls.

To learn how teenage girls manage to survive on their own away from home I went to Greenham Common, where youngsters are drawn, initially at least, more by comradeship than any fervently held political belief. It was a cold day in late autumn and there were no more than twenty-five women camped in groups of four or five around the perimeter fence. The majority of the women were aged between 16 and 20. All of the teenagers to whom I spoke had families. Apart from two girls, one of whom came from Australia and the other from New Zealand, all had left home against their parents wishes. When I asked the youngest of the group (aged 16) why she had run away, she replied: 'Oh, lots of things I suppose, but mostly I just couldn't stand my Mum's roasts day in, day out. The food up here's much better!'

The girls seemed to thrive on the extraordinarily caring relationships that shared hardship often produces. No outward-bound course ever devised could be as tough as the lives these young girls had elected to lead and yet they appeared fit, well and perfectly happy. Although many had run away from home in the first place, they had later contacted their families, most of them knew of their whereabouts. Generally speaking, as one girl put it to me, they weren't too keen but they just let us get on with it'.

Stealing

Mrs Baker accompanied her husband on a business trip to France, leaving their two sons, Mike, 19, and Thomas, 17, in charge of the house. When she returned, she discovered that £300 had disappeared from her bank account. Thomas had forged her signature using her credit card and cashed cheques to that amount. Far from being penitent, he merely stated, 'Well, I needed the money. If you had been here, you would have given it to me.'

I have talked to a number of teenagers, who all, without exception, admitted to having stolen something in their lives, whether it was an ashtray from a pub or a handful of sweets from a tray in a shop. They knew that what they were doing was wrong, but just 'did it for a lark' and 'because there didn't seem much harm in it'. More seriously, one boy of 16 admitted that he had on two occasions stolen his mother's car. The last time, he drove it into a lamppost and turned it over where it lay in the middle of the road just two streets away from his own front door. I spoke to the boy's mother, a single parent whose relationship with her son was fraught with tension and difficulty. She said that in order to claim on her insurance, she had been forced to lie about the crash. 'To this day, I don't know how I got away with it,' she exclaimed. 'It was a terrifying experience.'

Forgery, shoplifting and driving without a licence or insurance are criminal offences and parents may not be in a position to shield their children from the due process of the law, but most parents who discover that their child has been involved in a criminal offence, whether within the home or without, deal with it as an internal matter (as did Elizabeth and Michael when they discovered George's thefts; see Chapter 1). Sometimes it may seem appropriate to invoke the law in order to provide a youngster with a stern object lesson. One father I know became so angry and frightened for the safety of his errant son, who had taken his car for the third time without permission and for the third time, to use his own phrase, had 'wrapped it around a tree in a country lane', that he sought legal advice, with the result that the boy was banned from driving for two years and ordered to pay his father substantial damages.

If a teenager steals persistently, some kind of professional counselling is necessary in order to prevent the act becoming a habit for life. Stealing at this level is often a cry for help and as such should not go unheeded.

Lying

Young children are basically honest and straightforward and it comes as something of a shock to parents of adolescents to discover that lies and deviousness are characteristic of the age group. In fact, the more authoritarian and rigid the discipline in the home, the more lies are likely to be told. When asked to comment on the moral standards of his teenage son and daughter, one father gave me this view:

> It seems to me that the adolescent conscience remains pretty rudimentary for two or three years before the low threshold of morality rises above the level of 'honour amongst thieves'. True, my daughter wants to turn our home into a hostel for down and outs and drug addicts; my son comes up with a new idea each week to raise money for the handicapped; there is a lot of dreaming, much talk, but very little action. On the other hand, they are quite happy to remove bottles of wine from my cellar for a party, or lift the odd pound from their mother's purse, and, once cornered, getting them to tell the truth is like drawing a sabre tooth from a prehistoric tiger.

As the child moves into adolescence, his world becomes less public. More time spent away from home means that he is beginning to build a life of his own – a private life, which he can allow his parents to share only as much as he is willing. If he is asked, on returning home late for a meal, 'Where have you been?', he may reply, 'I've been down to the library with Bill and we missed the bus.' This statement may be true, partly true or entirely false. If false, it doesn't necessarily mean that he has been in trouble. Perhaps he lies to protect his privacy or to protect himself from a family row. His parents, on the other hand, have demanded to know his whereabouts less for reasons of curiosity than a desire to make sure that he was safe during the time spent out of their sight. They in turn, are anxious to protect him.

When a 16-year-old girl was asked by her father, 'Are you a virgin?', she responded, 'It's none of your business' and ran to her mother, tears of indignation blackening her cheeks with rivulets of mascara. 'How dare he ask me that!' she stormed. 'I wouldn't tell him the truth if he paid me. Anyway,' a small grin spreading over her face, 'I am a virgin as it happens, but I'm not going to give him the satisfaction of knowing it.' Once again, the father's question was prompted by concern for his daughter, but it cannot be denied that he had no right to expect a straight answer. Gradually, a teenager learns to tell his parents just enough to make them feel secure in the knowledge that they are at least aware of his activities, but not enough for them to violate his privacy. As long as parents have an outline, they should not necessarily expect the details. If they insist upon details, they may be fobbed off with lies.

Coming to terms with teenage lying is an important step in establishing a new relationship with a child. Once the process has been understood, it forms the foundation on which confidence between child and adult can be built. To acquire mutual trust on the basis of lies sounds paradoxical, but the fact is that in order to keep the lies to a minimum, parents have to learn to curb direct and awkward questions. If they show interest rather than curiosity, trust rather than suspicion, they will begin to receive more honest information about the life of their teenager than they know what to do with! As one mother told me:

> Not only does my daughter bring me her problems, for which I am very grateful, but I get the problems of all her friends, which often involve me in a great deal of trouble and moral soul-searching. My daughter trusts me with a confidence – a friend thinks she might be pregnant; she can't tell her mother, so what should she do? I explain the various alternatives and tell my daughter that she must try to persuade her friend to confide in her parents or another member of the family the truth about her condition. Advising her friends is a responsibility I would rather not have.

If teenagers adopt lying as a form of defence, they most certainly do not expect their parents to do the same! There is no doubt that *we* are expected to be scrupulously honest at all times. Which of us, during a heated argument has not been summarily defeated and side-tracked by an accusation of false-hood. 'But that's not what you said to me before. *You lied!*'

While lying in teenagers can be a problem, it is also a normal step towards the development of their own lives and personalities; but excessive lying is not normal. There are some youngsters for whom the habit becomes a compulsion. They lose the sense of what is real in everyday life and are often given to wild and extravagant fantasies about themselves or their families, which may begin to affect relationships with their friends. If parents are anxious that their child is being taken over by his own lies, they would be wise to consider professional advice.

Staying out late at night

Another problem that affects almost all parents with teenagers also revolves around the desire to protect them. Where teenagers go at night and what they do has profound significance for their safety. Few parents sleep soundly while their youngster is out late at night, even if they have been told the plans for the evening. If the teenager is particularly difficult and uncommunicative, refuses to give any information and storms out of the house, there is really very little that the worried and despairing parents can do, except wait until the key turns in the lock, the light is switched on and footsteps herald the child's return. Once again, it seems to be a question of confidence. As teenagers begin to trust that their parents will not attempt to prevent them going out and do not wish to pry into their private lives, but are merely anxious that adequate steps are being taken to ensure their safety, parents will be rewarded with a more reassuring picture of adolescent night-life.

Babysitting

Babysitting becomes a problem when young teenagers feel they are capable of being in the house alone in the evenings before their parents are willing to leave them unattended. Many 13-year-olds are themselves babysitters and rely on the job as a source of income; indeed, parents whose youngsters are sensible, reliable and responsible will wonder how the matter can present such serious consideration, but to those who have been through the unco-operative, uncommunicative, wilful, headstrong period with their teenagers, where anything can happen – and frequently does – the difficulties are all too familiar. To return after an evening out to find the house vibrating with noise, littered with cigarette butts and dirty crockery is enough to erase the memory of the happiest occasion (see pp. 47–50).

Of even greater concern, perhaps, is the fact that if teenagers leave the house during the evening – and not all promises to remain indoors will be kept – and then find themselves in trouble, stranded, or in any situation in which they would normally telephone home for help, they may not have anyone to turn to.

In Scotland it is against the law for children under 12 to be left on their own, but elsewhere in Britain it is an offence only if they are neglected in a way that is likely to cause unnecessary suffering, as, for example, leaving small children without food for a period of time or leaving them in a room with an unguarded fire. Young teenagers frequently resist the company of a babysitter even though they may, in reality, be quite terrified to be left in their homes alone. One response to this, of course, is to encourage them to have a friend over for the night, but then there is always the risk of double trouble – especially if the friend happens to be considered 'unsuitable'. So what can parents do? In the first instance the answer is probably to ride out the storms of protest and continue to employ the services of a trusted and responsible babysitter. This will work for a while, but there may come a time when the next tactic in the line of protest will take the form of a flat refusal to remain in the house in the company of a babysitter. If, as has been suggested elsewhere, it is virtually impossible to keep determined teenagers in the house against their will, then parents might find that while their home is being kept safe from marauders by a redundant babysitter, their stubborn, infuriating youngster is, at best staying at a friend's house or, at worst, out roaming the streets until they return, thus ensuring one way or the other that they have a rotten evening.

There are two practical solutions to the problem. The first is a decision by the parents not to go out, which can surely be appropriate only in exceptional circumstances; otherwise, by giving in to this not uncommon form of teenage blackmail, they invest in their children a most unnatural amount of power, which will probably render any other attempts at control useless.

The second was suggested to me by a father:

> When in doubt, appeal to their better natures; they almost always have one. My wife and I had been through the terrible experience of returning to find a party in progress and a substantial part of the house in need of repair and redecoration, and it was a while before we were able to summon the confidence to dispense with the help of a sitter. After a long period of protest, during which the sitter had become a lonely and expensive house guard, we decided that it was time to give our 16-year-old her independence. We understood that she was embarrassed by being 'looked after' in our absence, when many of her friends were allowed to remain in their homes alone. Although we knew where she would be while we were out for the evening, there was always a risk. We told her that the time had come to trust her in the house alone and suggested that her friend could stay the night for company but if once that trust was broken, then it was back to the babysitting days with a vengeance. She was actually very nervous on her own, so her friend was an important part of the package. We gave her the same warning as we had delivered to our daughter. Four months and several outings later I can report complete success, but I wouldn't leave her alone with a friend overnight. There's always a risk of something going wrong.

Homework

'Have you done your homework?' is a question that is familiar to parents of teenagers throughout the country, and constant, daily repetition robs it of its potency. The answers may include 'Yes' (meaning no), 'I don't have to give it in until next week' (meaning 'It should have been in last week but if I wait long enough, the teacher will forget all about it'), and 'I've forgotten my textbook/exercise book/pen/pencil/rubber/ruler/compass' – whichever is least likely to be readily available in the home.

In a survey conducted by the Schools Health Education Unit at Exeter University in 1984, 2,780 pupils at thirteen secondary schools were given a questionnaire to complete concerning their health and habits. The question 'How many hours did you spend doing homework yesterday?' produced the following response:

NUMBER OF HOURS	BOYS	GIRLS
	(PER CENT)	
None	48	32
Up to 1	31	39
Up to 2	14	18
Up to 3	5	8
Up to 4	1	2
Over 4	1	1

Across the country, it would seem that homework rates fairly low on the teenage list of priorities! Parents can only remind and encourage their children to do their homework: it cannot be forced from them. If children are not motivated to produce work for their teachers, they are even less likely to write an essay for the benefit of their parents. Although homework can become a major source of conflict in the home, parents of troublesome teenagers often find that it is the very least of their worries.

Television and video

Parents' concern over television centres around two main areas: the amount of time spent viewing television and the effect of daily doses of sex and violence on the screen. In the Schools Health Education Survey teenagers were asked 'For how long did you watch television after school yesterday?' The findings were as in the table on page 39.

These figures are interesting because they reveal, somewhat unexpectedly perhaps, that the nation's teenagers spend a relatively small period of their day watching television. However, current anxiety about children's tele-

NUMBER OF HOURS	BOYS	GIRLS
	(PER CENT)	
None	6	8
Up to 1	18	23
Over 1	19	26
Over 2	21	18
Over 3	16	14
Over 4	11	6
Over 5	9	5

vision is concerned less with the number of hours youngsters spend in front of the television and more with the possibly damaging effects of what have been described as 'video nasties'. Whereas intervention may be relatively easy in the case of young children, parents alone cannot control the viewing habits of teenagers. Therefore in 1984 Parliament passed the Video Recordings Act, the main intention of which is to protect children and young people from 'video nasties'. The term is somewhat subjective, of course, depending on the perception of the spectator, but it is generally taken to mean a gratuitous display of sex, horror and violence. Videos are now classified into categories according to content and it is an offence to supply or offer to supply videos to young people under the age specified in the classification. Penalties are limited to fines with a maximum of £20,000.

Does violence on television inspire violence in youngsters themselves? Since there are no definite answers, it remains for parents to make up their own minds on the matter after weighing up the evidence on both sides. In 1984 a study involving 10,000 children emerged from the University of Stellenbosch in South Africa after the popular television series 'The A-Team' was blamed for inspiring acts of mindless destruction by white South African schoolchildren. Television had been introduced to the country eight years previously – much later than in other industrialized countries – so the field for research remains relatively uncluttered. At Stellenbosch 100 children newly exposed to television were fed a diet of programmes containing varying degrees of violence over a three-week period. One-third of the group saw only violent programmes, others were shown programmes with a 'neutral' content, while the remainder were shown programmes of a social and socializing nature. The results suggested that only the children exposed to violence exclusively were noticeably affected: they apparently became much more aggressive.

American psychologist Dr Ed Christophersen asserts that most television is, at best, a waste of time and can actually be harmful to children, while Dr

W. A. Belson, author of *Television Violence and the Adolescent Boy*, a study of 1,565 adolescent boys in London, found that there was a connection between the amount of viewing of television violence by adolescent boys and the extent of their aggressive behaviour, and strongly recommended that there should be a cutback on the amount of violence shown on television.[7] On the other hand, *The Times Educational Supplement* reported the views of Huddersfield psychiatrist Dr Tobarek Hossain, who defended violent television. Dr Hossain claimed that 95 per cent of children quickly forget about violent episodes in television films or news programmes. 'It might play on their minds for a day or two,' he said. 'They could have a nightmare or a sleepless night; but the same happens with everything in life. It would not have any permanent effect and be most unlikely to cause illness or breakdown twenty years later.'[8] In the interview Dr Hossain suggested that television violence should not be viewed in isolation from other social and family pressures, and claimed there was no evidence to suggest that society had become more violent over the preceding fifteen years under the influence of television. He also suggested that a small percentage of children (about 4 to 5 per cent) already prone to aggression might be made more aggressive by watching violent films or videos, but these are children, he maintained, who would probably find other outlets for their antisocial behaviour. Despite his theoretical view, however, Dr Hossain did not permit his own children to watch 'video nasties', feeling that more research needs to be done on the effects of excessive violence and sadism.

In September 1983 the British Broadcasting Corporation published its own report on violence on television, in which it justified the portrayal of violence in some instances:

> In many cases the details of violent action should be avoided, although it is important not to diminish the significance of violence by treating violent episodes too summarily. There may be occasions when the consequences of violence should be shown at some length, in order to make its hideousness clear and perhaps arouse a compassionate response from viewers, e.g. 'Grange Hill'.[9]

At the centre of the controversy over 'video nasties' is Dr Brian Brown, the Director of the Television Research Unit at Oxford Polytechnic. In November 1983 a Parliamentary Video Enquiry Group horrified parents and teachers with their report *Video Violence and Children*. Dr Brown was involved in the group's research at the time, but later disclaimed its more sensational findings, which led to such newspaper headlines as the *Daily Mail*'s 'SADISM FOR SIX YEAR OLDS – Videos replace baby sitters ...

and the children's party conjuror'. On talking to Dr Brown, it was evident to me that he is anxious to promote a positive image for television and video. He watches a great deal of television for pleasure and believes that the medium is enriching, has improved the quality of our lives, enhanced our ability with language, heightened our awareness and added to our store of knowledge. Although 'parents worry that their children never open a book, and that they do nothing but watch television,' he said, he feels strongly that the rewards and pleasures of television viewing are as valuable as book reading, which he believes is essentially associated with middle class values and the need for academic achievement. He also believes that the concern about the effects of violence and video nasties is greatly exaggerated, agreeing with Dr Hossain that the vast majority of children forget about television violence and that it has no lasting effect on them. He suggests that television and videos are both sociable, socializing and an adjunct to family unity, adding that video machines are more controllable than television. 'You can choose which film to plug into the video, but you can't blot out a horrific rape scene that comes upon you unannounced when you are in the middle of watching a play.'

However, Dr Brown does not allow his own teenage children to watch 'Dallas' because he feels that the dubious morality portrayed in this immensely popular series is harmful, particularly to young teenagers. I discovered that he was by no means alone in his view. Writing in the *Guardian* about teenage pregnancies in Ireland, reporter Ronit Lentin quoted a girl from County Kildare who had had a baby at 17:

> I got pregnant after the first time. I was drunk. They tell you at home and at school that sex before marriage is sinful and that if you keep the child, you'll go to hell. Then you watch 'Dallas' and see Sue Ellen jump into bed with men she just met and your values get all mixed up. You think life is really like this; you want to be an adult, go out and have sex – and end up pregnant.[10]

Eileen Turner, the mother of two girls, told me:

> I don't like them watching 'Dallas'. I feel that the programme trivializes relationships, but if I had forbidden them to watch that particular type of programme, they would resent it. They would want to watch it even more. Their friends were all watching it and they would feel left out. So what I do is to sit through as many episodes as I can stand and I make comments, sometimes to their irritation, as to the immorality or morality of a situation. We discuss it afterwards and mostly the girls agree with my point of view. I try to find positive

things to say about the programme – parts which I might have enjoyed. All in all, I feel that this is the best compromise I can make.

Mrs Turner's solution is an ideal one, according to Patricia Marks Greenfield, Professor of Psychology at the University of California in Los Angeles and author of *Mind and Media*:

> Almost no research has been done on what parents would probably most like to know: how to counteract the influence of the social information children get from television. We do know that by discussing shows with children, parents or other adults can increase the benefits and decrease the negative effects of watching commercial television programs.[11]

Although researchers may not agree on the effects of screen violence on the teenage psyche, there does seem to be general agreement that television reinforces stereotypes. Margaret Heaton, senior research assistant at the Television Research Unit, felt that there was indeed a link between the violent image of the pop world macho-man and weak woman, and the perpetuation of the stereotypic gender roles. The Stellenbosch study also found that very little had been done to try to alter stereotypic images, and the notion that married women should stay at home and not work was being perpetuated.

The adolescent passion for music

The fact that teenagers love music is hardly a problem – it's just that they are addicted to LOUD music, and loud popular music has an inexorable beat that forces its way into the parental consciousness with all the subtlety of a pile-driver. How peaceful and unobtrusive the medium of television can seem to parents whose adolescents are permanently tuned in to the latest fashion in pop sounds. But just as the noise and din of a pop record can be an excruciating experience for parents, preventing them from thinking calmly and tying them into tight physical knots, the same noise and din is able to tranquillize teenagers, dispel black moods and release pent-up energy. A mother whose 14-year-old daughter was in a highly emotional state, told me that the girl would sit on the floor of her room rocking herself to music for hours on end. The volume was never anything less than full, except for a few minutes after each of the many occasions it had been forcibly lowered by her mother. Eventually the family decided to buy her a set of headphones, but these were rarely used. When asked why she always listened to the sound at full volume, the girl replied, 'The louder the music, the more it blots out my problems.' Another mother I know became so incensed by the noise from her teenager's record player that, after several requests to lower the volume were ignored, she strode into his room and kicked the machine to pieces – thereby hurting her foot and her purse, but at least restoring her sanity.

Perhaps of even greater concern to parents (who hardly need reminding of the influence of pop music and culture on their teenagers) is the content of the songs, which often are either sexually explicit or calculated to encourage a spirit of anarchy and violence. Pop music has a tradition of sexual innuendo – even the term 'rock and roll' was originally slang for sex – but parents are concerned when the lyrics are explicit rather than oblique. In Washington, D.C. an organization called Parents' Music Resource Centre (PMRC) has persuaded the American record industry to label particularly outspoken records with a 'health warning' similar to the one on cigarette packets. Although the PMRC is generally opposed to censorship, it hopes to achieve a rating system that would label cassette covers and record sleeves with warnings such as V for violence and X for profanity and lewdness. It wants explicit records to be kept behind the counter in shops and lyrics to be printed on the covers so that they can be read by parents.

Fashion and foul language

Why do some teenagers seem to go out of their way to create squalor? Why does the air turn blue with unending streams of X-rated vocabulary? Why do they choose to dress in rags, shave their heads, paint their lips black or adorn their ear-lobes with safety pins? The headmistress of a Middlesex comprehensive school told me that her staff could always pinpoint the rebellious and troubled youngsters by the way they dressed. 'The school uniform – if we can actually get them to wear it – usually contains elements of their own creation and, against the rules, they continue to wear make-up and jewellery,' she said.

The way teenagers dress, behave or wear their hair symbolizes the way they feel, and the more extreme the 'statement', the more likelihood there is of a confused and anxious individual who feels insecure and may suffer from low self-esteem. Adults learn to understate their emotions to hide their anxieties from the world, but teenagers, without the benefit of experience, make huge overstatements that conceal nothing. Theirs is a language of externals. They are concerned to display an image that best expresses their feelings, their enthusiasms and their taste at a particular moment in their lives, and that disguises the disquieting lack of self-confidence they are

43

trying so hard to overcome. The 'disguise' is apparent not only in dress and hairstyle, but also in gesture, language and, perhaps, sexual identity. Punks, rockabillies, casuals and skinheads are all examples of groups distinguished by their dress. It is evident that the 'uniform' of cult fashion does not necessarily flaunt sex; on the contrary, it may conceal even gender.

Studying the lives of adolescent girls in the 1980s Sue Lees found that girls between the ages of 15 and 16, far from being sexually liberated, were seriously worried about their reputations.[12] In the coeducational secondary schools involved in her survey the verbal abuse by boys to which the girls complained of being exposed appeared to threaten their freedom, self-esteem and development. The girls reported being called variously 'bitch', 'cow', 'dog', 'slut' and 'slag' (prostitute), irrespective of their actual sexual availability or experience, and complained that they have no means of redress. There appear to be no similarly generally demeaning words for boys; on the contrary, a boy referred to as a 'stud' is usually greatly admired by his peer group for his alleged sexual prowess. Such language, indicating, as it does, peer group acceptance or rejection, is a powerful form of control and one, Lees found, that girls also applied to each other to reinforce conformity not only in terms of sexuality, but also behaviour, clothes, friendships, school work and social life.

Fortunately for parents, even the most extreme and bizarre appearance or behaviour is subject to rapid change. Yesterday's punk can be tomorrow's Sloane Ranger, and the parents' own tastes will determine which style they can best tolerate. Nevertheless, punk culture is alarming to most parents because it has a tendency to be associated with anarchy, violence and drugs. While these associations cannot be denied, parents need not fear the worst just because their teenager dresses in a leather jacket adorned with zips and chains, carefully torn jeans, earrings and hair half shorn or crested and dyed to resemble a pink cockatoo.

But there is a lighter side to the problem of teenage dress. Now that their daughter is well past her teens, Geoff and Betty Williams could reflect on her adolescence with amusement, although at the time, they both agreed, 'it was sheer hell'. On one occasion, Geoff reminisced,

> we were going out to dinner at a restaurant – quite a formal occasion. Betty and I were changed and ready to go when Wendy emerged wearing a scrap of a mini-skirt which scarcely covered her behind, purple fishnet tights and a blouse through which an assortment of underwear was clearly visible. 'You can't come with us dressed like

that,' we said, but Wendy flatly refused to budge, at which point I took off my shoes and socks, and rolled my trousers way up above my knees. 'What are you doing, Daddy?' asked the horrified teenager. 'Well, my girl,' said I, 'if *you* can go to the restaurant showing your backside, *I* can go showing my knees.' Quite what I should have done if she had decided to call my bluff, I don't know, but as it was, she scuttled away upstairs and returned wearing something a little more conventional.

Most teenagers modify extremes of fashion and adapt a style to suit themselves. Their efforts are often intensely creative. What to a parent's eye might be an unacceptable and unsuitable mode of dress, (formed perhaps, from a plastic bin liner, an old corn sack or an outsize T-shirt) will probably be the result of considerable ingenuity and imagination. Who knows that they are not witnessing the makings of a Bruce Oldfield or a Mary Quant! The problems of teenage fashion become less of a worry when parents learn to tolerate the styles and recognize the statements. If however, the statement indicates that there may be cause for concern – that, along with other symptoms, a youngster seems to be showing signs of being deeply troubled or unhappy – some help and advice from one of the organizations listed at the end of the chapter might prove useful.

A bedroom like a pigsty

For parents who are house-proud or who simply like to live in clean and orderly surroundings, the teenage bedroom can be a nightmare. Last week's dirty clothes mingle with yesterday's clean laundry; ashtrays overflow, cigarette butts swim in the remains of unidentifiable liquids in mugs and glasses beside plates of mouldy food and empty crisp packets. Schoolbooks lie in scattered piles over the floor beside torn pieces of paper, the discarded results of days of half-completed homework. The bed is unmade and there is a damp patch on the pillow where a wet towel has been thrown down and left to rot. No one is allowed into this inner sanctum of filth and squalor: it may not be touched; it may not be cleaned – at least, that is, not without excessive scenes of conflict and emotional exhaustion. Such a bedroom is a statement. 'It is my life and I shall live it how I like,' it says. 'It's my private world and you can't come in.' How parents deal with the problem of the teenage bedroom is as individual as the family unit itself. Some are prepared to wage a constant battle, which they manage to win by 'breaking and entering' with a vacuum cleaner and disinfectant. Others, apart from insisting that the family china and glassware make their way back into circulation, shut the door and hope that time will clear up the mess – which it does, eventually.

Pocket money

Pocket money or an allowance is a tangible symbol of personal freedom. The problems involved are always how much and on what should it be spent? In deciding how much, parents must consider on what the money is to be spent. If a teenager is given the freedom to buy his own clothes, then the money must be enough to realistically cover his needs. It is best to be absolutely clear that the allowance is to cover particular items and not others. It may, for example, be used to cover the costs of clothing and entertainment but not food and travel; pens and pencils for school but not dinner money. Although weekly pocket money is suitable for small children, adolescents benefit from a monthly or regular allowance. It encourages them to budget and learn about money as well as adding to their self-respect and sense of independence. A bank account not only encourages saving, but also places an adolescent in the adult world. Some parents, if they can afford to do so, suggest to their teenager that they will double whatever he is able to save by a certain time.

It is important that the allowance is presented as regularly and promptly as a wage packet or monthly salary. If a financial crisis hits the family and the allowance can no longer be afforded, then it is only fair to discuss the matter, confiding in the teenagers and helping them to understand the problems involved. It will be an unwelcome stride into adulthood, and one that teenagers would rather put off, but it will nevertheless be a test of maturity and strength of character that may produce positive results. When money is especially scarce, parents' anxiety is increased by the fact that they are unable to give their children enough to cover their needs. They may feel that the risks of teenagers stealing what they want are increased. A hard-up and hard-working mother of four teenagers all living at home told me that her 17-year-old son had been on the dole for a year.

> He always gives me ten pounds a week from his dole money, but the rest never seems to go far and by the end of the week, he's always broke. Because I'm afraid he might go and steal something if he's desperate, like a packet of cigarettes or something, I always try to make sure he has at least some money in his pocket whenever he goes out of the house, even if it's only a couple of pounds.

Parents who feel that their teenager should not receive money unless it is in payment for work done have the difficulty of finding a task and setting a fair price. In *You and Your Adolescent* Dr James Hemming writes:

> Many parents supplement their children's income by paying them something for additional chores. But every member of the family should take a share of the regular chores without payment. No mother should ever let herself become a drudge. It trains the children in thoughtlessness and exploitation and leaves the mother lonely and lost when her services are no longer required.[13]

On the other hand, American psychologist Julia V. Allen advocates a payment for chores system, in which children are awarded a certain number of points for each household chore they perform during the week. At the end of the week, they are rewarded with the relevant amount of money, upon which a maximum has been set. Dr Allen suggests that parents should pay out only when they are satisfied that the job is completed and has been done properly. Until that time, all privileges, including telephoning, television, outings and free time should be suspended, she recommends.

It seems, however, that youngsters are increasingly taking matters into their own hands by finding 'Saturday jobs' or working after school in order to supplement their pocket money. Sometimes they are prompted by their parents. One mother told me:

> I give my daughter ten pounds a week in order to allow her enough to buy clothes and things from the chemist. I still have to help her out with major items of clothing and shoes, but when I learned that she spends about six pounds of her allowance each week on cigarettes, I thought it was about time she found herself a Saturday job. She now earns a basic six pounds working at a hairdressers, so that at least I don't have to fund a habit of which I don't approve!

Nevertheless, as one teenager moaned – having just made one of life's most painful discoveries – 'However much money you have, it never seems to be enough.'

In an attempt to help them 'think before they spend', the BBC School Radio Shop has a series of four programmes, *Value for Money*, available on cassette. Originally prepared for teachers and designed to promote classroom discussion, it can also be put to good use at home.

Parties

'House burned to ground after teenage party' ran the headlines in a local newspaper. Conditioned as we are not to believe everything we read in newspapers, I went along to examine the facts for myself. The story was indeed true. What had once been a very large and expensive house in an exclusive London suburb was now a remnant of twisted metalwork, charred wood and blackened bricks. The owners of the house had gone away for a weekend, leaving their two teenagers, aged 16 and 18, at home. The party itself was not particularly boisterous and all would have been well had it not been for two youngsters who had slipped upstairs to make love in one of the guest bedrooms: a cigarette carelessly placed during the proceedings set the curtains alight and the fire spread to the rest of the house. Mercifully, all the party-goers escaped unhurt, but for the parents it was the beginning of a long nightmare.

Parties can also be a terrifying ordeal for teenagers. Fifteen-year-old Marion M. persuaded her parents to allow her to throw a party while they were out of the house. In the ensuing chaos of the evening the stair bannister was ripped off its base, two doors were broken, and vomit, faeces, spilt drinks, discarded food and cigarette ends covered the furniture and floors. Unable to face the thought of her parents returning to the devastation, Marion went to the family medicine chest and swallowed as many pills as she could find, preferring oblivion to parental fury. Fortunately, a few friends were sober enough to call an ambulance and her life was saved.

One 15-year-old girl told me: 'I'd never give a party in my house because you couldn't relax. You know it's all going to get fucked up.' Others have said: 'I would never give a party if my parents were going to be at home' and 'Getting rid of guests is too difficult'. In a letter to a newspaper a 17-year-old boy wrote: 'There is absolutely no way they [teenagers] should hold parties in their parents' houses' and pointed out that, 'with a bit of organization (and even aid from their parents), they can find a place to call their own, dissolving inhibitions of the "generation gap" and leaving room for enjoyment.'

Most parties attended by adolescents from the age of 15 run on alcohol. Cider and lager form the base of the merriment, but, depending on the amount of money available, there sometimes is wine, and occasionally spirits turn up as a result of a raid on the family liquor supply. The many teenagers to whom I spoke on the subject of parties agreed that they were not places at which to eat. Food tended to provide party-goers with ammunition when the evening livened up: 'If you find food, it usually just gets chucked about.' 'Parties are just somewhere to get nice and pissed and have a good laugh' a 16-year-old boy told me, and his friends generally agreed. One girl described how parties affected her:

When you get pissed – at a time before you actually get sick – you feel happy and can just talk and talk and talk. You seem to have lots of confidence. I can be violent and merry at the same time. It depends on what happens at the party which way I'll turn. Parties are a way of releasing energy. Sometimes I nick things at parties – little things like tapes or something. You see, if the people who own the house don't mean anything to you, you don't care what happens to the place and you don't feel guilty about taking things.

In 1975 James Hemming wrote, 'Meaningless destructiveness is an almost entirely male propensity.'[14] More than a decade later, Dr Hemming agreed with me that, this no longer seems to be the case. Times have changed and 'There are more opportunities for girls to express feelings of aggression. Girls are capable of such dedicated concentration to gain their own emotional ends, and are no longer reticent in achieving those ends by violent means,' he said.

Many of the adolescent girls I interviewed were as delighted as the boys with the prospect of a violent evening – provided of course, that the excitement did not take place in their own homes. Violence is most frequently the product of boredom, frustration and a sense of personal inadequacy. The more teenagers I talked to about parties, (about 100 in all, between the ages of 13 and 16), the more it became apparent that there was a correlation between the less secure, less confident adolescents and parties where mayhem was likely to erupt. Not surprisingly, the idea of going to a party to get drunk appealed most to youngsters in this category.

Of course, it must be said that parties do not spell mayhem for all teenagers, as this extract from a conversation with a Midlands schoolgirl with close family ties and a great deal of self-confidence reveals.

I gave my first party when I was 15. My parents didn't mind what time the party ended, just as long as we turned down the music after ten o'clock. I have always made the rules about my parties because if they come from your parents, it weakens your case. I say, 'You may bring a friend, but if you bring more than one, you don't come in.' I try to use as many rooms as possible because one room gets a bit claustrophobic. I never allow anyone to go into my parents' bedroom though. I just tell them that they have no right in there, and I don't care who it is, if they go in, they will have to leave the party. If my parents come back early and the party is still going on, kids often drift over and talk to them. If the guests won't go, I usually say something

49

like, 'I'm tired – I've got work to do.' Once, my sister got so fed up that she left the room and returned wearing her pyjamas. I've never known anyone smoke dope at a party. One friend asked me if he could smoke some, but I said no, so he didn't.

Guests seem to enjoy the parties and want to come again. I think it helps to organize them carefully. I usually put away anything in the room which might be breakable, not that I don't trust my friends, just that I don't want things broken by mistake. There has to be a high point in the evening though, otherwise people get a bit bored. For my eighteenth birthday, I have put aside thirty pounds for fireworks, and we are going to have a barbecue. We have just bought a video, and this is a great help because it means that if anyone feels bored or lonely during the evening, they can watch the screen, while others can dance or just listen to the music and talk.

Gatecrashers can be a problem, but it's easier for us because we live in a flat. If there is trouble though, I generally ask a couple of friends who are heavy rugger-playing types to deal with it. Sometimes people get drunk, but so far, no one's been sick on the carpet.

However, so dire were the warnings I received from teenagers in general that I was forced to conclude that perhaps the safest solution to the problem of parties lies in never leaving the family home in the charge of youngsters!

Friendships

Very often it seems that a difficult adolescent will compound his or her difficulties by choosing friends who parents believe have the worst possible influence on him. It also often follows that the less secure and confident the youngster is, the more passionate the friendship will be. Rather in the same way that a teenager's bedroom can be seen as a statement, so can his or her friendships.

My best friend is about as different from my parents as you could possibly imagine. She's messy, untidy, rude, uses awful language, smokes dope, gets sick at parties and sometimes steals things, but she's the best friend I've ever had and I love her.

Not infrequently, such a declaration of loyalty, particularly in the case of girls, is reinforced by an attempt at a physical transformation to make herself look like her friend's twin. The transformation itself can present a considerable problem. A head of long, naturally dark, straight hair can be changed to a cropped, permed, brassily bleached blond. When a daughter returns home one day yelling to her mother, 'Be prepared for a shock, Mum', Mum would be wise to take the statement seriously and reach for a chair!

Boys are not immune to the 'twinning' syndrome either, as I discovered for myself when my 16-year-old son turned up one day with the most astonishing hair-do (one could not describe it accurately as a 'cut') I have ever seen. The hair was shorn at the back of the head, while in the front it was brushed forward and hung over his chin, tending to mingle with food and drink. The sides, sticking up in all directions, were carefully held in place with a mixture of soap and gel. I thought the style had to be unique until he brought a school friend to stay wearing the same strange '*coiff*' and a similarly odd collection of designer-torn clothing. It was hard to tell them apart.

In the case of friendships deemed by parents to be 'unsuitable', it is difficult to see what can effectively be done about the problem except to move to the opposite end of the country – and then, of course, there is no guarantee that another, perhaps even more unsuitable, friend will not be found as a substitute! Most parents I talked to about this particular difficulty felt that the best advice was to ensure that all friends were always welcome in the home so that the parents could exercise some moderating influence and enforce the house rules, and have the advantage of knowing that their own teenager was safely under their roof.

In one instance a mother who was particularly concerned about the friendship between her 15-year-old daughter, her daughter's best friend and a 22-year-old man, made it her business to get to know the young man well. She took him into her confidence and appealed to his sense of responsibility with some astonishingly positive results. After a while it became evident that the rather good-natured youth had landed himself with a somewhat unrewarding handful. Being a car driver, the girls used him as a taxi service and called him up day and night to extricate them from numerous scrapes. On one occasion, he intervened on the daughter's behalf when she found herself out of her depth at a party. When a 26-year-old man pressed the girl for her address and phone number, her young protector told him sternly, 'You had better not mess around with that girl; she's only 15.'

Broken romances

The broken romance is a common human experience, and most people manage to survive the terrible feelings of desolation it creates. Parents should take their adolescent's reactions to broken romances seriously and with the utmost sympathy and understanding. Some young people find themselves unable to cope with the extreme emotional upset that can be caused by a shattered romance and need professional counselling to help them through the crisis. Occasionally, depression and anxiety can become so acute that they lead to a suicide attempt (see p. 130).

Special problems

There are certain family situations that tend to make the adolescent more vulnerable – divorce, remarriage and the stepparent relationship, death, serious illness and change of environment for example. Many of these factors are, to some extent, apparent in the case histories in the previous chapter, but it also should be emphasized that problems arising during adolescence are not unique to children in broken homes, nor does divorce or single-parenthood necessarily always create the difficulties. Children are often adversely affected by change, sometimes at apparently the simplest levels; not surprising then that traumatic change often produces traumatic results in a child's behaviour. Gill Gorell Barnes, family therapist and senior social worker in the Department for Children and Parents at the Tavistock Clinic and at the Institute for Family Therapy, suggests in her book, *Working with Families*, that 'more alienation from parents correlated with increased parental and marital difficulty so that it could be argued that the impact of such difficulty "matured" during these early teenage years'.[15]

The effects of divorce

The number of divorces in Britain doubled from 80,000 in 1971 to 157,000 in 1981. In that year 159,000 children under 16 in England and Wales experienced the shock of divorce – and the trend shows no sign of slowing down. It is estimated that 2 million children in the United Kingdom are growing up with parents who are divorced or separated – some in single-parent families and many more in stepfamilies. As divorce occurs in almost one in three families, it may seem commonplace, but to the individuals concerned it is a catastrophe. One of the most immediate effects is isolation – the family turns inward upon itself, as each of the protagonists becomes obsessed by present pain and fear for the future. Anyone who has been through the misery of a divorce knows how difficult it can be to apply a tired and anxious mind to the everyday demands of children. Suddenly, after years of 'putting the children first', a mother may become self-absorbed and distant; a tolerant and kindly father can metamorphose into a tyrannical bully. Often, under great stress, people change, perhaps as a defence, perhaps because the concern for the future is so all-consuming.

Although parents worry and feel intense guilt that their children's lives have been thrown into disorder by their actions, they may not have the necessary mental energy or flexibility to cope with the children's demands. Teenagers who one day will refuse to communicate with their parents on any level, on the very next day will demand their undivided attention and co-operation. But parents cannot always give them the additional reassurance and security they need at such times, because they themselves are so extremely vulnerable. In consequence, adolescents, already in the throes of great physical and mental change and naturally anxious to break away from the pattern of parental care that informed their childhood, may become so insecure that instead of wanting to assert their independence, they cling even more fiercely to the family apron-strings. The more rejected they feel, the more violent will be their attempts to gain the reassurance that they at least are still loved.

Although some people describe the divorce or separation as relatively easy compared to the agonizing conflict that led up to it, others feel that the final break bears all the devastation and finality of death itself. Children drifting about in the wake of the disaster cannot fail to be affected, and the most parents can hope for is that they will recover quickly, since it is in the nature of children to be resilient. Research seems to suggest that only a few will show obvious signs of lasting disturbance and the damage is seldom irreversible, but there is no doubt that during the unstable teenage years the effect of divorce is likely to produce greater anxiety and greater insecurity, which can lead to serious behavioural problems. Divorce is a situation manufactured by the adult world, and if adults find it hard to cope with, how much more so will the teenager, already struggling with a host of his own worries. Most people who work with divorced and separating families recommend an open approach. Youngsters suffer more when they are kept in the dark concerning the breakup of their parents' marriage. They will be well aware of the unhappiness that surrounds an unstable relationship but, not knowing the cause, they may feel themselves in some way to blame. 'It is better to explain to adolescents fully than to cover up' is the advice of a social worker in the field.

In a study of 100 children, the writers Yvette Walzak and Sheila Burns concluded from their research that 'in the long run children's adjustment is significantly influenced by communication and post-divorce, rather than the pre-divorce, relationship with both parents'.[16] Divorced parents who can manage to submerge their differences and work together on behalf of their children do best for them. Courtroom battles, where parental motives become blurred and distorted by bitterness, only add to the children's sense of confusion and disorder. Parents should ask themselves if they are fighting for care and control of the children because they genuinely believe that they can provide the best care for them or, perhaps motivated by revenge, they want to prevent their ex-partner from gaining access at all possible cost irrespective of the children's needs.

Because isolation and lack of communication within the family following divorce can add to the distress of the parents and make the children more prone to serious behaviour disorders (for example, 60 per cent of referrals to the Brookside Family Consultation Clinic in Cambridge are children experiencing the effects of divorce, separation and custody conflict), sympathetic and objective advice from outside the family could help to reduce conflict and build a firm base for a new future.

The single-parent family

An American family therapist, Marion Walters, has argued a strong case in favour of the single-parent family in general. Since mother and father frequently disagree as to how their children should be brought up, she regards the single voice of authority as a positive advantage in many cases. Carolyn Douglas, family therapist and founder of Exploring Parenthood (see pp. 75, 219–20), supports this argument to a certain extent, as a result of personal experience. The mother of three children, she found herself in the role of a single parent when her husband's work took him to France for a year. She told me:

> During that time, my word became law. When my husband is at home, I usually refer to him if there is an argument – 'we'll see what your father thinks', or 'yes, you may stay out late if your father agrees'. While he was away for that year it was almost a relief to be able to rely on my own judgement. I think the girls (aged 15 and 16) benefited too from our cosy evenings together, which tended to be relaxed and centred around them rather than their father.

On the other hand, Mrs Douglas felt that the already heightened sexual tension that exists within families with adolescents becomes more problematical for single parents.

It seems, too, that even where relationships between teenager and parent are exceptionally hostile, it is more difficult for the youngster to break away and become independent. Up until the age of 17, Sam's relationship with his mother had been loving and friendly. As the only child, he felt a great sense of responsibility for her. When it came to the time that he wanted to move away from home to share a flat with some friends, he could not bring himself to make the break because he felt guilty about leaving his mother. He was especially anxious about leaving her alone in the house at night. He solved the problem in his own way by bringing friends home after parties equipped with sleeping bags in order that they might spend what was left of the night in his room. Excluded from the scene, his mother lay awake listening to sounds of merriment and what she assumed to be sexual activity. Far from feeling happy that her son had returned home to be with her, his presence served merely to increase her sense of loneliness and isolation. He became angry and frustrated and their relationship deteriorated to such an extent that Sam's mother sought professional help.

In talking to single mothers during my research I found that it was not unusual to be told: 'Children really do need a father, you know, especially when they become teenagers.' These are the parents who, in times of crisis or stress, find that their situation is worsened by not having a partner with whom to share the burden. They feel that with the benefit of a partner to share the difficulties, a tense and stormy relationship might have been defused more easily.

A mother whose teenage son was 'the kind of boy who would set fire to the furniture or break a window if he had a mind to' would, in moments of anger and frustration, set off in her car and 'drive for miles and miles' until she thought he would have left the house. If, on returning, she found him still at home, she would drive away again until she felt the tension disappear. 'It was on those occasions,' she said, 'that I wished there had been someone to leave him with. Even though I had to escape from him, there was always the feeling that he might do something irresponsible.'

Although in the majority of cases the single parent is a mother, many fathers raise their children alone and face similar problems. Indeed, their problems may be greater because our society still does not condition or prepare men for a parental role in the same way as it does women, and is not organized to help them in the same way. Although there are many agencies, organizations and informal groups designed to help the single parent, they are usually directed at women, and a single father must first find them and then overcome any prejudice he encounters simply because he is a man.

Research based on information gained by the National Council for One-parent Families shows that, as a general rule, the problems concerning adolescent children are common to all families, whether the parents are single or partnered, mothers or fathers. Nevertheless, it is found that the greatest concern of most single parents is poverty and this concern becomes all the more acute during the children's teenage years, when the demand for clothes, entertainment and travel expenses reaches its peak. Tension between parent and adolescent can be greatly increased: on the one hand, a parent has the feeling of having failed to provide adequately for his or her children's needs, while the youngsters feel deprived and resentful beside the relative affluence of the peer group. It is true that more single mothers in the 1980s work full time than in previous years, but, nevertheless, about 50 per cent of all lone parents depend on supplementary benefit as their sole source of income and currently this is at subsistence level. While contributions are made towards rent and rates, deductions are made against earnings and maintenance payments.

The current lack of jobs for school leavers is a particular problem for single parents already caught in the poverty trap.

Discipline (see pp. 26–7) is seen as a particular problem by many single parents. Although it could be argued that the role of the father as family disciplinarian is stereotypic and somewhat old-fashioned, it is nevertheless a great relief for a tired mother at the end of a bad day to be able to say: 'Your son has been impossible. He's sworn at me, refused to do his homework, plugged the cat into the electric light socket and burnt a hole in the sofa with one of your best cigars. Will you please go and deal with him!' Whether or not the father is actually perceived by the family as the main arbiter of discipline is not so much the issue as the fact that after a day's absence, and unaffected by the current family arguments and tensions, he will be in a better position to arbitrate in the situation than a mother who has been at home and constantly involved in the quarrel. It is this relief of being able to throw the burden of quarrels or disciplinary action on to the shoulders of an understanding partner, even for a short while, and then to be able to share and discuss the decisions involved that single parents often feel they miss.

Psychologist James Hemming maintains that 'In single-parent families, even more than in the other kind, discipline in adolescence depends on co-operation, not domination.'[17] He cites homework as a particular area of conflict, and suggests that 'the best solution is for the parent to share the adolescent's feelings on the matter and then to arrive at a sensible arrangement for dealing with homework.'

Without the teenager's co-operation, however, it must be said that no amount of nagging by the parent will force a textbook to be opened or a sentence to be written. Then, it may well be the time to adopt the recommendation of American psychologists, Robert and Jean Bayard, themselves parents of five teenagers. They recommend that, having attempted to discuss a problem with their youngsters and having pointed out the dangers and pitfalls involved in not following a certain path, if parents are still met with a stubborn wall of non-cooperation, they should try to relax and allow the teenagers to take responsibility for their own lives. The Bayards have much sound and sympathetic advice to offer in their book *Help! I've Got a Teenager! A Survival Guide for Desperate Parents*.

On the other hand, there is a limit to the amount of responsibility young teenagers can handle and the law is very clear as to the responsibility of the parents during this youthful period (see Chapter 6).

The stepfamily

In 'The Adolescent as Problem, Patient or Therapist?'[18] A. I. Cooklin lists eight factors – which I have expanded on below – that either singly or in combination can increase the problems of a teenager in a stepfamily.

1. Dealing with loss. Not all stepfamilies are brought together by a previous divorce. The loss may have involved the death of one parent and subsequent remarriage of the other. In a divorce situation, whichever parent leaves the family home without the children is in a sense 'lost' to them. In the former case a stepparent may find it easier to establish a close relationship with the teenager whereby he or she becomes a substitute for the lost parent, but in the case of divorce, where the natural parent is seen on a regular basis, there is the problem of divided loyalties.

2. Divided loyalties. Although some stepparents are fortunate in being able to form a loving relationship with their stepchild or stepchildren, most find it extremely difficult. Even when the potential for a close relationship exists, with evidence of fondness for each other shown on both sides, there will more often than not be a reserve on the part of the teenager, which may be impossible to break through. The teenager may find that he or she relates better to a stepparent than the natural parent, but to admit it or to show it by demonstrative affection is tantamount to admitting that 'I love you better than I love my mother/father.' When it comes to the problem of divided loyalties, parents themselves are often guilty of increasing their children's burden by complaining with great bitterness about the shortcomings of their erstwhile partner – once loved, but who by now may be seen as a deadly rival for the children's affections.

3. Where do I belong? In a stepfamily, youngsters may have to adapt in ways that are particularly difficult for them. A 15-year-old boy used to being the oldest of three siblings, let us say, now has to make way for an older stepbrother and a new baby. He may feel isolated and disregarded.

4. Membership in two households. Every household has its traditions and regulations. The stepfather or -mother, stepbrothers and -sisters bring their own set of traditions to bear in the teenager's life at the very time that he is trying to develop a life of his own. If both mother and father have remarried, an adolescent may also have the additional confusion of having to adapt to living conditions in two stephouseholds.

5. Unreasonable expectations. Perhaps the most unreasonable expectation of all is that in these difficult circumstances parents should expect their children to behave reasonably and without complaint.

6. Fantasies of natural parents remaining. It is not uncommon for couples contemplating remarriage soon after a divorce to delay marriage or living together 'for the sake of the children'. One couple to whom I spoke had lived apart for two years before they brought the family under one roof. A year after living together in the same house they finally married. Their reason was given to me by the mother:

> We thought that if we gave the children of both our previous marriages (five in all) a breathing space, they would have time to get over the shock of the separation period and divorce. It would also, we hoped, give them time to get used to the idea of us as a couple. Unfortunately, two years later, when we bought our house, there was a hold-up over the divorce proceedings. We decided to live together anyway, but we were worried that the older children (13 and 15 years) would be upset and embarrassed that we were unmarried. In the end I think we probably prolonged their agony. I couldn't understand at first why my son and daughter seemed so unhappy about my remarriage after such a long period of time. When I questioned them separately they both came up with more or less the same answer: 'But Mum, don't you see that while you weren't actually married, there was always the chance that you and Dad would get together again.'

7. Guilt over causing the divorce. One of the saddest and most common factors involved in divorce is that teenagers, who are capable of reasoning and have an understanding that is part adult yet still part child, blame themselves for somehow causing their parents divorce.

8. For adolescents, there are the additional problems associated with identity and sexuality.

The following two case histories illustrate some of the problems associated with setting up stepfamilies.

When Katrina married Jack Martin, five children, four boys and one girl, were brought together to form the stepfamily. Jack's sons, Tom, Mark and Joe, were 15, 13 and 6 respectively; Katrina's daughter, Deborah, was 13 and her son, Bill, 11 years old. Deborah and Bill lived with their mother and stepfather, while Jack's three sons lived close by with their mother and were frequent and regular visitors to the new home. From the start the boys accepted and adapted to the changes without any obvious signs of difficulty. Deborah, however, tried every means at her disposal (and there were many) to break the bonds that seemed to hold her mother and stepfather so closely together. She played her natural father off against her mother with consummate skill. 'I hold things back – store them up – and wait for the right moment when I know they are likely to hurt the most,' she told her mother with extreme frankness.

At home and at school (from which she was twice suspended) Deborah's behaviour was aggressive, disruptive and uncooperative. She disassociated herself from her stepbrothers, refusing to eat with them or remain in the same room. She refused to speak to her stepfather and verbally abused her mother with as much vehemence and foul language as she could muster. She wore thick make-up, a leather micro-skirt and black fishnet stockings and frequently disappeared in the evenings. When she returned late at night, she would not say where she had been. She painted her bedroom black, created a slum of dirty clothes, cigarette butts, rotting food and an occasional used tampon or sanitary towel. Any attempt by her mother to make a path through the mess was greeted with torrents of abuse and finally this message written in bright red paint across the blackened front of the bedroom door: PISS OFF MOTHER. Mrs Martin remembers:

> My daughter was definitely not easy to live with. Nevertheless, we recognized her intolerable behaviour as a cry for help and there was nothing we could do but hold tight and ride out the storm. My husband, infinitely supportive and patient, decided to maintain a low profile after the first 'Don't tell me what to do; you're not my fucking father.' I, on the other hand, tried to show Deborah in a variety of ways that she was still loved and wanted as much as ever and that I would never give up on her, no matter how cruel or outrageous her behaviour. After three years of hard work and heartbreak there were

the first signs of a truce: the vacuum appeared voluntarily in her
bedroom one day; on another, a white duvet cover was constructed
out of an old sheet; on another, a red mattress was placed on the floor
as a sofa, and a matching red beanbag was requested. School reports
were returned with encouraging comments: 'Some hard work at last!'
and later, 'Excellent work'. A pleated skirt was worn on a school
outing and the colour of the hair was changed from bright orange to a
relatively acceptable black. A Saturday job was obtained and the
work taken seriously and without complaint. Progress was slow and
there was much backsliding but we felt that at last there was a more
confident girl in the making.

One of our main problems was to make sure that the boys did not
suffer as a result of Deborah's overweening demands for attention.
We tended to make something of a joke of her behaviour to them,
taking them into our confidence. We never allowed her to come
between them and any promised outing or treat. She has remained
close to her brother, however, and he admires her greatly. I try to
spend a lot of time with him to make sure that he does not feel left out
but we have been told by his teacher that the seeds of rebellion are
already showing signs of taking root. If we are in for trouble from him
in the future, it will be entirely different and there's no point
anticipating it.

Mrs Martin's story suggests how extremely difficult discipline and family
rule-making can become in a stepfamily. In this case Deborah's stepfather
felt that the best line of defence was withdrawal rather than attack, but he
managed to place all his strength behind his wife so that no matter how
miserable and desperate she became, she could at least rely on his support
and advice. Deborah was almost 16 before her behaviour began to show
signs of improvement. In some families such fierce rebellion might well have
destroyed the marriage; certainly Deborah had high hopes of achieving such
an end.

Robert Jones and Mary Fielding were less fortunate. Four years after
separating from previous spouses and setting up a new home with the
intention of getting married when their divorces became absolute, Mary
decided that their relationship had suffered irrevocably as a direct result of
differences between the two families. From the outset Robert's three young
adolescents – the 'visitors' to the home – were so hostile that Mary found it
impossible to communicate with them. Eventually, she felt that it was better
for all concerned if the visits ceased. Instead, Robert alone took them out

each weekend and away for longer periods during the holidays. Far from relieving the tension, this arrangement seemed to increase it as Mary found herself becoming resentful of the time Robert spent away from her. Although he had formed a happy relationship with her children, Mary felt that he was dominated by an ex-wife and teenagers who could not bring themselves to address her. 'I lost respect for him,' she said. 'It did not seem right that he should always be at the beck and call of his ex-wife. I somehow felt cheated. I certainly would not contemplate marriage now.'

Generally speaking, it is found that the younger the children at the time the stepfamily is formed, the better the chance of their making a successful relationship with the stepparent. Boys seem to find it easier to manage their mother's new relationship than do adolescent girls;[19] but Elizabeth Hodder, founder of Stepfamily, The National Stepfamily Association and author of *The Step-parents' Handbook*, advises stepfathers that

> stepchildren can show delayed reactions to the hurt they experienced earlier in their lives and this can lead them to behave in the most disturbing way just when you as a stepfather feel you are making real progress with the relationship and deserve some reward for your efforts. You must console yourself that they would be behaving in this way whether you were behaving badly or well towards them and that your job is not to take personal offence at their behaviour but to turn a blind eye. Be patient and positive.[20]

She also advises stepmothers:

> If you have inherited an impossibly disruptive stepchild and he or she is old enough (16 +), your husband and you may quite reasonably and properly decide that they would be better off – and so would you and the rest of the family – if they left home. There is nothing more soul-destroying than trying to mould the rest of the family around a disturbed teenager's wilful and persistent destructiveness. Much will depend on the circumstances as to what alternatives are available in terms of local authority provision, local hostels or friends and relatives, but if your family's survival depends on this break, then it is not selfish to consider it.[21]

The circumstances surrounding divorce and remarriage leave children with a strong sense of having been rejected, even if it is not true. One parent, for whatever reason, leaves the family home: the children wonder what they may have done to provoke such a drastic action. One or perhaps both parents' attention is focused on another partner: the children feel left out and unwanted. Researchers are unanimous in their findings that this sense of rejection plays a major role in aggressive behaviour. In these circumstances it is difficult to overestimate a teenager's capacity for hatred. Teenage girls particularly find it hard to come to terms with a stepparent. Horror stories abound. In one instance a psychologist, whose patient was the distressed mother of two sisters, aged 13 and 15, described how the girls had planned a long campaign of hatred to oust their stepfather from the home. Sadly, they finally succeeded after they cut up and tore to shreds every single item of clothing in his wardrobe.

If a stepfamily is under siege and relationships are seriously threatened by the actions of unhappy children, it is time to seek help both for their sakes and the sake of the harrassed and despairing adults.

Coping with death

Phillip Johnson lost his wife, Miriam, and his 11-year-old son, Paul, in a car crash six years ago. His daughter, Jane, aged 13, survived, but her best friend was crushed to death. Fortunately, as he says himself, he was working at his office when the accident took place:

> Had I been driving, I think I should have been a very different man today. As it was, I decided to carry on without seeking professional help, but perhaps should not have been able to do so without the assistance of many friends and acquaintances who responded to my loss in quite remarkable ways. I had more support from the pub than the pulpit – probably because I spent more time in the pub than I should have done at that stage where drinking partners became surprisingly compassionate friends.

Phillip's first priority was how to tell his daughter, then in hospital with a broken pelvis and cracked ribs, that her mother and brother were not going to survive. Both were in intensive care in the same hospital. 'I felt instinctively that it was best to talk about death with Jane from the outset,' he remembers. 'I began slowly by warning her that her mother and brother were seriously ill and that we had to face the fact that they might not survive. My wife was the first to die, then my son a couple of days later.' Phillip feels that children are remarkably clear-sighted and practical about death. When he told Jane about the loss of her mother, she asked 'Why has she died?' He replied, 'Perhaps God needed her now,' to which Jane responded, 'But so do we!' Phillip thinks that his daughter's practical, down-to-earth nature helped her to come to terms with her loss. About ten days after the accident she asked her father whether he had written to Paul's school 'to tell them he won't be coming back this term'.

Phillip says,

> My advice to parents who find themsevles in this awful situation is, while your judgement is so off-balance, don't make any major changes initially. Keep things as normal as possible. Jane pretty much directed me into maintaining our way of life by telling me that if ever I sold our house, she would take it as an indication that I no longer loved her mother. As it was, I found a curious comfort in doing the housework and the cooking. It was a challenge to keep the home going, and I was determined not to turn Jane into a 'mother substitute'.
>
> I think it is important to tell youngsters that other people are missing the dead as well as just the members of their immediate family. For me, the most difficult thing to handle was not so much telling Jane that her mother and brother had died, but meeting my son's friends after the event. One of the worst moments was when his best friend came round to the house for the first time. This boy and I have felt bound to each other ever since. I was very close to Paul and I miss him almost more intensely as the years go by. Had he lived, he would be a teenager now, and we could have done so much together. The friendship which has built up between Jane and myself, though, is perhaps even greater than it would have otherwise been; it's a bit like the difference in the relationship between battlefield comrades and the friendship of raw recruits who have seen no action.

Jane's aunt, Christine (her mother's sister), has fulfilled the role of a mother figure. She herself was 14 when her own mother died and it took a year before her father could bring himself to tell his children of his wife's death. She was either 'ill, convalescing in the country' or 'staying with an aunt', but never dead. Jane's uncle was 6 at the time, and in retrospect feels that the prolonged delay in telling him and his sisters of their mother's death did him a great deal of harm. He finds it 'abnormally hard to trust people in adult life'. Christine says that her experience of loss as a child has been invaluable in helping and supporting Jane through such a difficult period. She looks after her niece, together with her own children, during the holidays while Phillip works.

As for the future, Phillip is soon to remarry, which will mean Jane sharing her home with a stepbrother. Their relationship to date has been wary, but Phillip expresses more concern about his own reaction towards the boy, than his daughter's. 'We get on very well as a rule,' he said, 'but sometimes, when I'm angry with him, I have to bite back unjust words such as, "Paul wouldn't have done that."' Although Jane and her stepbrother-to-be do not appear unhappy about the new family arrangements, Phillip and his fiancée are acutely aware of the difficulties involved for the future.

When a member of the family dies, the bereaved unite in their grief and gather together in order to support each other through the period of mourning, but as in divorce – which is after all, bereavement in another form – there is a tendency for the grieving parent to withdraw and thereby inadvertently leave the children to cope with their confused emotions on their own. Dr Dora Black, a consultant child psychiatrist who specializes in the problems of the bereaved, explains:

> A death in the family is a frightening and unnerving experience for a
> child. To prevent it forming the basis for future problems, the child
> will need help in understanding his loss and in expressing his grief.
> Although the adult instinct is to protect him, the truth (in manageable
> doses) is the wisest course . . . For children, the conspiracy of silence
> can be bewildering and frightening. They find themselves alone with a
> tearful, withdrawn parent whom they cannot contact or comfort and
> who no longer appears to meet their needs . . . when they grow up,
> bereaved children are twice as likely to develop depressive illnesses
> needing psychiatric treatment as people from intact families . . .
> Adolescents should rarely be denied access to a dying parent but again
> must be prepared – preferably by the family doctor – for what they
> will experience and given repeated opportunities to ask questions and
> make sense of their experiences.[22]

In 1985 Dr Viera Bailey of the West Middlesex Hospital told an international conference on bereavement at Royal Holloway College that she was surprised how often parents failed to inform the school when there had been a death in the family. In several cases schools had referred children to her for seemingly inexplicable behavioural problems and it had emerged that teaching staff had not been told about a death, or, in some cases, a long illness preceding a death.

> Parents coping with their own grief often deny that children are
> affected. Children react to loss very like adults and it is important that
> schools are informed of a death; but the majority of bereaved children

do achieve a normal adjustment and are certainly less disturbed than children of families where there is severe marital discord.

However painful it may be for parents to bring to the school's attention the fact that problems at home may be the cause of their child's erratic behaviour, Dr Bailey emphasizes the importance of communicating with the school particularly in times of family crisis. Very often, the behaviour that is cause for concern at school may not be evident at home.

Because of the volatile nature of adolescence, it sometimes happens that the pain of loss, dulled for a while, re-emerges at a time of crisis – typically in consequence of a broken romance or pressures from exams. A bereavement counsellor told me that in her experience young people responded very quickly to counselling. They seem able, she said, to express their feelings in such an honest and forthright way that it is easier to get to the root of their problem. She had recently visited Mary, a 16-year-old girl, whose best friend had been killed instantly in a road accident. Mary had been walking back from school with a small group of friends. As they prepared to cross a road, her friend, who was standing beside her, stepped out a little ahead of the others and was hit by a car. Mary herself was slightly hurt and required a couple of days in hospital. Once home, although she was willing to return to school. Mary refused to accept invitations or leave the house to spend time with her schoolmates for any social occasions. It was as though she had resolved to block all the fun from her life.

Her parents consulted their GP, who suggested that they try bereavement counselling before the situation became more serious. After only three visits from the counsellor, the crisis passed and Mary resumed her normal, busy social life. The counsellor said,

> She seemed to need permission to start going out again. She remembered vividly the terrible thud of her friend's body against the car and felt terribly guilty – 'Why did it have to be Sally and not me who died?' was the question which concerned her most. After talking in great detail about the incident, about her friend and about her feelings, it was possible to reassure her and give her the 'permission' she seemed to crave.

Long-term and terminal illness

If an adolescent has an illness that, while not terminal, keeps him or her confined to bed or home for more than a few days, parents will find that their child's problems will be more than just the obvious physical ones.

Even while he is too ill to do anything, a normally active and sociable young person may well feel frustrated at missing his normal round of activities. If it takes him a substantial time – several months, say – to fully recover, he may worry about falling behind at school and become increasingly restless, which may result in aggressive behaviour or depression. If he was unable to receive visits from his friends and has been restricted to the company of a very few people, he may seem to become unnaturally shy when his recovery is completed. A young person, particularly one in the early stages of adolescence, who has been isolated in this way may find suddenly returning to a busy and crowded school overwhelming. He may fear that his friends have 'forgotten' him or, if he was just starting at a new school, find it difficult to make new friends.

Parents can help by being aware of these problems and taking steps to alleviate them. They can, for example, consult the headteacher and the education welfare officer for help and advice about missed schooling and home tuition (see pp. 164–5) if appropriate. As soon as the child is well enough, parents should encourage his friends to visit so that he can regain his social confidence.

Perhaps there is no greater tragedy for parents than to have their child become terminally ill. Increasingly, children with terminal cancer and, to a lesser extent, those with other incurable cardiac, respiratory and renal illnesses are living out their final days or months at home rather than in a hospital. However, no matter how devoted they are, some adults cannot care for a child in a critical condition. They may need the resources or prefer the security of the hospital and its staff. But for those who feel they can cope, research has shown that the rewards to both family and patient can be great and can even lessen the trauma of death when it comes.

Dr Ida Martinson, professor and chairman of family health-care nursing at the University of California, has conducted a study for the American National Cancer Institute to determine whether home care for the terminally ill was both feasible and desirable. Talking about her research in 1985, she said:

> We tend to think that doctors in hospitals can do better, but there is no way that we, as health professionals, can compete with the quality of individualized personal care. A parent knows if the child prefers a red ice-lolly to an orange one. A parent will not just bring a lemonade to the child – she will bundle that child up and take him to the drink stand.

Dr Martinson made it clear that essential to the success of care at home is round-the-clock availability of competent, sensitive support, most often from nurses, but also from social workers, therapists, counsellors, home health aides and clergy. Parents have to learn to perform certain medical procedures as well as providing emotional support for the child. The option of readmission to the hospital must also be kept open.

Whether a terminally ill child is cared for at home or in a hospice or hospital, parents and siblings will also need counselling and help to cope with the illness and their ultimate loss.

Loners, bullies and the bullied

The ability to make friends comes so easily to some, yet for others it remains an elusive and seemingly unattainable quality. It is estimated that about one child in ten has difficulty in making friends. When asked why they thought some people found it hard to make friends and were often cruelly shunned, a group of teenagers gave two main reasons: 'Some kids try too hard and in the wrong way, while others don't bother to try at all and are exceptionally quiet.' In the first instance they cited examples of someone who 'arrives on the scene, barges in and won't go away' or 'thinks he is so big – he tries to dress and act like the boys who are really important and just makes a fool of himself', behaviour of which girls could also be guilty.

In the second instance the teenagers said sometimes the problem was the parents, and cited the example of a girl they knew:

> She's quite a nice girl really, but so subdued. Her mother doesn't allow her to eat sweets, watch television or go out. She did have a friend once, but the mother didn't like her and wouldn't have her in the house, so they had to meet secretly after school in the park. It was too difficult after a while – the friend got bored and gave up.

It can be almost as painful for parents to witness their child's isolation as it is for the child to experience rejection. Helping a young person to make friends is not easy, but according to James Hemming, 'Such young people can nearly always be helped to escape from their social isolation if someone cares enough and patiently helps to build their social confidence. It must be positive help; chivvying and criticism only make things worse.'

Counselling may be helpful, but since friendship begins at home perhaps the most effective way to break the pattern of loneliness is to encourage a child to bring friends home. Teenagers are often at a loose end and enjoy a place to meet after school. Some parents are unwilling to allow such meetings in their homes and, although this alone will not ensure friendships, a child who can offer a base may find it an asset. Parents have to maintain a balance between being careful that the hospitality is not abused and that the visitors do not get out of hand, and remaining unobtrusively in the background. Teenagers whose parents insist on 'joining in the fun' are likely to withdraw into their shells in embarrassment. They must have the encouragement but also the freedom to develop social relationships in their own way.

The problem of friendlessness is linked to the problem of bullying, as the same kind of children are often the victims. The girls and boys most likely to be bullied are those who are regarded as not 'fitting in'. They may be considered too pacific, too studious, too pretty, too smartly dressed, prim, spoilt, nervous, quiet or timid. Bullying can range from verbal harrassment and intimidation to physical assault, and may be more difficult for parents to discover if the child is at boarding rather than day school. Generally, boys are more likely than girls to be involved in bullying – on both the giving and receiving end – and tend to attack their victims verbally or physically, while girls tend to ostracize them.

'Swots' have always been a prime target for bullies. Glenn Turner paints a bleak picture of the pupil who is working hard to pass his exams and please the teacher. If he is to escape bullying from the 'dossers' – children who spend their time 'messing around', disrupting lessons and doing the minimum of work – he must find a way to disguise the fact that he is working so hard. Turner discovered that in an effort to solve this problem some pupils tried to build up a reputation for being carefree and enjoying themselves and then studied at home in secret; others worked hard in class as a rule, but occasionally participated enthusiastically in bouts of 'messing about'; while still others found scapegoats among their classmates, labelling them swots for fear of being so described themselves.

Glenn Turner expressed his concern to me that 'so many parents strongly push their children to do well academically but forget that at the same time they must learn how to fit in and get along with the peer group.' His advice to parents whose children are being bullied is first to talk through the problems with the child and see if there is any way in which they can help. If the bullying persists, parents should make a strong representation to the headteacher. In *most* schools bullying, when it is detected, is treated as a serious offence worthy of the severest punishment; in *some* schools, teachers turn a blind eye. James Hemming's view is that:

> in cases of bullying at school it is, of course, always wise to talk the matter over with the headmaster, tutor, school counsellor or whoever else knows all the children concerned. The aim should not be to get

the bullies punished, which may only make matters worse, but to get the whole relational situation studied and worked through. The causes of bullying are complicated: a school that has a bullying problem has a good deal more to attend to than the suppression of a few individuals. Just as happy boys aren't too often bullies, so happy schools don't often have problems of bullying.[23]

If the head's response is 'I'm afraid there's very little we can do about the problem. I suggest a transfer to another school', parents should take their complaint to a higher authority.

Young people to whom I spoke who had been victims of bullying, particularly at the time of transfer to senior school, indicated that they had coped with the problem in their own way. At the first sign of trouble they went out of their way to cultivate the friendship of someone considered by all to be 'tough, hard and not someone to mess about with'. Some of the smaller boys, who felt themselves to be more vulnerable because of their size, made sure that they found a larger, stronger 'protector', even though the relationship might have placed them in a position of subservience. Not everyone was in favour of asking their parents for help. 'If you're being bullied, it's very difficult to ask anyone to help you, because if it were known that you had sneaked, the bullying would probably be made worse. I wouldn't dare tell my parents; they'd almost certainly interfere,' one youngster confided.

It is just as distressing for caring parents to find out that their child is a bully rather than a victim, and their initial reaction may be anger and revulsion. They have to overcome these feelings in order to help their child, whose aggression is often an indication of deeper problems. Like their victims, many bullies are children who don't seem to 'fit in', in this case perhaps because they feel inadequate socially, physically or academically. Their behaviour may be a way of attacking those who reject them and at the same time a means of gaining acceptance with another group. Parents need to talk to their children to try to get to the root of the problem, and may need to seek counselling through the school or independently (see Chapter 7).

Adoption and adolescence

Dr Michael Humphrey has stated:

It could be maintained that adopters are commonly more anxious in the parental role and would therefore be more inclined to seek advice early in the child's life. Our findings showed that, on the contrary, adopted children were more likely to be seen for the first time at the approach or onset of puberty than were children brought up by their own parents. This bears out the common assumption that the real difficulties of adoptive parenthood do not become manifest until adolescence.[24]

Of course, one might also add that the 'real difficulties' of parenthood in general do not become manifest until adolescence. No large-scale study has proved conclusively that adopted children as a whole are more prone than children who live with their natural parents to be emotionally disturbed. However, because adolescence involves the quest for identity, it seems reasonable to suggest that adoptees are going to find the process of adolescence that much more difficult; but as with all teenagers, their passage to adulthood will depend to a large extent on the relationship that exists with their parents, adoptive or otherwise.

Dr F. H. Stone, former consultant in child psychiatry at the Royal Hospital for Sick Children in Glasgow, writing about the problems of identity experienced in adolescence by adopted children, says:

When there are emotional problems, really basic problems connected with identification, something is likely to happen. Instead of the young person playing at roles, he may very actively take on a particular favoured role, which he then proceeds to live, and this role tends to be the one least in favour with the parents or other adults who care for this young person.

And so we see again and again in our clinics the parents of teenagers who come to us in utter despair and say 'Not only are we worried about this child, but the very thing we have always been most afraid of: that's what he is doing.' If that was drugs, then it's drugs; if promiscuity, then it's promiscuity; if failure to learn, then it's failure to learn. How does the young person isolate exactly the area of parental concern which is likely to be most effectively attacked? I don't know, but he does. This, psychologist Erik Erikson . . ., calls a 'negative identity'. One can readily appreciate the relevance of this to the adoptive situation, because here we see the danger, in the confusion or embarrassment of explaining to the child about the natural mother or father, of denigrating them either as people who abandoned him, who did not care for him, or who had certain attributes of personality or behaviour; the danger here is that this will backlash, and later on, especially in adolescence, this is precisely the mode of behaviour which the child adopts in his 'negative identity'.

Erikson also makes one other observation which I suggest is highly relevant to adoption, and that is by showing in his case studies how important it is for the adolescent to know about the past in order to plan the future. Where the past is a void, there is an inability to make decisions about the future, and the teenager just drifts. It is not that he looks at the occupation, interests, or personality traits of the parents or grandparents, and then says 'That's what I'm *not* going to do or be.' Sometimes boys and girls produce the most elegant compromises between their wishes for themselves and the actual traditional occupations or interests in their families. But where there is no past, the adolescent often seems to lack a signpost to the future.[25]

Cults

For unhappy teenagers who may have great difficulty in identifying with their parents or peer group and in consequence feel lonely and alienated, the idea of the cult can be an attractive one. The more impressionable and psychologically vulnerable they are at the time, the more chance they have of falling into the hands of a cult figure who demands total devotion and absolute, unquestioning obedience; who may also deny access to their parents and former friends; and who may exploit them through unpaid employment and poor working conditions. According to Deo Gloria Outreach, a Kent-based organization that helps parents whose children have been 'lost' to a cult, 'Given the right circumstances, a condition which varies according to an individual's character, sophisticated mind control techniques will work on *anyone*, even those who think they are immune.'

The Unification Church, or 'Moonies', are one of the most publicized of these cults; they are also one of the most highly organized and successful in terms of recruitment, both in Britain and in the United States. The fact that a young person is being approached by a cult member intent on winning him or her over is by no means always obvious. It is a case where to be 'forewarned' does not necessarily mean to be 'forearmed'. The Unification Church, for example, has at least 115 pseudonyms with very plausible 'fronts'.

Dr Eli Shapiro of Boston University Medical Center in Massachusetts writes:

> Adolescents in their formative years have been especially susceptible and, as a result, the futures of many young people have been devastated. Such teenagers are lured into destructive cults by

behaviour modification and mind control techniques which result in depersonalization and complete mental and physical control by the leaders. This leads to a marked change in the personality and lifestyle of the individual, who becomes dependent on and subservient to his leader. In most cases denouncement of, as well as separation from, the family follows entry into a destructive cult, resulting in great emotional turmoil.[26]

Opinions may vary as to what constitutes a 'destructive cult' but Dr Shapiro defines its characteristics as follows:

1. Demands complete obedience to and subservience to one individual, who purports to be God, the Messiah or some form of, or a messenger of, the deity.
2. Requires separation from society. Association with non-members is discouraged, except to gain money or to proselytize.
3. Discourages any form of self-development. Education is scorned and the self-image is totally destroyed.
4. Teaches hatred of parents, organized religion and, sometimes, the (US) government.
5. Does not have concern for the material body; feels only the soul is important.
6. Takes all material possessions (past, present and future) for its own use. Members are not permitted to own anything in their own names.
7. Makes it almost impossible for a member to leave, either through physical restraints or psychologic fears.
8. Maintains the member in a 'brainwashed' state through destructive behaviour modification techniques.[27]

Using the Unification Church as an example of pernicious cult activity, Michael Eidel of Cornell University, Ithaca, New York, offered the following advice to students and parents in the *Cornell Daily Sun* in 1982:

They were bound to show up sometime and now, under the not-well-enough-known cover name of CARP (Collegiate Association for the Research of Principles), Unification Church members have set up camp in Ithaca. The debate concerning cults usually embodies questions such as 'Aren't all religions cults?' or 'Don't parents, teachers and media engage in the same type of indoctrination/brainwashing?' or 'Doesn't everyone have the right to freedom of speech?' But questions of merit about a particular philosophy and of freedom of speech are subordinate to the central issue; we must examine the methods with which a group operates. My emphasis is on community awareness rather than on the question of whether or not cults should be outlawed. The only person who can outlaw cults for him or herself is that individual. As is the case with anyone or any group claiming to have new answers and unbounded love for you, all of us – all potential victims – must think critically and be aware. Beware of any new acquaintance who invites you to a group dinner where you will be sure to meet 'many interesting and loving people'. Beware of people who express scepticism about the goodness of your family and/or friends: people the sceptic does not even know. Beware of invitations to isolated weekend workshops with nebulous goals. These workshops involve sleep and food deprivation, hyperactivity, constant peer pressure and bombardment of the groups' doctrine. And, most of all, realize that at times when you or a friend are in states of temporary depression, you are especially vulnerable to cult deception.[28]

Mr S. is an active member of FAIR (Family Action Information and Rescue, see p. 79). He and his wife were anxious to publicize their experience in order to encourage and give hope to the many families who have suffered or are suffering from the loss of a child to a so-called 'destructive' sect. For the most part, however, parents are concerned to guard the secrecy of their actions during the course of the prolonged and delicate negotiations involved in rescuing offspring, who are frequently most unwilling to co-operate. Mr and Mrs S.'s son, Timothy, a university student, was on holiday with a friend in the United States when they were both befriended by members of the Unification Church. For almost a month they heard no mention of the Church or the cult's leader, the Reverend Sun Myung Moon, and by the time they did, the process of indoctrination was well under way. Typically, the young men had been isolated from the community at large and each other in a camp in Boonville. They were kept short of food and sleep, and subjected to a diet of rigorous physical activity and constant peer pressure. While his friend left the camp at this stage to meet his parents, Mr S.'s son agreed to remain behind, apparently enjoying collecting money for 'worthy causes' and distributing food to the poor. In increasingly uncharacteristic letters home he informed his distraught parents that he had become a member of the Unification Church.

Turning to FAIR for help, Mr S. was given the telephone number of one of the Moonie bases and was able to talk to his son. In retrospect, he says,

73

I used quite the wrong approach. I became angry and denounced the Moonies as evil, which of course gave them the opportunity of persuading him [Timothy] that Satan was working through his parents. We soon learned to moderate our tactics. Eventually we devised a plan whereby my brother and younger son flew to San Francisco to contact the boy in person with the news that my health had seriously deteriorated. As a regular patient at the National Heart Hospital over a number of years, the excuse was perfectly plausible. At the time, in London, the *Daily Mail* were on trial for libel. They had described the Unification Church as the 'religion that destroys families'. The proceedings brought many important members of the cult to the city and two young women came to see me to say that Timothy was worried about my health. Afraid of adverse publicity, they must have reported back that I was a very sick man because Timothy agreed to come home with his uncle and brother.

At this point, the family acknowledges they made a bad mistake. They allowed their son to return to the camp to clear up his things, during which time he was persuaded to reverse his decision and his uncle and brother returned to England alone. Their visit had not been in vain however. Desperately anxious about his father, not only because of his apparent ill-health but also because Timothy had been told that his parents were causing the 'Church' a great deal of trouble and embarrassment, the young man finally arrived home 'a different person. Painfully thin and exhausted. His clothing was poor and ill-fitting, but worse than that, he had developed a nervous and hesitant manner and seemed completely lost, as though he were in the house of a stranger.' While at home Timothy was in constant touch with the Moonies' headquarters in London, and was visited by them on several occasions. Gradually, with counselling and advice from ex-Moonies, he began to make his own judgements and, according to his father, 'saw the cult in its true light and settled down to a normal working life amongst an extremely happy and thankful family'.

Forceful abduction from a cult is illegal in Britain but not in the United States, as Susan and Anne Swatland's book *Escape from the Moonies* makes clear. On 17 March 1981 Moonie-convert Susan was taken from a San Francisco street by professionals and forced into a car in which her mother was waiting. It was a traumatic experience for mother and daughter and although evidently successful, it tends to illustrate the potential harm that agencies such as FAIR and Deo Gloria Outreach feel might be the result of shock tactics.

Where to go for help and advice

The organizations listed below are open during normal office hours unless stated otherwise. Many of them will supply lists of their own publications – factsheets, leaflets, magazines, books – on request.

General

Church of England Children's
  Society
Old Town Hall
Kennington Road
London SE11 4QD
Tel: 01–735–2441
  A Christian charity operating throughout England and Wales. Offers children and young people, regardless of religious belief, help with problems of isolation and loneliness, truancy and delinquency, despair of unemployment, separation from parents, homelessness, and mental and physical handicap.

Exploring Parenthood Trust
Omnibus Workspace
39–41 North Road
London N7 9DP
Tel: 01–607–9647 and 01–700–4822

Families Anonymous
5 Parsons Green
London SW6
Tel: 01–731–8060
  Self-help groups for concerned families of individuals with behavioural problems, including drugs, truancy, running away, delinquency and hostility. Cannot be recommended too highly for the effective support it offers parents.

Family Services Units
207 Old Marylebone Road
London NW1 5QP
Tel: 01–402–5175
  National organization that provides services to prevent the breakdown of family life.

Family Welfare Association
501–505 Kingsland Road
London E8
Tel: 01–245–6251
  National organization offering help, advice and information.

National Association of Young
  People's Counselling and
  Advisory Services (NAYPCAS)
  Provides addresses of local counselling and advice services.
REGIONAL OFFICES:
102 Harper Road
London SE1
Tel: 01–403–2444

75

17–23 Albion Street
Leicester LE1 6GD
Tel: 0533–554775 ext. 22/36

Wheels Youth
14 Justice Street
Aberdeen
Tel: 0224–21956

2A Ribble Street
Belfast
Tel: 0232–658708

45 Hardwick Street
Dublin 1
Tel: 0001–745–398

National Marriage Guidance
    Council
Herbert Gray College
Little Church Street
Rugby, Warwickshire CV2 3AP
Tel: 0788–73241
    Help, advice and information
about local branches.

OPUS: Organization for Parents
    Under Stress
26 Manor Drive
Pickering, Yorkshire WF5 0LL
Tel: 0751–73235
    An umbrella organization for
various bodies offering help to
parents. Can advise on help
available locally.

Parents Anonymous (London)
6 Manor Gardens
London N7
Tel: 01–263–5672
Lifeline tel: 01–263–8918

Runaways

Alone in London Service Ltd
30 Mount Pleasant
London WC1
Tel: 01–278–4224
    and
69 Rosoman Street
London EC1
Tel: 01–837–5710
    Advice and counselling centres for
homeless young people up to the age
of 21. Offers a comprehensive range
of housing options. Staff are willing
to counsel parents, but cannot liaise
with them without the full
agreement of the young person.

Centrepoint Soho
57 Dean Street
London W1V 5HH
Tel: 01–434–2861
Message Home Service: 01–799–
    7662
    See p. 30.

The Passage
St Vincent's
Carlisle Place
London SW1
Tel: 01–828–4183;
    01–821–6980 after 5.30 p.m.
    A day centre for single homeless
people.

Salvation Army
International Headquarters
101 Queen Victoria Street
London EC4
Tel: 01–236–5222

The Salvation Army's experience in looking after the homeless is without parallel. They can also help trace missing persons.

Separated, divorced and one-parent families

Children Need Fathers
18 Green Lane
Grendon
Atherstone, Warwickshire CV9 2PL
Tel: 08277–2427

CRUSE (National Organization for the Widowed and their Children)
Cruse House
126 Sheen Road
Richmond, Surrey TW9 1UR
Tel: 01–940–4818
   Offers counselling, advice and information on practical matters, and opportunities for contacts with others.

Families Need Fathers
37 Garden Road
London SE15 3UB
Tel: 01–639–5362
   A national self-help organization concerned with the problems of maintaining a child's relationship with its parents during and after separation and divorce.

Gingerbread
   A national network of more than 300 self-help groups for one-parent families. Provides information and advice on financial, social and legal problems, and organizes activities. Regional headquarters are at the following addresses:

35 Wellington Street
London WC2 7BN
Tel: 01–240–0953

9–11 Fleet Street
Liverpool L1 4AR
Tel: 051–708–8848

4A Lauriston Gardens
Edinburgh EH3 3HH
Tel: 031–229–0923
Office hours: 10 a.m.–2.30 p.m.
Mon., Wed., Fri.

291 Ormeau Road
Belfast BT7
Tel: 0232–693701

Mothers Apart from Their Children (MATCH)
64 Delaware Mansions
Delaware Road
London W9
Tel: 01–892–9949

National Association of Widows
Stafford District Voluntary Service Centre
Chell Road
Stafford ST16 2QA
Tel: 0785–45465

National Council for One-parent Families
225 Kentish Town Road
London NW5 2LX
Tel: 01–267–1361
   Offers help and free and confidential advice on housing benefits and legal matters.

The National Family Conciliation
  Council
155 High Street
Dorking, Surrey RH4 1AD
Tel: 0306–882754
  Represents voluntary Family
Conciliation Services throughout
Britain, which help divorcing
couples with children reach
agreement on future parenting.

Northern Ireland Women's Aid
143A University Street
Belfast 7
Tel: 0232–249041

One-Parent Family Holidays
25 Fore Street
Praze An Beeble
Camborne, Cornwall
Tel: 0209–831274

Scottish Council for Single Parents
44 Albany Street
Edinburgh EH1 3QR
Tel: 031–556–3899

Stepfamilies

The National Stepfamily
  Association
329 Mills Road
Cambridge CB2 2QT
Tel: 0223–246861

Stepfamily
Maris House
Maris Lane, Trumpington
Cambridge CB2 2LB
Tel: 0223–841306
  Practical help, support,
information and advice to all
members of stepfamilies: married

or unmarried, full- or part-time,
parents and children.

Bereavement counselling

General practitioners, social
workers and Citizens' Advice
Bureaux can provide information
on, and referral to, local
bereavement counselling services.

Compassionate Friends
6 Denmark Street
Bristol BS1 5DQ
Tel: 0272–292778
  Headquarters of national
organization helping parents and
adolescents through bereavement;
will put teenagers in touch with
others who have had similar
experience.

CRUSE
See p. 77.

Adoption

The British Agencies for Adoption
  and Fostering
11 Southwark Street
London SE1 1RQ
Tel: 01–407–8800

The National Organization for the
  Counselling of Adoptees and
  Their Parents (NORCAP)
49 Russell Hill Road
Purley, Surrey CR2 2XB
  Enclose s.a.e. for reply.

Cults

Council on Mind Abuse (COMA)
BM COMA
London WC1N 3XX

An organization of concerned families and individuals, all of whom have experienced cult involvement in some way.

Cultists Anonymous
BM Box 1407
London WC1N 3XX
Tel: 0482–443104

Deo Gloria Outreach
7 London Road
Bromley, Kent BR1 1BY
Tel: 01–464–9500

Although it works closely with other groups involved in the problem of cults, Deo Gloria is a Christian organization committed to upholding the aims of the Church. It counsels by consent with the cult member and is anxious to keep open as many lines of communication as possible with individual cults. It disagrees emphatically with forcible abduction.

EMERGE (Ex-members of Extremist Religious Groups)
BM Box 1199
London WC1N 3XX

FAIR (Family Action Information and Rescue)
BM Box 3535
PO Box 12
London WC1N 3XX
Tel: 01–539–3940

A voluntary body, not committed to any religious or political stance. In counselling cult members it does not seek to convert them to any other belief, but to restore them 'to a state of mind where rational judgements can be made'. It maintains contacts with cults and their leaders in order to attempt to influence and modify their policies. It does not advocate coercive de-programming or illegal rescue techniques.

Housetop
39 Homer Street
London W1
Tel: 01–402–9679

A Roman Catholic organization.

Notes

1. Anna Freud, *Psychoanalytic Study of the Child*, New York, International University Press, 1958
2. Michael Rutter *et al.*, *Fifteen Thousand Hours: Secondary Schools and Their Effects on Children*, Shepton Mallet, Open Books, 1979
3. Michael Rutter, *Changing Youth in a Changing Society: Patterns of Adolescent Development and Disorder*, London, Nuffield Provincial Hospital Trust, 1979
4. Gary May, *Child Discipline: Guidelines for Parents*, Chicago, National Committee for Prevention of Child Abuse, 1979

5. Ibid.
6. Judy Dunn, *Sisters and Brothers*, London, Fontana, 1984
7. W. A. Belson, *Television Violence and the Adolescent Boy*, Farnborough, Saxon House, 1978
8. Mike Durham, 'Doctor Defends Violent Television', *Times Educational Supplement*, 1982
9. BBC, *The Portrayal of Violence in Television Programmes*, London, 1983, p. 22
10. Ronit Lentin, *Guardian*, 11 April 1984, p. 8
11. Patricia Marks Greenfield, *Mind and Media*, London, Fontana, 1984
12. Sue Lees, *Losing Out*, London, Hutchinson, 1986
13. James Hemming, *You and Your Adolescent*, London, Ebury, 1975
14. Ibid.
15. Gill Gorell Barnes, *Working with Families*, London, Macmillan, 1984
16. Yvette Walczak and Sheila Burns, *Divorce: The Child's Point of View*, London, Harper & Row, 1984
17. Hemming, op. cit.
18. A. I. Cooklin, 'The Adolescent as Problem, Patient or Therapist', *Journal of Adolescence*, vol. 2, 1979, pp. 113–26
19. Walzak and Barnes, op. cit.
20. Elizabeth Hodder, *The Step-parents' Handbook*, London, Sphere, 1985
21. Ibid.
22. Dora Black, 'Early Help for the Bereaved Child Avoids Later Problems', *Modern Medicine*, 17 May 1979
23. Hemming, op. cit.
24. Michael Humphrey, 'Factors Associated with Maladjustment in Adoptive Families', *Child Adoption*
25. F. H. Stone, 'Adoption and Identity', *Child Adoption*
26. Eli Shapiro, 'Destructive Cultism', *AFP*, vol. 15, no. 2
27. Ibid.
28. Michael Eidel, *Cornell Daily Sun*, 7 February 1982

Chapter 3

Addictions

Drug use and abuse

Because of the tragic consequences involved in drug addiction, there is nothing that strikes more fear into the hearts of parents than the thought that their teenager might be participating in the drug scene. It has been estimated that up to 40 per cent of children under the age of 16 have tried drugs at one time or another but the secrecy that surrounds such habits means that the true numbers may be far greater. The difficulty in obtaining comprehensive statistics on drug abuse among young people is perhaps best illustrated by the comments of researchers working on a survey for the Strathclyde Resource Unit for the Youth Enquiry Service 1983 Youth Survey. They asked a sample of 551 males and 463 females whether they had ever tried drugs. They write: 'We did not quantify the regularity of usage, nor did we try to find out what sort of drugs were being tried. We found that young people were quite happy to discuss this issue. There was a high level of acceptance of the use of drugs as being normal.' On the other hand, when the research team asked 'Have you ever sniffed glue?' they found young people reluctant to admit to using the substance. They comment:

> Of all the questions asked in our survey we would consider the returns on this question to be the least accurate because of the reluctance of young people to talk about this subject. If they had used glue they were embarrassed to admit it, as it was viewed as a childish activity. If they had not used glue, they were quite often insulted to be asked if they had.

Drugs are now widely available – at pubs, clubs, shops, schools, street corners and parties. For the young person determined to experiment with drugs, it requires only the minimum of effort – a word to a friend of a friend or to an older brother or sister – to acquire 'speed' (amphetamines), 'blow' (marijuana) or 'acid' (LSD), and only slightly more of an effort to find a source of heroin.

Drug users almost invariably argue that marijuana, amphetamines and cocaine are much less harmful in their effects than alcohol. Their argument is not convincing. The teenager who forms a psychological habit of taking marijuana whenever the problems of life become unbearable or who wants to give a 'lift' to a life that seems to have become intolerably dull, will become less resistant to the subsequent use of more harmful drugs. Almost all heroin addicts will admit that the first drug they used was cannabis. What youngsters do not always admit is that these so-called 'soft drugs' are taken in combination with alcohol or other drugs (thereby increasing the strength of each), which can produce medically catastrophic effects on both mind and body. It is easier to overdose on stimulants and tranquillizers than on heroin, and sudden withdrawal can lead to repeated convulsions (*status epilepticus*) that can result in death.

When John, aged 15, started vomiting after drinking heavily at a party, his friends thought he was drunk, but he began to vomit blood and 'blacked out' and they later learned that he had arrived 'stoned' on 'speed' and 'blow'. As he was evidently seriously ill, the first concern of his friends was to telephone for an ambulance. However, they decided that if he were taken to hospital, the police would necessarily be informed of his condition, which might result in embarrassing questions for them and trouble for John. Instead, they half carried and half walked him home, but he 'blacked out' several times on the way and was in such obvious distress that a passing motorist stopped and offered to give him a lift to his house, where it was left to his anguished parents to pick up the pieces.

Home Office figures released in September 1985 showed that since 1980 there had been a 200 per cent increase in the number of notified addicts, with the figure rising at a rate of 32 per cent a year. The figures also showed that the percentage of drug offenders under the age of 17 had risen by 20 per cent. While there is every reason for parents to be worried about their children in the light of the current increase in teenage drug abuse – and there certainly is no room for complacency – the situation must be looked at in perspective.

There are three main reasons why teenagers take drugs. Firstly, succumbing to peer group pressure, they hope that indulgence will help them gain acceptance and admiration of a particular group of friends. Secondly, for precisely the same reason that many adults feel more comfortable after the first drink at a party: drugs break down the barriers of shyness and anxiety that so painfully afflict the teenage years. Thirdly, teenagers take drugs as part of the search for new experience and excitement to dispel boredom. Although less usual, teenage drug abuse can also be a cry for help, in which case the consequences are likely to be more problematic. Of the one in three youngsters who experiment with drugs, only a small minority will become 'hooked' (although there is no precise information available to indicate just how many do escape dependency). Most young drug takers use drugs occasionally, often giving up after the first tentative experiment. One 15-year-old girl describing her first experience with marijuana said that it caused such a violent bout of vomiting that she decided never to try it again. Others who take drugs regularly, perhaps as an integral part of their weekend's entertainment, are obviously those for whom the dangers of becoming addicted are greatly increased, but, again, not necessarily. Some experienced workers in the field to whom I spoke felt that individual body chemistry played the same role in drug addiction as it would appear to do in alcoholism; in other words, certain people can use drugs regularly for long periods without becoming addicted, while others become 'hooked' very quickly.

Given that the vast majority of young people are content to confine their experiments with illicit drugs to the odd occasion, what are the factors involved in a teenager moving from occasional to regular use, or from regular use to addiction? They are not easy to pinpoint, but it would appear that certain characteristics are common to those youngsters who are more likely to be at risk. Firstly, parents should perhaps examine their own habits and their own medicine cabinets since research has shown that teenagers whose parents use significant amounts of alcohol, tranquillizers, tobacco, sedatives and amphetamines are more likely to take marijuana, alcohol and other drugs themselves. Secondly, many people who work with addicts feel that the tendency toward addiction is grounded in a personality that is inadequately prepared to cope with the everyday pressures of life. Addicts have little confidence and a particularly low self-esteem. If they feel that their parents have given up on them and that their lives offer no evidence of support, then the temptation to cocoon themselves in the blanket of drug-induced security can be hard to resist. An unstable home background can produce the kind of instability in a teenager that in times of conflict might provoke him to seek instant relief from his troubles.

Also at risk are the unemployed teenagers and those who have chosen to 'drop out' of the educational system. A survey begun in 1979 and carried out by Dr Martin Plant with a team from Edinburgh University showed strong links between drugs and the dole. In the Edinburgh region more than half of the unemployed boys and more than a third of the unemployed girls had used illegal drugs. Drug use among students and young people who had jobs was found to be much lower. Adolescents with too much time on their hands and without direction or purpose find that by using drugs they can create a fantasy world that blots out poverty and boredom, and provides them with a sole purpose – that of acquiring more drugs. 'No dole, no dope; no dope, no hope' is a slice of baleful teenage wisdom, but even this twilight zone is a social world of sorts.

Matthew, who has been out of work since leaving school at 17, is attempting to set up a pop group. The competition to play in pubs and clubs is so great that there doesn't seem much likelihood of being heard in public, but the incentive to do so brings the group together in a shared interest, which also involves regular use of a variety of drugs. Drugs are seen as an adjunct to sociability and appear to Matthew and his friends to cheer up a world of poverty and uncertainty. It may not be an enviable or desirable existence, but it is still some way from the desperate, secretive and lonely life of the heroin addict who would sell his soul – and his friend's too, if indeed he has a friend – for a 'fix'.

Michael became a heroin addict at 18 after four years of regular drug-taking and experimentation. Now 26, he is a registered addict and is served by the National Health Service with a daily supply of methadone – a chemical substitute, no less addictive but a great deal cheaper and safer to use. Michael's home background is affluent, caring and middle class. He is an intelligent, talented and handsome young man and his story is profoundly sad.

> I started experimenting with drugs when I was about 14. We used to mix barbiturates and alcohol at parties and the effect was a knock-out. You felt like you'd been hit with a sledge hammer sometimes; it was more dramatic than heroin. When people talk about 'soft' drugs and 'hard' drugs it can be misleading because the soft drugs are often quickly addictive and can have devastating effects. The use of drugs at parties is amazingly widespread, particularly hash [cannabis – the resin from the marijuana plant] and pot [the leaves of the plant]. In some pubs the publican turns a blind eye, and you see people 'snorting' off the tables. Young teenagers, under age, often go to pubs – I began drinking in pubs when I was 14 – and they are very vulnerable, although I have never actually seen pushers work on young kids. You usually have to have an introduction to a pusher before you can get the stuff. My first experience with heroin was in a back alley with a couple of addicts my friend and I had met in a train coming home. I wasn't afraid. It was rather disappointing really – different to what I had imagined and not nearly as exciting or dramatic as LSD. I continued having a fix once a fortnight or once a week.

There is a kind of comradeship amongst addicts, but it is based more on a certain sharing of guilt than real friendship. If your friend is desperate, he will steal from you without hesitation. Addicts tend to keep their addiction secret, because they can be spurned by non-addicts and regarded as social outcasts or criminals. When you're hooked, the only thing you worry about is money. For those who don't pay the dealer, there can be serious consequences. I have a friend who owed £4,000 and his life was threatened; it was 'pay up in two weeks or else . . .' He sold everything he had and he's the only addict I know who managed to kick the habit. I was spending about £80 a week on heroin. I managed to get an overdraft at the bank, but things became so bad that I had to involve my parents, who then were able to placate the bank manager. For their sakes, I kicked the habit for a month or so, but the withdrawal symptoms were so bad that I couldn't continue. It felt like a prolonged dose of very bad flu. The idea that most people have of addicts withdrawing with terrible stomach cramps and violent nausea with vomiting is not always the way it really is. There is a terrible lethargy – you just feel like you want to spend all day in bed. The muscles seem weighed down and the limbs feel constantly irritated so that you always want to stretch them out, but doing so never relieves the discomfort. The trouble is that this terrible feeling never seems to go away. If it lasted for a day or so, it would be easier to bear, but after a month, I couldn't stand it any more and went back for a fix. My mother can always tell when I've taken a fix because she says I become white-faced and sweaty, and the pupils of my eyes become like tiny pinpoints.

After the month spent trying to withdraw, I decided to become a registered addict. The moment you go to your GP he is obliged to register you. It takes about two and a half weeks to become attached to a clinic and this is a crucial time for addicts, because often they find the waiting too stressful and they return to the dealers for a fix. Once you attend the clinic, heroin is withdrawn and methadone is substituted. I was prescribed methadone under strict supervision; it's mostly given in the form of a linctus. This cuts out the dangers of dirty needles. The dose, which is rigorously controlled in that you have to drink the stuff down in front of a doctor or a nurse, lasts for about thirty hours, whereas the effect of heroin in a seasoned addict lasts only about four hours. The withdrawal symptoms from methadone are far worse for me, though, and although there is little chance that I will ever kick the habit, it has allowed me to rely on myself and my own judgement more.

If things go really wrong, I will still have a fix in order to boost my morale. To me it seems not much more than having a couple of beers, or at the end of a day, saying, 'God, I need a drink.' The habit will always rule you though. I can never go away on the spur of the moment because I am totally reliant on the chemist who holds my prescription. If I travel, then it takes about two weeks to prepare the way; I can't store methadone. It is prescribed in daily doses and if I want to travel around, I have to arrange pick-ups in other parts of the country.

There are strict rules surrounding the use of methadone. The clinic insists upon urine tests to see whether or not you have had an additional fix, but there are always ways around the problem. I was standing in a cubicle at the hospital, peeing into my bottle, when a hand reached over the partition bearing an empty glass. 'Here,' said a voice, 'pee in this for me mate. I've just had a fix.' 'I can't,' I replied, 'I don't have any more left!'

Apart from being tied to a clinic, there are other disadvantages in registering as an addict. First, it goes down on a public record and, second, it restricts your movements. The trouble is, most addicts really believe they can give up the habit by themselves but giving up is like losing a girl-friend – like missing something vital inside you. I feel more normal on methadone, though. I have a job working as a dishwasher, but I also play the tenor sax in a rock group and am deeply committed to my music. On heroin it is almost impossible to lead any kind of normal life; one is either on a great high or a fearful low and, of course, you're constantly searching for money. I have lived for days on a small tin of baked beans in order that all the money I had should go on the drug. It is a habit which is very isolating, but since 'chasing the dragon' has become popular, taking heroin can be a more social business.

Private medicine has really boosted the drug trade. There are some private doctors with a special licence to deal in controlled drugs and sometimes they prescribe up to five times the necessary dose. They even prescribe to people who aren't addicts. Although you have to be pretty convincing, all the doctors are interested in is the money. Addicts sell the remainder of their heroin or methadone, and there are huge sums to be made all round.

I have been stopped and questioned by the police six times now. On the first occasion, I was on my way home and a couple of officers stopped me. They found an empty syringe but no drugs, so I was taken to the police station, strip-searched and put in a cell for three hours to await a CID bloke. Most police think drug addicts are scum, and the two who picked me up were thoroughly unpleasant. Eventually, I was driven back to my flat and my room was searched. I was then taken back to the police station and told I had to walk home, which seemed hard going after having worked fourteen hours the day before. One time, I asked, 'Why have you stopped me?' 'Because you look like a student,' came the reply, 'and students often have drugs on them.'

Michael's impressions of his world – his addiction, the police, rogue doctors and the underlying violence that exists for those who cannot find the money to pay for their habit – are common to most addicts, but his experiences, sordid and affecting though they are, are made more tolerable by the fact that since his family discovered his habit, they have stood by him and given him every support. Others are less fortunate.

According to the Reverend Adele Blakebrough-Fairburn, who helps her father, Eric Blakebrough, run the Kaleidoscope Project in Kingston-upon-Thames, Surrey, once it is discovered that youngsters have become addicted, they are often thrown out of the parental home. This comes after a long and difficult time, during which the family may well have found that the amount of thieving – usually the result of an addict's desperate attempt to finance his habit – has become insupportable. At such times, Adele Blakebrough-Fairburn explained,

> it may well be in the best interests of teenager and parents alike that young addicts are forced to move away from home, and parents should never feel guilty. Middle-class parents find it particularly hard to come to terms with the reality of their children's condition, in part because they had such high expectations for them. There is also the element of shame which they feel attaches to the parent of a teenage addict, they care deeply about what friends and neighbours might think. Parents usually telephone us anonymously for help and hope that we will be able to 'cure' their child in return for payment; but of course it isn't as easy as that.

Parents going to Kaleidoscope for help are counselled separately from their children: 'If parents become overtly involved, a kid would never agree to come to us.' Unlike many of her colleagues working in the field of drug

A PARENTS' GUIDE TO THE PROBLEMS OF ADOLESCENCE

abuse, Adele Blakebrough-Fairburn feels that ex-addicts are too close to the subject to make reliable helpers and she is more sceptical than others concerning an addict's ability to stay off drugs. In her experience the next fix is never far enough away and will almost always be needed in a time of crisis. It is therefore the policy of Kaleidoscope to look less towards a cure than to maintaining the addict on a regular, daily dose of methadone in order to achieve a more stable and ordered existence. Adele describes the change from heroin to methadone as 'dramatic'. 'It is astonishing,' she says, 'how quickly the addict's appearance alters for the better as his health improves. Also, it is rare that thieving continues to be a problem after the substitute drug has been introduced.'

Kaleidoscope is essentially a community project that offers sanctuary not only to drug addicts but to all teenagers whether they have acute problems and need special help or merely want to find a place to go after pubs and cinemas have closed. On Friday nights the club is open from 10 p.m. and stays open until breakfast time on Saturday morning. The education unit offers courses to GCSE and A level, but also concentrates on basic skills for teenagers who dropped out of school before properly learning to read or write.

No less impressive is the work being carried out by other organizations, often on a shoestring budget in less attractive surroundings. About half the country's drug population is now centred in the London area and the director of the Crisis Centre for Multiple-Drug Users in London spends the majority of his time finding the money to keep the project open. The deputy director told me:

> Generally speaking, we deal here, with youngsters who have drifted away from home, and our bias is towards those who are in severe crisis. In fact, you might say, the worse their predicament, the more points they score with us. Many of our 'clients' are without shelter and seriously at risk, either from violence within their family or prostitution on the streets. Although we do receive addicts via the social services or hospitals, the vast majority are referred direct from the street, where we have the reputation of being tough and difficult, but they know we'll do the job.

In this instance 'the job' involves an eight-to-ten-day detoxification process during a stay of three weeks, after which the 'client' is referred to an appropriate agency for rehabilitation.

> The real problem is not so much getting the person off the drugs – that's relatively easy. It's giving him enough self-confidence and will

to stay off. Typical addicts are lonely, isolated and anxious, have a low self-esteem and feel quite unable to cope with life without drugs. It is our job to lessen their anxiety and make them feel comfortable and relaxed and get them to enjoy being drug-free. To this end, we give the minimum of the substitute, methadone, during the detoxification process and concentrate on non-medical ways of reducing the addict's fears. We use massage and acupuncture and relaxation hypnosis, and since insomnia is a symptom of drug abuse, we also teach self-hypnosis.

There are twenty-six members of staff at the Crisis Centre. Working on a twenty-four-hour rota system, they include nurses, social workers, and volunteers, some of whom are ex-addicts and who must be drug-free for three or four years before being accepted into the work force. The volunteers are used to comfort and support addicts during their three-week stay at the centre and hopefully to persuade them that the world is a happier place without drugs. 'The centre has three main aims,' the deputy director stated:

> Firstly, we offer a sanctuary which is absolutely drug-free, where addicts can come to stop and think. If there is any suggestion that addicts are using drugs while staying with us, the place comes to a complete halt while we ransack every corner of the building to discover the evidence. If it is produced, they are thrown out. Secondly, we offer medical care and health education to people who are often physically debilitated and have not visited a doctor in years. Addicts are checked for signs of hepatitis, AIDS and venereal disease; for the last, they are given a course of antibiotics, which, if previously prescribed, may not have been taken correctly or may have been sold as drugs on the street. And, thirdly, we offer the maximum social support in the hopes that by obtaining details of their background and personalities, we will learn the best way of helping them as individuals.

The Crisis Centre is one of the few places where addicts can go for help while actually suffering from the effects of drugs. Most centres require the addict to be drug-free on admission. Although addiction centres may differ in their emphasis and the methods they adopt in order to achieve detoxification and rehabilitation (and this is an important factor to consider when deciding on the kind of help a parent feels to be most appropriate for both themselves and their teenager), wherever I went I found the dedication,

kindness and sympathy of the many professionals and other workers involved second to none.

Signs and symptoms of drug abuse

Many of the tell-tale signs that a youngster is using, or has used, drugs are not easy to differentiate from those that are generally symptomatic of adolescence; hence it would not be surprising to learn that Elizabeth (Chapter 1) did not know of her son's drug abuse and addiction for at least four years after his first experiments. On the other hand, along with the mood swings and related symptoms that are characteristic generally of adolescence, there are some more obvious symptoms, which Helen Bethune, in her excellent book *Off the Hook: Coping with Addiction* makes very clear. Her guidelines are printed below. It is important to stress that many of the symptoms taken on their own (hyperactivity, excitable movements, diminished appetite, for example) may be the result of causes other than drug abuse, where several if not all of the symptoms may be present.

PHYSICAL AND BEHAVIOURAL SYMPTOMS OF SPEED (AMPHETAMINE SULPHATE) USE

1. Hyperactivity, inability to sleep, wandering round house all night
2. Fidgety, jumpy, nervous, excitable movements
3. Sometimes dilation of the pupils of the eyes
4. Rapid, rambling, repetitive speech
5. Sudden enthusiasms – which die equally suddenly
6. Very heavy cigarette smoking and/or chewing of gum
7. Need for a great deal of liquid – tea, coffee, anything
8. Frequent sniffing – without symptoms of the common cold
9. Diminished or non-existent appetite
10. Inability to concentrate for more than a few moments at a time

After prolonged or heavy use:

11. Occasional dizziness
12. Blotchy skin, drained pallid appearance
13. Swollen lips with a blackish deposit at corners of mouth and sometimes on the lips themselves
14. Rapid decay of teeth [1]

The physical and behavioural symptoms of cocaine use are similar to those of 'speed' use in terms of the swings of moods experienced: from great enthusiasm, cheerfulness and nervous energy to depression, exhaustion and lack of energy. Because of the high price of the drug, lying and stealing are as common to the cocaine user as the heroin addict. Frequent sniffing with or without a cold is also a characteristic, and after prolonged and excessive use, coke-snorters risk destruction of the bridge of the nose and even the nostrils.

Generally, it is not possible to differentiate between the symptoms of 'crack' use and those of other forms of cocaine, although rapid changes in behaviour are probably the most reliable indicators. 'Crack' is the street name given to tiny chunks or 'rocks' of freebase cocaine, a smokeable form of the drug extracted from cocaine hydrochloride powder in a simple chemical procedure using baking soda, heat and water. Dealers prefer to sell 'crack' rather than cocaine powder because it is more profitable, easier to handle and highly addictive. The potent, rapidly produced 'high' lasts only 3–5 minutes and is followed by an equally forceful 'crash', characterized by feelings of agitation and depression, and by cravings for more drugs. Most users say they became addicted to 'crack' within six months.

Bethune identifies the following tell-tale signs of heroin use.

PHYSICAL AND BEHAVIOURAL SYMPTOMS OF HEROIN USE

1. Change of behaviour, aggression, cockiness
2. Withdrawal from family life. 'I couldn't get through to her,' says a mother. 'She began isolating herself in her room.'
3. Diminishing appetite

With increased heroin consumption, the symptoms increase too:
4. Lying
5. Stealing
6. Total isolation in room away from family
7. Extreme thinness
8. Beautiful, ethereal facial appearance and fragile look
9. Rarely bothering with clothes, perhaps two outfits. Seldom eccentric, since it is particularly important for heroin addicts to appear 'normal'
10. No interest in family, social activities, or school
11. Late-night telephone calls
12. Coming home late at night or not at all
13. Staying in bed all day, watching TV if possible
14. Refusing to lie in the sun or even, if possible, to go into sunlight

(pinhead-sized pupils – 'pinned-out' pupils – make bright light positively painful – hence the frequent use of dark glasses by addicts, and their preference for night and low lighting)

15. Always wearing long sleeves, high necklines and jeans (these cover injection marks)

16. Hate to be touched, hugged or embraced (highly sensitive skin – also the reason for simplified and few clothes)

17. Extreme aggression, irritability and insensitivity to others

18. If addiction can be described as creating the Jekyll and Hyde syndrome (as it often is), then Hyde now predominates except when the addict wants something. Then Jekyll appears, all sweetness, promises and light – which lasts only until the demand has been met

19. 'Gouching out' – sleepy appearance occasionally snapping awake

20. Sweaty face (when withdrawing) and shaky hands [2]

Bethune's book is extremely forceful in its presentation of the unacceptable face of marijuana, stating that the drug not only interferes with the production of RNA and DNA and with the body's immune response system, but it is also known to cause sterility in males.

Another book that reinforces the view that marijuana has a dangerous side to its 'harmless' image is *How to Get off Drugs* by Ira Mothner and Alan Weitz. Concerning the adverse reactions of cannabis, the authors write:

> Many users become fearful and confused, others suspicious or aggressive. Paranoid reactions are frequent, and many users have experienced 'panic attacks'. Although usually brief, anxiety builds quickly during these attacks and victims become fearful of losing control. They may feel an intense need to get home or to some other safe place; sometimes they will just get into bed and hide under the covers. They can become highly agitated but will usually respond to being 'talked down' by someone they know and trust . . . Generally, it is younger and less experienced users who panic, though some older former users cite these attacks as the reason they gave up the drug. [3]

I gave the book to a group of young people aged 16 to 17 years who are regular (about twice a week) cannabis users and asked them for their comments on this section. The adverse reactions were common to all of them in one way or another and they seemed so astounded to witness their symptoms in print that they could not wait to articulate their experiences. A 16-year-old girl described her own frightening experiences while taking marijuana, which she had begun to use at the age of 14. It was her story that seemed to best illustrate the potential dangers of the altered state of mind inherent in any form of drug-taking.

> When I get stoned at a party, I sometimes have this dreadful need to get home. It's all I can think about to do. Whatever time of the night, I have to leave the place and find my way home. It's sort of paranoid I suppose but when I'm in the train, every time it stops, I have this terrifying urge to go on to the platform even though I really know it isn't my station. To stop myself I have to bite my hand or arm so that it hurts.

Dr Peter Bruggen and Charles O'Brian's book *Surviving Adolescence* is very useful. Dr Bruggen is a consultant psychiatrist at Hill End Adolescent Unit and although I would not challenge his authority, his advice to teenagers concerning marijuana seems more sanguine than perhaps parents would like it to be. He writes:

> Marijuana is, in our view, probably less dangerous physiologically than either the above two [alcohol and tobacco]: but it is illegal. Therefore we recommend that you do not take marijuana. We add the obvious warning, that through its illegality, you may be introduced to the hard drugs which we know are dangerous. You will know that many people are making money from the distribution of hard drugs to young people.[4]

Most parents who have seen the effects marijuana has on their children would suggest that while the physiological effects may not be deemed to be as hazardous as alcohol or tobacco, the psychological effects can be fraught with danger. One mother who knew that her son had used marijuana on and off over a long period told me that she always recognized when he had smoked pot. 'When you live with someone and know them really well, it's obvious when they're smoking the stuff. My boy becomes moody and aggressive and has sometimes been violent, but when he's been off it for a while, he's a different person.'

On 30 December 1987 *The Independent*'s medical editor, Oliver Gillie, reported on two new studies that linked cannabis smoking with schizophrenia and lung problems later in life. In the first study 4,000 Swedish army conscripts who admitted to smoking cannabis were followed up over a period of fifteen years. Results showed that 1 in 185 developed schizophrenia in that period. In other words, those who smoked the weed regularly were six times more likely to develop schizophrenia. However, it should be added that less than 10 per cent of schizophrenics are or have been regular cannabis users and in the same study other factors, such as parental divorce and other disturbances of upbringing or schooling, were associated with doubling the risk of schizophrenia. The second study concerned the effects cannabis smoking had on the lungs. It found that the adverse effects of cannabis on the body were greater than those caused by tobacco.

The language of drugs

Since lack of communication can so often be not only the cause of problems between parents and teenagers, but also the barrier that prevents a solution, listening to young people talking amongst themselves is a good way to gain access to their lives without questions or demands for explanations. In no way does one advocate deliberate eavesdropping – that would surely be disastrous – but adolescents' voices are so loud and the language so uninhibited that it is very difficult to avoid 'tuning in' on occasion. Underneath the obvious exaggerations and flamboyant boasts there is frequently a wealth of useful material for the concerned parent – the current street terms for various drugs being just one example.

One mother, whose son's many and varied friends were frequent visitors to the family home, would admit privately to her teenager that she had overhead a particular conversation and ask him to interpret various words and expressions. She was usually accused of being hopelessly naïve and out of date and explanations were delivered with a good deal of mirth; as a result her vocabulary and knowledge increased. One day she discovered a small bottle containing a single bead in her son's bedroom. Having been 'educated' by him as to the meaning of 'poppers', she realized that she had stumbled across amyl nitrate. Still with the bottle in her hand, she immediately questioned the boy, and was told that the drug had been bought by 'a friend's brother' and that he had 'only sniffed it once or twice but it wasn't much good and the smell was disgusting'. In fact, amyl nitrate is potentially extremely dangerous because it greatly increases the blood pressure, thus straining the heart. It was a frightening experience for the mother and her wariness has since increased, but she feels that the knowledge gained from teenage talk together with her son's confidence helped her to approach the crisis without panic.

The table of jargon on pp. 96–7 might prove useful to parents whose teenagers have not educated them. As fashions change, new terminology is introduced, often varying according to the area of the country in which the user lives.

How can parents help?

If parents suspect or discover that their teenager has become involved with drugs, fear for their child's safety may lead them to panic but such a reaction is counterproductive. Nothing can be achieved amidst scenes of anger and bitter recrimination. Initially, it is most important to discover which drug or drugs are being used, how often and why. A true picture will emerge only in a calm atmosphere, which is likely to promote confidence rather than hostility. Young people must feel that their parents are on their side whatever the consequences. If a 'joint' has been smoked at a party, parents need not feel that there is any immediate danger of their youngster becoming an abuser. On the other hand, it is important to talk about the experience, to reaffirm their own values, beliefs and concerns and, above all, to stress their care for the child. If the signs and symptoms would seem to point to the fact that a teenager is using drugs regularly, then professional help should be sought immediately. It is important that the adolescent is made to feel that this particular course of action stems from love and compassion and not from the desire to punish or humiliate.

Mrs C. knew that her daughter and her daughter's friend smoked 'pot'. In preparing the 'joint' it is usual to combine the weed with tobacco and roll both in a cigarette paper. The 'roll-your-own' cigarette papers in the bedroom combined with shreds of tobacco, unused cork filters and cigarette husks gave the game away, as did the peculiarly sweet smell given off by the drug when smoked. The carelessness and untidiness of teenagers can sometimes be an advantage. Mrs C., while accepting that the girls were occasional users, expressed her disapproval, stressing the illegality of possessing marijuana, and forbade the girls to use it in her home. Since she knew that the drug could be readily supplied, there seemed nothing to do but keep a careful watch for any change in the situation that might indicate a more serious problem. One weekend she noticed that there seemed to be a significant increase in the amount of tell-tale debris on the carpet in her daughter's room. Mrs C. asked her daughter whether she was using more of the drug than usual. The girl reassured her to the contrary, but said, 'We're making them to sell at school.' After Mrs C. explained the terrible consequences if they were caught – which they most certainly would be in time – the girls swore that they would no longer sell their wares to playground customers. Mrs C. knew there were no guarantees, but felt sure that the girls had been sufficiently frightened by her graphic description of juvenile court and the dire punishments meted out to drug pushers not to continue their dangerous venture. Why did they do it? Not, it seems, for money, although that was

Drug jargon [5]

JARGON	DEFINITION	JARGON	DEFINITION
Opioids: naturally occurring opiates and their synthetic analogues			
amps	methadone	morf	morphine
DFs	DF 118	palf	Palfium
dike	Diconal	peth	pethidine
H, junk	heroin	phy, phy pills	methadone
linctus	methadone	smack, stuff, £10 bag	heroin
Stimulants			
blues, bluies	blue amphetamine pills	rit	Ritalin, methentermine
coke	cocaine	speed	amphetamine,
crack	smokeable form of cocaine		methylamphet-amine, methedrine
dex, dexies	dexedrine		
meth	methedrine	sulph	amphetamine sulphate
poppers	amyl nitrate		
prellies	Preludin	uppers	any amphetamine
Sedatives			
barbs	barbiturates	Mickey Finn	chloral hydrate
ciba's	Doriden	mogies	Mogadon
downers	depressants	nembies	Nembutal
green and blacks	Librium	red chicken	heroin on a barbiturate base
hem, heminev	Heminevrin		
knock-out drops	chloral hydrate	seckies	Seconal
libs	Librium	sleepers	depressants
ludes	Quaaludes, methaqualone	tuies	Tuinal
		vals	Valium
mandies	Mandrax		
Psychedelics and cannabis			
acid, a tab of acid	LSD	joint	cannabis cigarette
blow	cannabis cigarette	Lebanese or Acapulco gold	high quality cannabis
brick	kilo of compressed marijuana	pot	marijuana
dope	marijuana	resin, sausage, THC	cannabis
dots	microdots, LSD		
ganja	West Indian hashish	smoke	cannabis cigarette
		tea, weed	marijuana
grass	marijuana		

JARGON	DEFINITION	JARGON	DEFINITION
People			
barb freaks	barb addicts	junkies	heroin users
contact, dealer	drug pedlar	pusher	drug pedlar
hog, pig	one who uses all he can get	speed freaks	heavy amphetamine users
hype	addict		
Drug taking			
brewing up	preparing an injection	quill	folded paper used for inhaling
chasing the dragon	inhaling smoke of heroin burnt on silver paper	scoring	getting drugs illegally, taking drugs, injecting
cranking up	taking any drug	scrip	prescription
Doctor Scrip	doctor who prescribes copiously	set of works	syringe and equipment
dropping a tab or cap	swallowing	shooting up	injecting
		skin-popping	subcutaneous injections
fixing	injecting		
gear	syringe and equipment	sniffing	inhaling glue
		snorting	sniffing cocaine, heroin, etc.
joy-pops	subcutaneous injections	spike	syringe
main lining	intravenous injection	track marks	signs of injections in veins
Drug effects			
buzz	intoxicated feeling	have a habit, hooked	addicted
cold turkey	complete withdrawal from drugs without drugs substitute	high, hit	intoxicated feeling
		horrors	bad hallucinations
		kick the habit	give up drugs
coming down, crashing out	withdrawal phase from dose	sick	withdrawal symptoms
detox	give up drugs	trip	drug experience
Trouble with the law			
goof	give oneself away to the police, spoil an injection	hot	wanted by the law, stolen
		pusher-upper	internal concealment
holding	possessing drugs	rumble	police nearby

Mrs C.'s assumption and she took pains to stress that, if they were that desperate for funds, they should turn to her for help; no, it was done, they said, 'for fun; for a laugh'.

Some professionals in the field, particularly those who specialize in the day-to-day care of addicts often in a critical condition expressed a view that may appear to some to be overly sanguine, but offers a degree of comfort to parents who know that their youngsters are no strangers to pot and suspect that they may have experimented with other drugs. They point to a distinction between the 'drug user' and the 'drug abuser'. They suggest that 'abusers' have generally reached a stage whereby they are emotionally and physically dependent on drugs, have difficulty in maintaining relationships with their family and friends, are often in trouble legally or financially and are unable to hold down a job. They stress that the vast majority of young people who 'use' a variety of drugs from time to time do so without becoming dependent upon them. Other professionals, however, would argue, more conservatively perhaps, that all 'use' is 'abuse'. Whereas the line between dependence and addiction is narrow, the difference between experimentation and dependence is very wide, and it should be emphasized that a very small minority of young people move on from a phase of experimentation to become drug dependent.

Solvent abuse

The history of solvent abuse is as old as the oracle of Apollo at Delphi whose prophecies were accompanied by the effects of intoxicating gases that escaped from the Earth's crust. The ancient Hebrews inhaled fumes from burning spices as part of their religious ritual. In the eighteenth century the students of Friedrich Hoffman took pleasure in inhaling his discovery – ether – long before it was used as a general anaesthetic. After the First World War ether became a fashionable substance to 'sniff' at parties, and during the Depression some of the unemployed dulled their misery by inhaling petrol-soaked rags. Glue-sniffing became a problem in America in the 1960s and was adopted by British teenagers a few years later. Although initially publicity centred around glue, the substances used by the sniffer are widely varied and readily obtainable. They include industrial solvents and dry-cleaning fluids; glues and cements; paints, thinners and strippers;

lacquers; nail polish and remover; lighter fuel; petrol; surgical spirit; hair spray and aerosols. Solvent abuse is the term commonly used to describe the habit, but it is also known as *volatile substance abuse* (VSA) since it is the volatile substance, found not only in solvents, that is responsible for the 'high'.

Most solvents and gases used place a dangerous strain on the heart by increasing its sensitivity to adrenalin. Death frequently occurs through heart failure, although a number of sniffers die through inhaling their own vomit. (Doctors advise turning a victim on his side if he is found lying on his back in a critical condition.) In an article in the *New Scientist*, Omar Sattaur states:

> Sniffing aerosols is potentially more dangerous than sniffing solvents. This is because by concentrating the vapours from an aerosol, in a plastic bag, for example, it is possible to produce a vapour containing close to 100 per cent of the volatile compounds. There are additional hazards for those who have a penchant for butane gas, as contained in the small cylinders of cigarette lighter refills. Sprayed directly into the mouth, the 'freezing cold' gas accumulates as a liquid at the back of the mouth. The tissues are chilled and begin to produce large quantities of liquid. Fluid can build up in the lungs and the person can die by 'drowning from the inside out'.[6]

The typical 'sniffer' is between 8 and 17, and twenty times more likely to be male than female. As with drugs, the most frequent cause of inhaling solvents stems from the desire to experiment, either through curiosity, boredom or bravado. As 'sniffing' tends to be a group activity, it has the added attraction of being a shared experience, but, fortunately, as with most forms of drug abuse, the occasional experience proves to be enough to satisfy most youngsters well before it can become a habit. Dr Joyce Watson, writing in *The Practitioner*, concludes:

> Solvent abuse should be regarded as a passing phase or fad. It is something that adolescents are likely to test and try rather than a phenomenon that will endure . . . There is no physical addiction to these volatile substances. However, some individuals become dependent on the habit.[7]

She also cites the study she and Dr D. Campbell published in 1978 in which they stated their opinion that

> solvent abuse should be considered part of the normal experimentation process of adolescence for some individuals. In itself this

experimentation is not pathological and it is not exclusively carried out by children from deprived homes. The most important factor in determining whether an individual chooses to indulge is the influence of his peer group.[8]

Although death from glue sniffing is rare, the leaflet put out by the National Campaign Against Solvent Abuse makes it clear to parents that the problem should not be ignored as just a passing fad. The long-term effects of the fumes inhaled, it suggests, can lead to permanent brain damage and kidney failure, both of which could be fatal. Glue-sniffing is particularly dangerous on a full stomach, when victims have been known to pass out and choke to death on their own vomit. The leaflet also maintains that glue-sniffing is addictive and 'falls into the same category of depressant drugs as tranquillizers and barbiturates'.

Two 15-year-old girls described to me what happened to them when they inhaled typewriter correction fluid thinner: 'I inhaled a few times, but it didn't seem to have much effect,' one of them said. 'But then,' continued the other, 'I stopped you going on because the effect it had on me was so frightening. My heart seemed to be beating all over the place – sort of out of time. It was horrible. Also, I had a headache and felt sick.' The solvents in such thinners have been known to cause heart failure after the first few attempts at inhalation.

Alan Billington of the National Campaign Against Solvent Abuse began working with solvent abusers after discovering that his own son had become addicted to glue. 'At the time, it was a terrible experience' he remembered.

> There seemed to be no one to turn to for help, so I fell back on my own resources. Following an article which I wrote for the *News of the World*, the reponse from desperate parents in a similar predicament was overwhelming. This was the beginning of the National Campaign Against Solvent Abuse, which is now a registered charity. Long after my son was completely cured, I found myself so involved that I gave up my job to work on the project full time.

Alan Billington has become well known for his success in weaning addicts off solvents. He doesn't think in terms of success rates, though, but talks more of an 8 per cent failure rate, which does not include those solvent addicts who 'kick the habit the second time around'. He asserts that there are perhaps more adult addicts than has been realized, although the average age for solvent abusers in 1987 was 13.2 years. He cites as an example, a 23-year-old woman who has been addicted to solvents since the age of 14. She now inhales half a pint to a pint of glue each day.

Signs and symptoms of solvent abuse

Because most of the substances used act as depressants on the central nervous system, the effects of sniffing in the early stages are similar to alcohol or anaesthesia. There is a short period of euphoria followed by depression, which can lead to disorientation, drowsiness and hallucinations. As with alcohol abuse, a sniffer may suffer a hangover and total amnesia is not uncommon. There are several obvious signs of solvent abuse. The breath, hair and clothing smell of chemicals. There are often signs of adhesive or cleaning material on the clothes, hair or round the mouth and nose, and spots, boils or a red ring around the nose and mouth where a bag, rag or bottle may have been used. The pupils of the eyes are frequently dilated and there may even be a loss of vision and lack of muscular co-ordination. Other symptoms are less easy to identify since, as with drug abuse generally, they also reflect some of the normal ups and downs of adolescence, such as restlessness, confusion, aggressive behaviour, moodiness, listlessness and general lack of energy.

How can parents help?

The National Campaign Against Solvent Abuse issues the following advice for parents:

1. Be realistic in your expectations of yourself and your son/daughter.
2. Try to keep the problem in perspective – remember, all adolescents are awkward and all of them do have good points despite present appearances.
3. Giving up solvents is very difficult (harder if they've been on it longer) – achievements may be small but watch out for them – give praise and encouragement for the good things they do as well as objecting to the bad things they do. (We all respond better to a pat on the back.)

REMEMBER:

You are not alone in this.
Others are doing their bit.
You do have the strength to cope.
You do actually love your child.

TRY TO:	TRY NOT TO:
Remain calm	Panic
Allow honest talk	Be secretive
Pick the right time to say/to act	Precipitate rows
Be supportive	Reject/eject
Accept your limitations	Give up/become depressed
Be available/observant	Opt out of the situation
	Forecast gloom and doom
Be clear as to what your problem is and what is his/her problem	'Take on' the problem
Be consistent	'Blow hot and cold'

Alcohol abuse

In the west of Scotland alcohol abuse is considered the most serious problem in the field of addiction. In 1979 the Social Work Committee of the Strathclyde Regional Council published a report stating, 'In so far as drugs are concerned, our information is that, although addiction is on the increase, it is not yet regarded as a major problem in the west of Scotland. Some would argue that this is because we manufacture the most effective drug of all, i.e. alcohol.'

According to research by the Health Education Council, more than half the boys and a third of the girls aged 11 have an alcoholic drink at least once a week, and the most popular place for them to acquire alcohol is in their own homes. Many parents would not panic if they found a bottle of gin under their teenager's bed, but would if they found marijuana. The former is legal and generally accepted as an adjunct to social life, while the latter is not. To most people alcohol use does not imply abuse. However, although it is true that only a small percentage of the millions of people who drink, drink to excess, for them and their families alcohol abuse is a problem no less serious than drug abuse.

Talking to teenagers between the ages of 13 and 16 it is possible to receive the impression that very great numbers of them do drink to excess. It is not unusual, it seems, for a youngster to consume a bottle of vermouth at a party and the next day be reminded by his or her friends where and over whom he or she had vomited. Although one bottle of vermouth does not necessarily produce or indicate an alcoholic, drunkenness is bound to make a young person more vulnerable, even when such drinking bouts are public occasions in the company of friends.

Alcohol has become part of the adolescent rites of passage and for many teenagers it is important to be seen by their peers indulging enthusiastically in this more licentious symbol of the adult world. One school counsellor told me:

> Since the decline of the 1960s coffee bars young teenagers have taken to using pubs as their meeting place, where alcohol is never difficult to obtain, if not from the publican, then from an older friend or acquaintance. Fortunately, though – and rather to my surprise – we have had very few problems. Mostly, kids learn to handle drink very quickly and keep well within the socially acceptable limits. After the initial experiments, they soon become wary of the consequences of excess.

Ann Hawker, of the Medical Council on Alcoholism and author of the comprehensive study *Adolescents and Alcohol*, also reported that the majority of teenagers in her survey drank without problems. However, she pointed out, 'There are a number, boys and girls alike, who were showing signs that they were drinking excessively on frequent occasions and some were experiencing drink-related symptoms.' She found that 10 per cent of boys and girls interviewed had episodes more than once during a year where they had no memory of the previous night. Several said that they drank 'because they liked to get drunk'. Ms Hawker's study was carried out in 1976–7, and she does not feel that the pattern of drinking has altered much since then. Boredom, particularly in rural areas, where entertainment for young people is limited, is still a major factor, she says.

Because drinking alcohol is socially acceptable and within the law, it is usually viewed as safer for youngsters to take than drugs. 'I think both my kids drink too much – but at least it's better than drugs' one father told me. However, according to Dr John Janeway Conger, 'The fact is that alcohol is just as much a psychoactive drug as, for example, marijuana, and its dangers for a significant minority have been far more clearly established.' The general acceptance of alcohol can also make it difficult to convince those concerned that a teenager's 'social' drinking, often extremely unsociable in its results, is becoming a serious problem, as Mrs S.'s experience shows.

> Our son was 14 and at boarding school. He came home almost every weekend, usually with a friend, and it was during this time that I first noticed he had begun drinking. Sometimes bottles of alcohol would

be brought home while at other times they would disappear from the drinks cupboard. I telephoned my son's headmaster, who flatly denied that John was drinking, certainly not at school anyway. Gradually, as his work deteriorated, I became even more convinced that he was having alcohol at school. In desperation I telephoned the school matron and suggested that she check the contents of his bag when he returned after a weekend. Sure enough, she found a bottle of lemonade and a lemonade bottle which contained vodka. The headmaster still seemed reluctant to tackle the problem, and my husband flatly refused to consider the possibility of John's alcoholism – perhaps because there was some history of drinking in his own family. I was absolutely alone in the matter and could not at that stage bring myself to seek help outside the family. I decided to take John away from boarding school and send him to a local day school where I could keep an eye on him. It's early days yet but he's only 15 and I am very worried about his future.

The fact Mrs S. was the only member of the family to think that her son had a serious drinking problem left her feeling lonely and isolated in her battle against his growing addiction. Some months after our first interview, I talked to her again and learned that she had finally decided to contact Al-Anon (see pp. 106, 119) for help.

Mrs M.T. was fortunate in having the support of the whole family. In response to an advertisement placed in various local newspapers throughout the country asking parents to tell me about their more problematic experiences with their teenagers, she wrote:

We have five children and feel we are a 'successful' family. Some people say 'I never nag,' some say 'I nag them all the time.' I think nagging should be kept for the things that really matter, not things like doing homework or tidying the bedroom. One of the boys, at 19, was drinking too much; I think it took me a long time to realize it. I decided that if I didn't keep on at him about it, he might never know that it was a problem. Eventually he realized that he needed help and had to have therapy at a hospital. We felt we had rescued him from a life of misery. We told the rest of the family and they were very good and helpful to him – especially as we didn't want this news to be public knowledge.

These examples reveal not only how important parents' help is, but also reflect the concern that most parents feel to keep such problems hidden from friends and neighbours, a fact that organizations such as Alcoholics Anonymous (AA) and Al-Anon (see pp. 106, 119–20) clearly recognize. A Scottish spokesman at AA remembered his own crisis twenty years earlier at the age of 17:

> Alcoholics Anonymous in Glasgow was in a huge office block on a busy main road. There was no way I would be noticed going into that building, and yet I was so panic-stricken at the time that I waited forever for the street to be cleared of buses before I could be certain that no one who might recognize me would be able to glance out from the windows as they passed and see me diving into AA!

Signs and symptoms of alcohol abuse

Because of the social acceptability of drinking, it can be difficult to determine when someone needs help. AA produce this simple questionnaire, called 'How to tell when drinking is becoming a problem', which is aimed at teenagers.

1. Do you drink because you have problems? To face up to stressful situations?
2. Do you drink when you get mad at other people, your friends or parents?
3. Do you often prefer to drink alone, rather than with others?
4. Are you starting to get low marks? Are you skiving off work?
5. Do you ever try to stop or drink less – and fail?
6. Have you begun to drink in the morning before school or work?
7. Do you gulp your drinks as if to satisfy a great thirst?
8. Do you ever have loss of memory due to your drinking?
9. Do you avoid being honest with others about your drinking?
10. Do you ever get into trouble when you are drinking?
11. Do you often get drunk when you drink, even when you do not mean to?
12. Do you think you're big to be able to hold your drink?

The questions are simple and straightforward, and helpful to parents attempting to initiate a discussion with a young person who may be having problems with drink. In the end the parents must decide whether they need to seek help for themselves and their child. If they do, they can be assured of much kindness, concern and, above all, a good chance of success.

How can parents help?

There are a number of different approaches to the problem of alcoholism, and considerable debate as to their relative merits. Apart from alcohol treatment units in hospitals, there are counselling services based in the community, and detoxification centres and hostels, some of which offer therapy. Alcoholics Anonymous, the well-known world-wide organization run exclusively by ex-alcoholics, is open to all people of all ages and all religions; the only requirement needed for entry is a firm desire to stop drinking. There is no professional counselling service and, apart from following a suggested programme of recovery, which involves twelve spiritual and practical steps, the help and support derives from sharing experiences at regular meetings with others in the same predicament. Those members of AA who have learned to live without alcohol hope that their particular path to sobriety will be of use to other members struggling with their alcoholic illness.

Angela, who was working for Alcoholics Anonymous when I met her, is just one example. She began experimenting with drugs, particularly cocaine, when she was a young teenager but found that their effects were not as exciting or dramatic as those of alcohol. 'Alcohol knocked me out in a way that drugs did not seem to have the power to do. I became totally oblivious.' At 18, after a three-year history of drinking seriously, Angela realized she was an alcoholic. She had moved out of the family home some years earlier after trying to stab her brother with a penknife, and found that the only people prepared to put up with her 'going to bed with a bottle' and to take care of her as a 'more or less permanent drunk' were her grandparents. At first, she consumed at least two bottles of vodka a day, but gradually found that she was able to tolerate less while continuously craving more. A psychiatrist suggested that she try AA. 'It was a slow start,' she said, 'but it has been a tremendous success and I have been off alcohol for the past three years.'

Because the language of the twelve-step programme is grounded in the Christian faith, I questioned whether it might at first sight have little appeal for people of different persuasions. It was explained, however, that the emphasis is not religious in the denominational sense, and that the wording is intended primarily to encourage alcoholics to regain faith in themselves and use their inner resources in order to build up enough self-confidence and will-power to conquer their addiction.

Al-Anon was born out of AA in the 1930s and operates in the same way. It exists to help and support families with an alcoholic member, whether he or she is a parent or the child. A spokeswoman said that 'when a whole family elects to attend regular meetings, their chances of success are doubled'.

The Al-Anon booklet *To the Mother and Father of An Alcoholic* begins:

> The problem of alcoholism is often thought of as one that only concerns husbands and wives of compulsive drinkers. Too seldom does anyone consider the plight of the confused and sorrowing parents of an alcoholic child. Parents have a special relationship with their children. Theirs is a deep emotional tie coupled with a great sense of responsibility. Parents bring a child into the world, and watch it grow, under loving guidance. All their hopes for the future appear shattered when they realize their child may be in trouble because of drinking.

Teenagers with an alcoholic parent are encouraged to attend Alateen groups. Sponsored by adult Al-Anon members, who provide the necessary stability and guidance, at these meetings youngsters share their ideas and experiences in the hope that they will be able to develop and assert their own identity while becoming less preoccupied with their parents' drinking problems and less affected by the resulting family strife.

ACCEPT (Alcoholism Community Centres for Education, Prevention, Treatment and Research) has an approach to treating alcoholism that is radically different to AA's one-programme-for-everyone. It tailors each programme to the individual 'client' with the help of a multidisciplinary team, whose full-time staff are augmented by a sessional team of specialist workers, including counsellors; clinical, behavioural and research psychologists; psychotherapists; yoga, relaxation, art, marriage guidance and sex therapists; psychiatric social workers; and legal and financial advisers all of whom act together with trained volunteers. Their aim is to intervene at the beginning of the drink dependency process, but they will help anyone on request, whatever the stage of their dependency. About 5 per cent of ACCEPT's annual referrals are teenagers.

They extend their services to Drinkwatchers, a national network of groups operating on the lines of the more familiar Weightwatchers.

Libra is another approach to alcohol, drug and what it calls, associated life problems. Co-founders Ric Evans and Ronnie Maggs write: 'The Libra approach grew out of the combined experience over a number of years of a suffering drinker and suffering psychiatrist.' Libra offers befriending, weekly group meetings, special-purpose small groups, meetings for relatives and friends, and counselling before, during and after a stay in hospital or prison.

It works closely with other professionals – GPs, psychiatrists, social workers – and develops special resources to meet the particular need of group members – controlled drinking group, abstinent group, etc.

Smoking

In 1982 a survey carried out by the Office of Population Censuses and Surveys showed that 11 per cent of teenagers under 16 in England and Wales regularly smoked fifty or more cigarettes a week. Between them, they were buying cigarettes worth more than £50 million a year. In 1984 a repeat survey covering 3,600 pupils in almost 127 schools in England and Wales showed 22 per cent of all secondary school pupils smoked, and 13 per cent smoked regularly. In the fifth year 31 per cent of boys (compared with 26 per cent in 1982) and 28 per cent of girls (no change since 1982) smoked regularly. The 1984 survey suggested that 11- to 15-year-olds were smoking between 19.6 and 26 million cigarettes a week – at an annual cost of between £70 million and £90 million.[9] A survey carried out in Scotland found similar levels of smoking.

Children whose parents smoke are more likely to acquire the habit than children of non-smokers. Dr Howard Williams, a consultant physician at the Whittington Hospital in London, who has been running a 'stop-smoking' course in Islington for the past 25 years suggests that

> if children had not seen adults smoke they would have had no incentive to begin, no model to copy. Children start to smoke from curiosity and from the urge to experiment. Curiosity is soon satisfied and the sequel may be unpleasant, ending with nausea and vomiting, but bravado demands that the experiments continue. They see smoking accepted as normal behaviour, permitted in homes, schools, offices and hospitals. At first their smoking is infrequent, intermittent and irregular. Later it takes on a different significance. Older children look on smoking as a symbol of maturity. Classroom smokers are not uncommonly below average at lessons and games, and take to cigarettes to restore their self-respect, to liberate themselves from the pressure of school life or to anticipate the adult world in which they hope to shine socially. When they gather together in youth clubs, coffee bars or discos, smoking is predominantly a social pastime. But when daily smoking becomes a constant feature, practised alone

regardless of social pressures, then the smoker is becoming dependent on the drug nicotine in the tobacco smoke. Nearly all regular smokers arc drug dependent.[10]

For parents who are non-smokers, it is particularly difficult to live with a teenager who is a regular smoker. While some will manage successfully to banish all smoking from the house, others will find themselves accepting some form of compromise. Mr and Mrs M. were horrified to discover that their 15-year-old daughter, Joy, was smoking and their first reaction was to refuse to allow her to use cigarettes at home. However, since most of the girl's friends smoked and arrived for social occasions with ample supplies of cigarettes and matches, it proved to be impossible to prevent their daughter and everyone else from lighting up as soon as they thought the coast was clear. Eventually it was agreed that the smoking would be confined to Joy's room, and as far as her parents can tell, the rule has never been broken.

A number of teenagers interviewed insisted that they would honestly like to give up the habit, for the most part because they found it too expensive. It is not easy to withdraw from smoking on one's own, and parents who wish to encourage their child to give up the habit should contact the Health Education Office (listed under the local Health Authority in the telephone directory) or their Community Health Council to find out if there is a clinic or self-help group in the area.

Gambling

It is against the law for people under the age of 18 to enter betting shops or casinos, or place bets at the races, but there is no legal minimum age for entry to amusement arcades or for playing computer games and fruit machines (also called one-arm bandits) in cafes and shops. In 1984 London Weekend Television's 'The London Programme' investigated teenage gambling in the city's amusement arcades. In every arcade they visited – in all areas of the city – there were children under the age of 16 gambling, many of them during school hours. In the programme Robert Davis, speaking for the Amusement Arcades Action Group (AAAG), expressed its concern over the effect the arcades appear to have on children:

> ... it leads often to addiction to gambling at a young
> age, and we've obviously got evidence to prove that many children

leave school during the day to play on the machines. This often leads to them running out of the little money they have. What happens? They then turn to some form of crime to raise money to feed their addiction and play the machines again.[11]

The chairman of the British Amusement Catering Trades Association (BACTA), strongly disputed the allegations made by the action group:

> The allegations that children under the age of 16 are being permitted into arcades unaccompanied by adults is unfair. Our members have a voluntary code of practice which excludes unaccompanied minors under the age of 16, and they all use their best endeavours to enforce that in their arcades. Sometimes, as we all know, it's quite difficult to distinguish between a mature 15-year-old and a 16-year-old. So there are difficulties, but in general terms I find that our members are being successful in policing that activity and indeed following our code of practice.[12]

However, on the same programme Dr Emanuel Moran, consultant psychiatrist and chairman of the National Council on Gambling, reported that in a survey he conducted there was a high rate of gambling by schoolchildren and the most common form was fruit machines and computer games in amusement arcades. He felt strongly that the fruit machine

> is certainly a very dangerous form of gambling, which really shouldn't be available to young people at all. This is largely due to the fact that they use a principle – a psychological principle – of operant conditioning in which behaviour which is rewarded is encouraged, and this is the explanation of why in the case of fruit machines the gambling goes on, often irrespective of winnings or losses. The sort of problems that one comes across are, first of all, related to money . . . The children steal money in order to play and so you get extortion in the playground and stealing from home and stealing on a much broader base as well. But also you get disturbances of other types – in particular, of course, children will miss school because they're at an amusement arcade and therefore . . . there's truancy and difficulties of that type.[13]

A survey conducted by the National Housing and Town Planning Council in 1987 confirmed many of AAAG's and Dr Moran's findings. It indicated that more than half the nation's 13-to 16-year-olds go to amusement arcades every week, about one-third regularly gamble away their dinner money, and a significant number truant from school and steal money to play the machines.

Dr Moran believes that teenage gambling leads to problems later in life:

> I think there's a great danger that we're breeding a sort of epidemic of pathological gambling for the future. In the history of the majority of pathological gamblers whom one sees in adulthood, one almost invariably finds that gambling begins in adolescence.[14]

The director of the Merseyside Council for Gambling Addiction disagrees. He says there is little evidence that youngsters progress from fruit machines to other forms of gambling in adult life; the real problem is why children gamble.

> Monetary loss is usually the first thing which draws the parents' attention to the fact that their youngster is gambling, but to then label the child as a 'gambling addict' is to lead parents to the worst possible scenario. Over-indulgence on the fruit machine is more often than not an expression of an individual's inability to communicate anxieties which may be rooted elsewhere in the family.

If it becomes apparent that a child is frequenting amusement arcades during school hours or stealing in order to gamble there or in other places, parents should seek help and advice.

Where to go for help and advice

The family doctor is a primary source of help and advice concerning all forms of addiction. However, not everyone feels at ease with his or her doctor and may prefer to discuss the problem with someone else, perhaps anonymously.

The organizations listed below are open during normal office hours unless stated otherwise. Many of them will supply lists of their own publications – factsheets, leaflets, magazines, books – on request.

Drugs

Nearly all hospital drug clinics
operate a strict catchment area, most
have a waiting list and many require
all new patients to be referred by
their GP. Treatment varies
considerably: some offer only out-
patient treatment, others only in-
patient detoxification. In most cases
the service will be offered during
extremely limited hours, so
appointments are essential.

Addiction, Rehabilitation and
   Advice Service
Dalmilling Road
Ayr
Tel: 0292–260122
   Day centre, offering individual
and group counselling, help and
support during withdrawal.

Blenheim Project
7 Thorpe Close
London W10 5XL
Tel: 01–960–5599
   Specializes in self-help drugs
advice. Open 10 a.m.–5 p.m.
weekdays; please telephone first.

Denmark Street Day Project
Denmark Street Health Centre
Denmark Street
Glasgow G22
Tel: 041–336–5311
   Information, advice and
counselling for drug users and their
families.

Drugline Birmingham
Dale House

New Meeting Street
Birmingham B4 7SX
Tel: 021–632–6363   Line open
   10 a.m.–2 p.m. weekdays and
   7.30–9.30p.m. Tues., Wed., Thurs.
   Answerphone at all other times.
   Confidential counselling, advice
and support service for drug users
and their parents.

Drugline London
28 Ballina Street
London SE23 1DR
Tel: 01–291–2341
   Support and advice for parents of
drug users.

Drugline Sheffield
302 Abbeydale Road
Sheffield S7 1FL
Tel: 0742–580033   Line open
   10 a.m.–2 p.m. weekdays and
   7.30–9.30 p.m. Tues., Thurs.
   Answerphone at all other times.
   Confidential counselling, advice
and support service for drug users
and their parents.

Drugs Information Service
Glasgow
Tel: 041–332–0063   Line open 2–
   9 p.m. weekdays.
   Confidential information and
advice service for drug users and
their families.

Easterhouse Campaign on Drug
   Abuse (ECODA)
8–12 Arnisdale Road
Easterhouse, Glasgow G34
Tel: 041–773–2255

Information, advice and counselling for drug users and their families.

Families Anonymous
5 Parsons Green, London SW6
Tel: 01–731–8060
and
Charing Cross Clinic
8 Woodside Crescent
Glasgow G3
Tel: 041–332–5463
A chain of self-help groups; if there isn't one in your area, Families Anonymous will explain how to start one. See also p. 75.

The Gateway Exchange
Abbey Mount
Regent Road
Edinburgh
Tel: 031–661–0982
Day centre offering information and advice, individual and group therapy and counselling for drug users and their families.

Information and Resource Unit on
    Addiction
82 West Regent Street
Glasgow G2 2QF
Tel: 041–332–0063   Line open 2–10 p.m. weekdays.
Information and advice about all forms of addiction.

Leith Project
36 Henderson Street
Leith, Edinburgh
Tel: 031–553–5250
Telephone advice service and counselling for users on a drop-in basis.

Libra
Tel: 0903–33931
Round-the-clock helpline for alcoholics, drug and solvent users.

Lifeline Project
Joddrell Street
Manchester M3 3HE
Tel: 061–832–6353
Confidential advice and counselling service. Provides a needle exchange (dirty needles exchanged for clean ones) and runs a three-week intensive drug-free induction course. Fieldworkers will visit families and offer support during detoxification programme.

Merseyside Drugs Council
5 Mortimer Street
Birkenhead L45 5EU
Tel: 051–647–8633
    and
25 Hope Street
Liverpool L1 9BQ
Tel: 051–709–0074
    and
109 Corporation Street
St Helens WA1 1SX
Tel: 0744–30072
Confidential counselling for drug users and their families. Information on the misuse of drugs and new methods of treatment.

Narcotics Anonymous
P O Box 246
Milman Street
London SW10
Tel: 01–871–0505

Self-help group for drug users, holding meetings in various parts of the country.

NAYPCAS (National Association of Young People's Counselling and Advisory Services)
17–23 Albion Street
Leicester LE1 6DG
Provides addresses of the nearest counselling and advice services.

Parents Anonymous
7 Park Grove
Off Broadway
Worsley
Walkden, Manchester
Tel: 061–790–6544
A support group for families of drug abusers.

Release
169 Commercial Street
London E1
Tel: 01–603–8654
National 24-hour-a-day emergency telephone service, offering advice and information on legal and drug-related problems.

St Enoch's Centre
13 South Portland Street
Glasgow G5
Tel: 041–429–5342
Day project for drug users, open 10 a.m.–4 p.m. weekdays. Individual counselling offered.

SCODA (The Standing Conference on Drug Abuse)
1 Hatton Place
London EC1N 8ND

Tel: 01–430–2341
Can supply up-to-date list of helping agencies throughout the country.

Shada
Muirhouse Area Social Work Department
34 Muirhouse Crescent
Muirhouse, Edinburgh
Tel: 031–332–2314
Telephone advice and drop-in centre.

Simpson House
52 Queen Street
Edinburgh
Tel: 031–225–6028
Counselling for drug users and their families.

SWAPA (South Wales Association for the Prevention of Addiction)
111 Cowbridge Road East
Cardiff CF1 9AG
Tel: 0222–26113
A 24-hour-a-day nationwide counselling service for drug and solvent abusers, their parents and friends. Send s.a.e. for publications list.

Wester Hailes Hotline
The Harbour
Hailsand Road
Wester Hailes, Edinburgh
Tel: 031–442–2465
Telephone advice service.

The residential services listed below are available on the National Health

Service, do not operate a catchment area unless stated and are open to both sexes unless stated otherwise. The list has been compiled with SCODA's assistance, but inclusion on it does not imply their recommendation.

GENERAL HOUSES

Alwin House
40 Colville Terrace
London W11
Tel: 01–229–0311
Age: 18–25
    Long-term accommodation with resident support group and full-time staff. Voluntary referrals only. Drug-free from day of entry.

Bridges
Equity Chambers
40 Piccadilly
Bradford BD1 3NN
Tel: 0274–723863
    A relatively unstructured project for chaotic drug users who want to explore the possibilities facing them. Accepts residents on bail and conditions of bail. Drug-free on admission.

City Roads (Crisis Intervention) Ltd
Crisis Centre for Multiple-Drug
    Users
358 City Road
London EC1V 2PY
Tel: 01–278–8671
    See pp. 88–9. Short-stay detoxification for multiple-drug users in crisis. Greater London catchment area only.

Cranstoun Project
148–150 Penwith Road
Earlsfield, London SW18
Tel: 01–877–0211
    Provides details of residential resources in the south-east.

Crescent House
10 St Stephen's Crescent
London W2
Tel: 01–229–3710
    Age: 17+. A Richmond Fellowship house (see p. 225). Provides individual and group counselling. Drug-free before admission – no specific time.

Face to Face
Shirley Holmes Manor
Shirley Holmes
Lymington, Hampshire SO41 8NH
Tel: 0590–683454
    Age: 16+. Drug-free for 24 hours before admission. Will take couples.

Ferry Cross Resource Centre
27 Wensum Street
Norwich, Norfolk
Tel: 0603–61939
    Age: 15–25. Detoxification in young people's unit. Practical help, concentrating on life skills.

Kaleidoscope
40–46 Cromwell Road
Kingston-on-Thames, Surrey
Tel: 01–549–2681/7488
    Age: 16–22. See pp. 87–8. A supportive environment offering rehabilitation for people with a variety of problems, including drug

use. Capacity 23. Accommodation in cluster flats.

Parole Release Scheme
30 Sisters Avenue
London SW11 5SQ
Tel: 01–672–9464
    Age: 17+. A mixed hostel for ex-offenders and ex-addicts (drugs/alcohol). A minimum support unit that can be used as a stepping stone to independent living. Drug-free.

CONCEPT HOUSES

Have a hierarchical structure operated in conjunction with intensive group sessions in which all members of the community are equal. Residents in working through the programme, work their way up the hierarchy. (*See also* p. 217.)

Alpha House
Wickham Road
Droxford
Southampton SO3 1PD
Tel: 0489–877210
    Age: 16–40. Drug-free for 24 hours before admission. Can accommodate children while treating parents.

Inward House
89 King Street
Lancaster LA1 1RM
Tel: 0542–69599
    Age: 16+. Drug-free on admission.

Ley Community
Sandy Croft
Sandy Lane
Yarnton, Oxfordshire
Tel: 08675–71777
    Age: 18–35. Drug-free for 24 hours before admission.

Phoenix House
1 Eliot Bank
Forest Hill
London SE23
Tel: 01–699–5748/1515
    Age: 16+. Drug-free for 24 hours before admission. Has special family units to accommodate children while treating parents.

Phoenix Sheffield
229 Graham Road
Ranmoor
Sheffield S10 3GS
Tel: 0742–308–230/391
    Age: 18+. Drug-free for 24 hours before admission.

CHRISTIAN PHILOSOPHY

The nature of these houses varies. Their common factor is an emphasis, in varying degrees, on the importance of a resident's acceptance of, and faith in, Jesus as the Lord, and their healer.

Chatterton Hey (male only)
Edenfield
near Bury, Lancashire
Tel: 070–682–3698
    Age: 18–35. Drug-free on admission.

Meta House (female only)
The Bournemouth Project
133 Princess Road
Westbourne, Bournemouth
Tel: 0202–764581
Age: 16–40. Holding house for up to three months. Drug-free for two weeks before admission. Can accommodate children while treating mothers.

Teen Challenge (male only)
Bryn Road, Penygroes
Llanelli, Dyfed SA14 7PP
Tel: 0269–842718
Age: 18–35. Twelve-bed hostel based entirely on Bible study. Drug-free on admission.

Deliverance International
33 Aldersbrook Road
London E12
Tel: 01–989–4610
Age: Prefer under 40. Not required to be drug-free on admission, but must desire to stop using.

Life for the World Trust (male only)
Oldbury House
Oldbury Court Road
Fishponds, Bristol BS16 2JH
Tel: 0272–655582
Age: 20–30. Drug-free on admission.
and
12 Stanley Avenue
Thorpe
Norwich, Norfolk
Tel: 0603–39905
Age: 18–30. Extended family home for men and women, will take couples and can accommodate patients' children.

Pye Barn Trust (male only)
16 The Chase
London SW4
Tel: 01–622–4870
Age: 18–30. Drug-free on admission.

Yeldall Manor (male only)
Hare Hatch
near Twyford
Reading
Berkshire RG10 9XR
Tel: 073–522–2287
Age: 20–40. Drug-free on admission, or non-medical withdrawal immediately on admission.

HOUSES WITH CHRISTIAN STAFF

Coke Hole Trust (1 house for males, 1 for females)
70 Junction Road
Andover
Hampshire
Tel: 0264–61045
Age: 18–30. Drug-free on entry – no specific time.

ACCOMMODATION

Roma House
65/67 Talgarth Road
London W14
Tel: 01–603–8383
Age: 18+. Accommodation and care for notified addicts or those in the process of notification. Will consider couples without children. No restriction on referrals.

Solvent abuse

The National Campaign Against
  Solvent Abuse
Unit S 15
245 Coldharbour Lane
London SW9
Tel: 01–733–7330
  Round-the-clock telephone
helpline. Gives confidential help to
teenagers and will advise parents
and put them in touch with local
helping organization.

REGIONAL BRANCHES

Basingstoke Campaign Against
  Solvent Abuse
60 Gregory Close
Basingstoke, Hampshire
Tel: 0256–24354

Essex Campaign Against Solvent
  Abuse
42 Charles Pell Road
Colchester, Essex
Tel: 0206–869058

National Campaign Against Solvent
  Abuse (Rochdale)
53 Cloverhall Crescent
Belfield
Rochdale, Lancashire
Tel: 0706–56931

Preston Campaign Against Solvent
  Abuse
31 Thirlmere Road
Preston, Lancashire
  Write only.

Scottish Campaign Against Solvent
  Abuse
29 Sidney Street

Arbroath
Tel: 0241–74712

Shropshire Working Party on
  Solvent Abuse
117 King Street
Wellington
Telford, Shropshire TE1 1NV
Tel: 0952–53053

Yorkshire Campaign Against
  Solvent Abuse
119 Thornes Road
Wakefield, Yorkshire
Tel: 0924–374595

OTHER AGENCIES

The Avon Federation of PTA
60 Charnwood Road
Whitchurch, Bristol
Tel: 0272–834138

Bexley Solvent Advisory Panel
1A Pickford Road
Bexley Heath, Kent DA7 3AT
Tel: 01–304–6524

Community Links
81 High Street South
London E6
Tel: 01–472–6652

East Belfast YMCA
183 Albertbridge Road
Belfast BT5 4PS
Tel: 0232–57052

Greenwich Solvent Abuse Panel
Shooters Hill Police Station
Shooters Hill Road
London SE18
Tel: 01–853–8110

Harrow Group Against the Misuse
  of Solvents
Tel: 01–864–6099

Kaleidoscope
  See p. 115.

The Matthew Project
1 Willow Lane
Norwich, Norfolk NR2 1EU
Tel: 0603–619347

Merseyside Drugs Council
  See p. 113.

Oasis
9A Clarendon Road
London SW19
Tel: 01–540–7166

The Off Centre
25 Hackney Grove
London E8
Tel: 01–985–8566, 01–986–4016

Sandwell Health Authority
8 Grange Road
West Bromwich, West Midlands
Tel: 021–525–5363
Answerphone 021–525–8522

Substance Abuse Unit
Crossways
Whitehall Road
Uxbridge, Middlesex UB8 2DF
Tel: 0895–57285

Sunderland YMCA
1–3 Toward Road
Sunderland SR1 2QF
Tel: 0783–674307

The United Council on Alcohol and
  Other Drugs

112 Albany Road
Cardiff CF2 3RU
Tel: 0222–493895

Washington Youth Advice Centre
The Galleries
Washington, Tyne & Wear
Tel: 091–417–8163/4
Lines open 3–5 p.m. Wed.

Alcohol

ACCEPT
200 Seagrave Road
London SW6 1RQ
Tel: 01–381–3155
  See p. 107. Open 10 a.m.–6 p.m.
every day and by appointment.
Offers individual and group
counselling, group therapy and
activities, job and career planning
for problem drinkers and their
families. Operates National
Drinkwatchers Network.

Al-Anon Family Groups UK and
  Eire
61 Great Dover Street
London SE1 4YF
Tel: 01–403–0888.   Line open 24
  hours a day
  Help for relatives and friends of
problem drinkers (whether still
drinking or in recovery) through
confidential group meetings.
Contact this main office for details
of nearest local group.

Alateen
61 Great Dover Street
London SE1 4YF

119

Tel: 01–403–0888
Line open 24 hours a day.
Part of Al-Anon, providing support and help for people 12–20 with an alcoholic relative.

Alcohol Counselling Service
34 Electric Lane
London SW9 8JT
Tel: 01–737–3570/3579
Free confidential counselling service for anyone who sees his or her drinking as a problem. Women are particularly welcome.

Alcohol Problem Advisory Service
(APAS)
National Temperance Hospital
Hampstead Road
London NW1 2LT
Tel: 01–388–5962, 01–387–9300
ext. 498
Appointment necessary.
Individual and group therapy. Will refer those from outside catchment area.

Alcoholic Rehabilitation Centre
Woodbine Centre
Wanstead, London E11
Tel: 01–552–5532 Line open 7.30–10 p.m. Wed.
Individual and group counselling and medical advice for those in north-east London boroughs. Ring for appointment.

Alcoholics Anonymous
11 Redcliffe Gardens
London SW10
Tel: 01–352–3001/2/3 Lines open

10 a.m.–10 p.m. and 24-hour-a-day answerphone
See p. 106. There are about 870 AA self-help groups throughout the country. Contact this main office for details of nearest group.

Aquarius
Aquarius Centre
Pebblemill House
263 Bristol Road
Birmingham, B5
Tel: 021–471–1361
Voluntary agency linked to the Alcoholic Rehabilitation Research Group at Birmingham University. Offers day and residential counselling to people of all ages with different kinds of drinking problems.

Families Anonymous
See p. 113.

GLASS (Greater London Alcohol Advisory Service)
146 Queen Victoria Street
London EC4V 4BX
Tel: 01–248–8406 and answerphone
Information and advice service for problem drinkers and their families in Greater London.

National Drinkwatchers Network
See ACCEPT.

Robert Smith Unit
Walker Dunbar House
Clifton Down Road
Bristol BS5 4AQ
Tel: 0272–735004
Part of the Barrow Hospital Group. Patients referred after

detoxification for programme of daily treatment, counselling and therapies. Follow-up programme includes continuing visits to the unit and weekly checks in out-patients department. Weekly attendance at local A A group insisted on.

Smoking

ASH (Action on Smoking and
  Health)
5–11 Mortimer Street
London W1N 7RJ
Tel: 01–637–9843
  and
Royal College of Physicians
9 Queen Street
Edinburgh EH12 1JQ
Tel: 031–225–4725

Health Education Council
78 New Oxford Street
London WC1
Tel: 01–637–1881

National Society of Non-Smokers
Latimer House
40–48 Hanson Street
London W1P 7DE
Tel: 01–636–9103

Gambling

Gamblers Anonymous
National Service Office
17–23 Blantyre Street
Cheyne Walk
London SW10 0DT

Tel: 01–352–3060   Line open 24
  hours a day
  Contact national office for details of local self-help groups for gamblers of all ages and Gam-Anon support groups for families and friends of those with a gambling problem.

Eire
Tel: 010–353–21–502398

Glasgow
Tel: 041–445–1115

Manchester
Tel: 061–273–3574

Merseyside Council on Gambling
  Addictions
11 Rodney Street
Liverpool
Tel: 051–709–0110

National Council on Gambling
Chase Farm Hospital
The Ridgeway
Enfield, Middlesex
Tel: 01–366–6000 ext. 448

Notes

1. Helen Bethune, *Off the Hook: Coping with Addiction*, London, Methuen, 1985
2. Ibid.
3. Ira Mothner and Alan Weitz, *How to Get Off Drugs*, London, Penguin, 1986
4. Dr Peter Bruggen and Charles O'Brian, *Surviving Adolescence: A Handbook for Adolescents and Their Parents*, London, Faber & Faber, 1986
5. Adapted from A. Banks and T. A. N. Waller, *Drug Addiction and Polydrug Abuse*, London, Institute for the Study of Drug Dependence, 1983
6. Omar Sattaur, 'How Glue Sniffers Come Unstuck', *New Scientist*, no. 1399, 1 March 1984, pp. 29–33
7. Dr Joyce Watson, 'Solvent Abuse and Adolescents', *The Practitioner*, vol. 228, May 1984, pp. 487–90.
8. D. Campbell and J. M. Watson, 'A Comparative Study of Eighteen Glue Sniffers', *Community Health*, no. 9, 1978, pp. 207–10
9. Jay Dobbs and Alan Marsh, *Smoking Among Secondary School Children in 1984*, London, HMSO, 1985
10. Dr Howard Williams, *Facts About Smoking for Young and Old*, London, Chest, Heart and Stroke Association, n.d.
11. London Weekend Television, *The London Programme: Amusement Arcades*, 6 July 1984.
12. Ibid.
13. Ibid.
14. Ibid.

Chapter 4

Health and sex

Puberty marks the beginning of adolescence. It is a period of accelerated physical growth followed by the rapid emergence of sexual identity and function. It begins on average at about 11 in girls and at about 13 in boys, but can occur earlier or later. Occasionally puberty begins at a very early age; this may be a hereditary condition, but a doctor should be consulted in any case. A doctor should also be consulted if a child shows no signs of puberty by his or her late teens; if necessary, puberty can be stimulated by hormone injections.

Severe difficulties in adjusting, or failing to adjust, to sexual development and its implications of adult responsibilities can result in abnormal behaviour and physical illness. The mood swings that are an accepted pattern of adolescent behaviour may sometimes make it difficult to establish whether an individual is normally miserable or more seriously depressed, while obesity, anorexia, suicide threats or attempts and the use and abuse of drugs are more obvious indications of severe problems.

For parents whose children show signs of any of these problems, the first step might be to confide in their GP, who can suggest alternative sources of help if he is unable to be of help himself. If a teenager refuses to visit a doctor, which is not unlikely, it is still rewarding for parents to seek advice. It may be that simply by talking to them, a professional will be able to gather enough information to either allay their fears or suggest ways in which they might help their child overcome particular problems.

General health

Parents have the responsibility for their children's health care until the children are 16 (see p. 198) and often undertake it for longer. Generally, adolescents are full of energy and enthusiasm, and loathe to recognize or complain if anything is wrong with them; they may go to a doctor only if a parent arranges it. Although there are no illnesses that occur only in ado-lescence, teenagers may be more vulnerable than either younger children or adults because their life-style can lower their resistance. Their eating habits are a major factor.

As adolescents mature, eating becomes part of their social life. Their nutritional needs change as their bodies grow, but at the same time their diet is controlled less by their parents and influenced more by their peer group. School and social activities and jobs may also affect the pattern of eating, changing it from regular meals to an irregular series of snacks. As a result teenagers may often not consume a sufficient amount of the nutrients essential for good health. Concern about their weight – particularly, but not only, among girls – also leads some teenagers to follow unhealthy diets. Getting too little sleep and smoking are other factors that seriously lower their resistance to illness.

Parents may no longer be able to control every aspect of their children's lives – and it can be counter-productive to nag – but they can encourage their teenagers to follow a healthy life-style, for instance, by their own example and by providing tasty, nutrition-packed snacks to replace missed meals.

Physical problems

Acne

Not everyone suffers from acne, but it is a very common, often unsightly skin complaint that may start any time after the onset of puberty and can continue for some years. The hormone testosterone, which stimulates sexual development, also stimulates the sebaceous glands to increase their activity. These glands produce an oily substance, sebum, that lubricates the skin. The pathway by which sebum and various other materials, including dead cells, are passed to the skin's surface is the follicle.

Acne begins when conditions arise that block the passage of materials through the follicle and bacteria starts to grow. As the materials accumulate, they push against the wall of the follicle and cause it to bulge into a tiny ball. If the ball gets large enough, it may be seen on the skin's surface as a flesh-coloured bump, commonly called a whitehead. If the follicle wall breaks, the dead cells, bacteria and oil spill out and irritate the surrounding skin, and may result in a cyst. Sometimes the accumulating material can stretch the opening of the follicle – the pore – and the tip of the cells can be seen on the skin's surface. Its dark colour – giving it its common name of blackhead – is due not to dirt but to natural substances present in the skin. Whiteheads and blackheads can become inflamed to pustules or boils, which in severe cases can leave permanent scars.

Anything chemical or mechanical that obstructs a follicle – a fringe of hair, oil-based cosmetics and moisturizers – can cause acne to flare up. Stress, menstruation and certain medicines also sometimes contribute to an outbreak of acne, and certain clothing, such as polo-neck sweaters, can irritate the skin by rubbing it. Most experts now agree that diet does not contribute to acne, despite the long-held belief that fried foods and chocolate can aggravate the condition.

Although acne is not caused by poor hygiene, thorough cleansing helps remove surface oil that can trap sebum underneath. If blemishes appear, they should be left alone; squeezing can lead to more serious inflammation and scarring. The sun, or a course of sun-bed treatment, may have a healing effect and is worth trying in the first instance. If exposure to ultraviolet radiation is insufficient to control the condition, a doctor should be consulted. He may recommend antiseptic skin cleansers or prescribe antibiotics, and can advise on the availability and suitability of various treatments to remove scars after the acne has completely cleared up.

Obesity

Teenagers are very aware of, and concerned with, the shape of their bodies and can be deeply affected by being extremely overweight, which can also adversely affect their physical health. Obesity is only rarely caused by a glandular malfunction, but there is evidence to suggest that some people have a tendency to be overweight because of particular metabolic problems. Generally, however, obesity is the result of excessive eating, an unhealthy diet – too many fats and sweets – and insufficient exercise.

A doctor should be consulted to determine the cause of the weight problem and to recommend treatment. Even if obesity is the result of overeating, it is important to avoid extreme and nutritionally unbalanced diets, which may be popular and produce a short-term weight loss but can cause other health problems. Learning new, healthy eating patterns and taking exercise can be effective in controlling weight in the long term, although in some cases psychological help might be necessary to determine and treat the underlying reason for excessive eating.

Hirsutism

It is perfectly normal for sexually mature girls and women to have hair on their limbs and around their nipples as well as in the pubic area and under the arms. However, a *heavy* growth of hair on the body anywhere other than in the pubic area and under the arms may cause considerable concern to girls. If this hirsutism is hereditary, the problem is entirely cosmetic and can be treated by hair removal creams or electrolysis; the latter is available for teenagers on the National Health, although there may be a long waiting list. If hirsutism is not hereditary, it may be due to a hormonal imbalance, and a doctor should be consulted.

Cosmetic deformity

If during late adolescence it can be shown that there is a cosmetic condition – such as moles, birthmarks, a large, badly shaped nose, or overdeveloped breasts – that is causing the individual psychological distress, corrective surgery may be available on the National Health. The family doctor must be consulted in the first instance and can refer the individual to a reputable specialist. It cannot be stressed too strongly that unskilled cosmetic surgery can leave a patient with serious and permanent scars.

Some private clinics specializing in cosmetic surgery and non-surgical treatment for skin problems, such as acne, offer free advice about the treatments available and suitable to the individual, but private cosmetic surgery is very expensive. A reputable clinic will always consult with the family doctor before undertaking any form of surgery.

Mental illness and psychological problems

Mental distress can be as painful and potentially serious as any physical illness, but the symptoms are often more difficult to describe and explain. People who become mentally ill develop psychological problems that affect their emotional moods and behaviour, and the way in which they communicate with other people. MIND, the National Association for Mental Health, describes the differences between types of mental illness in the following way:

A division is often made between 'neuroses' and 'psychoses'. 'Neurosis' is the name given to the more common and usually less serious types of mental disorder – which can nevertheless be profoundly distressing to the sufferer. 'Psychosis' refers to those illnesses where the sufferer experiences, at times, such severe distress that he or she seems to lose touch with reality completely. People with psychotic disturbances often aren't aware that anything is wrong . . .[1]

Although this is a useful general guide to the complicated problems that can affect the mind, not all professionals agree with the accuracy of these labels. Instead, they tend to examine the symptoms of each disturbance – which can include anxiety, depression, intense fear, delusions and hallucinations – and look for the cause, which might be organic or psychological.

Depression

The symptoms of depression in adolescents are no different from those in adults, but are more difficult for parents to recognize because in many cases they resemble or form a part of the natural mood swings of this age group. For example, MIND indicates that

> mild depression may result in feelings of deep sadness and regret; a negative outlook and loss of enjoyment of life; indecisiveness or lack of concentration; feelings of guilt and failure; erosion of self-confidence; pessimism about the future. In more severe depressions the sufferer may experience chronic anxiety, sudden mood swings, fears of ill-health, poor memory and difficulty in organizing thoughts, and feelings of worthlessness and meaninglessness.[2]

Thoughts of suicide may follow such hopeless despair.

Depression can also produce physical symptoms, including disturbed sleep, headaches and dizziness, tiredness, exhaustion, loss of appetite and weight, all of which, again, may be naturally but incorrectly assumed to have a completely different cause.

There are many causes of depression, which for adolescents might include bereavement, separation or divorce of parents, difficulties in their relationships, pressure at school or work, unemployment, poor housing conditions and financial problems. MIND points out that

> underlying these potential causes of depression are the twin factors of failure and loss – loss of a loved one, loss of a role, loss of self-confidence. These are significant: the experience of failure and loss of

> self-esteem often result in feelings of guilt, gloom and lethargy – the
> hallmarks of depression . . . Vulnerable people . . . mentally withdraw
> from situations they can't accept or cope with.[3]

Physical changes resulting from ill-health, hormonal or biochemical imbalances, drug or alcohol abuse (see Chapter 3), dietary problems (see Anorexia and bulimia, p. 129) and allergies can also lead to depression.

Parents who suspect that their children's behaviour is more than the normal moodiness of the average teenager should consult their family doctor. One of the main difficulties they have to face is a lack of co-operation; even if they admit to having a problem, teenagers are quite likely to refuse any form of professional help. Nevertheless, parents themselves can benefit from guidance. At least they can come to understand the possible nature of their children's problems and then will be in a better position to help if and when they are allowed to do so.

Schizophrenia

Schizophrenia is a psychosis that usually shows its first symptoms when the sufferer is a young adult, but the range of symptoms is so wide that it can be difficult to distinguish between this and other forms of mental illness. However, there are three symptoms that are readily identifiable.

> Thought disorder: An affected person may come to believe that their
> thoughts, feelings and actions are under the control of an external,
> alien force. They feel that this external force is taking away their own
> thoughts and inserting others into their mind – their thoughts are
> being broadcast to the people around them.
> Hallucinations: the person may experience hallucinations – seeing,
> hearing or smelling things which aren't really there. Very often they
> hear hallucinatory things discussing their thoughts or behaviour or
> urging them to do certain things.
> Delusions: The person may form false beliefs which can't be argued
> away: for example, believing that they are being pursued by secret
> agents.[4]

Although a schizophrenic breakdown is a frightening experience, many people make a full recovery. As in most instances of illness, the obvious person for parents to turn to is the family doctor. If a diagnosis of schizophrenia is made, not only will the patient need specialist psychiatric help but he and his parents will also need long-term support.

Anorexia and bulimia

Anorexia nervosa is a disorder that arises most often during adolescence and is far more common among girls and young women than among boys. It is characterized by extreme dieting – limiting the amount eaten and vomiting or using purgatives to rid the body of food consumed. Anorexia results in extreme weight loss and can lead to the loss of periods, libido, hair and energy, and, if unchecked, to death.

Bulimia is a separate but similar disorder. The self-induced starvation of the anorectic alternates with bouts of uncontrollable eating, or bingeing. Although the psychological complexities of anorexia and bulimia are such that no single cause can be isolated, the prevalence of these disorders in Western society suggests that the influence of fashion may be a factor. The successful and desirable adult woman is usually portrayed in films, newspapers and magazines as slim, and some girls and young women may become obsessed with dieting in an effort to achieve this often unrealistic ideal.

In many cases psychiatrists see the disorder as a sign that an adolescent is unable to come to terms with independence and adult responsibilities, particularly sexuality, and is trying to remain a child. Such anorectic girls are likely to regard their lack of physical development and loss of periods as a triumph. In other cases anorexia and bulimia are seen as the means by which an insecure girl is able to exert some control over her own life.

Anorexia develops insidiously, and other members of the family might not be aware of a problem at first. Sufferers themselves appear quite unconcerned, rarely realizing that anything is wrong with them. However, as family and friends become more anxious and try to pressure them into eating, anorectics become firmer in their resolve and devious in their efforts to maintain their weight loss.

Medical help is frequently sought only after all other means of persuasion have failed, when the condition is very advanced and the adolescent has to be admitted to hospital for treatment. Medically controlled feeding may save an anorectic's life in the short term, but because the underlying cause is psychological, counselling or therapy is needed to effect a cure.

Bulimia is more apparent than anorexia, as on a binge a bulimic might eat the family's entire food supply and, being uncontrollable, make quite a mess. A bulimic's health is seriously at risk from the continued use of laxatives and repeated vomiting; like anorectics, bulimics need psychological help if they are to be cured.

Self-injury

The incidence of self-injury – a form of aggression – rises sharply during adolescence, particularly around the age of 14, and is seen far more often in girls than boys. Professor Erik Erikson suggests that boys tend more towards making aggressive attacks on other people than to mutilating themselves.

Perhaps the most common form of self-injury is cutting the wrists, arms and, sometimes, the stomach and face. Often the cuts are just superficial, inflicted with a piece of broken glass rather than a knife or razor, but they are still very frightening for parents, whose immediate instinct is to think that their child is suffering from a serious mental illness. Dr Erikson states, reassuringly, that this is not the case. Usually self-injury can be seen as an act of defiance and an expression of a need for help, perhaps in trying to achieve independence. 'Adolescents in general', Dr Erikson writes, 'often seem to have a disregard, even a positive loathing, for their bodies. They are capable of abusing themselves in a way that can be very perplexing for adults.'

Tattooing is an example of self-injury as a cult phenomenon. It is a means of impressing the peer group with a badge of courage because the process is known to be painful. It may distress parents, who will have warned their youngsters that such a mark is ineradicable and may become a severe embarrassment in later life. The danger that tattooing may be done with an infected needle and transmit AIDS (see p. 134) adds to parents' concern, but there is nothing they can do to prevent their youngster from being tattooed if he or she is determined.

Suicide threats and attempts

In a survey of adolescents between the ages of 15 and 19 suicide was shown to be the third commonest cause of death after accidents and malignant disease. The Samaritans say that 'Every month three people of 16 and under kill themselves.' The usual causes of absolute despair that lead young people to attempt suicide are conflicts with their parents, loneliness and unhappiness in relations with their boy- or girl-friends.

Some adolescents have a real desire for death and carefully plan it. More often, however, those who attempt suicide wish to draw attention to their plight – a cry for help. They do not really intend to cause their own death, but to be rescued from it at the last minute. Unfortunately, if their threats are unheeded, help may arrive too late to save them.

Threats of suicide and suicide attempts should always be treated seriously.

Parents may find that they cannot give their children the help they need, particularly if family conflict is the motivating force. Immediate help is always available from the Samaritans (see p. 138) and there are many sources of longer-term counselling and therapy (see Chapter 7).

Physical abuse

Physical abuse of a young person can lead to impaired family relationships, physical and mental handicap, and death. Youngsters who have been abused are more likely to abuse their own children. Adolescent behaviour can be infuriating – there's no doubt about it – and teenagers are capable of reducing their parents to levels of absolute rage, which, without firm control, could lead to physical violence. The practical solution is to walk away from any confrontation that feels as though it might degenerate into a fight. This is perhaps possible only if those occasions are few and far between, and there has been a cooling-off period. Parents who are worried about the violence of their own or their partner's actions towards their children should seek professional help.

Sex

Sex education

Sex education is essential and, ideally, should begin before puberty, around the ages of 10–11, so that young people understand and are prepared for the changes that will take place in their bodies, and not confused, worried or guilt-ridden by misinformation they pick up from other children. They need to be told about the sexual anatomy, feelings and behaviour of both sexes; the facts about reproduction, including contraception, intercourse and pregnancy; the importance of a loving relationship and sexual responsibility; the risks of sexually transmitted diseases; and the effect of alcohol on sexual behaviour. Girls may need reassurance about period pain, sanitary protection and pre-menstrual tension, and boys about 'wet dreams'; both sexes may have questions about kissing, fondling, foreplay and masturbation.

Regrettably, the very personal nature of sex often results in poor education. Some parents are too embarrassed to talk about it and, even if it is included in the school curriculum, some children may be too embarrassed to ask questions to which they desperately want the answers. The more relaxed and natural the approach by parents or teachers, the more easily sex will be discussed and understood by teenagers. It may be much easier for a mother to talk to her daughter, and a father to his son. There are many informative books available and parents may find them helpful in initiating discussion. If parents feel they cannot talk freely about sex, they should have an alternative ready. This could be a teacher, the family doctor or an independent self-referral agency such as a family planning clinic, where advice and help are freely available.

Sexual identity

Sexual feeling and behaviour have many variations. The majority of people are heterosexual: they are sexually attracted to members of the opposite sex. Transvestites, or cross-dressers, are heterosexuals who dress in the clothes of the opposite sex to obtain sexual excitement. Homosexuals are sexually attracted to members of the same sex. Adolescents may experiment with homosexual relationships during puberty as a normal part of growing up and finding their true heterosexual identity, but for some it is the sexual pattern they will maintain in maturity.

Homosexuals are often aware from an early age that they are somehow different from the majority of other children, but it can be difficult for them, as well as for their parents, to recognize and accept their homosexuality. They might find they are snubbed and even victimized at school by other children, and even by those who are gay. In *I Know What I Am*, a pamphlet published by the Joint Council for Gay Teenagers, the authors say:

> A vital part of helping gay people to lead happy and fulfilling lives
> (just as it is for heterosexual people) is to provide them from an early
> age with positive advice from others whose lives can act as models for
> their own and the opportunity to experience relationships and
> emotions.[5]

Parents and children alike may benefit from counselling directed at helping them to adjust to their situation rather than trying to alter it.

Contraception

Young people should learn about contraception as part of their basic sex education. The majority of effective contraceptive measures – the oral contraceptive pill, the intra-uterine device (IUD or coil), the diaphragm or cap – are for use by women and obtainable only through a doctor. Sixteen is the age of medical consent (see p.198) and girls of that age and older can receive contraceptive help without the knowledge of their parents; in most circumstances girls under 16 cannot.

The condom, or sheath, which gives the male the responsibility for contraception, and the sponge are available on the chemist's counter.

Pregnancy

Pregnancy can and does occur in adolescence. A young girl who is pregnant needs a great deal of help in order to overcome feelings of fear, confusion, guilt and isolation. She needs careful counselling as to whether the pregnancy can and should be terminated or allowed to continue, whether to keep the baby or have it adopted. Confronted with perhaps the first major adult decision of her life, the outcome will be crucial to her and it is important that she is involved in as much of the decision-making as possible.

If termination is decided on, the sooner it is done and the fewer people involved within the family, the better. It will spare the girl added embarrassment and anxiety if she feels that her troubles have been kept a private matter. Parents should keep a caring eye on their daughter for some time after an abortion in case of a depressive reaction and to ensure that contraception is fully understood for the future.

If the pregnancy is to continue, antenatal care should begin as soon as possible. There are no special features for a pregnant adolescent; she is treated the same as a pregnant adult. However, because of her youth, she needs guidance at school and at home to cope with the consequent social problems.

If the pregnancy is discovered too late for a termination and the girl does not want to keep the child, she can have it legally adopted. The arrangements are made before the baby is due to be born, and the girl will be counselled by a social worker. The baby is usually separated from the mother immediately after birth.

Sexually transmitted diseases (STD)

The moment sexual intercourse begins, the possibility of catching an STD arises. There are a great many STDs, and their effects can include mild discomfort or extreme pain, structural damage, sterility, blindness, paralysis, insanity and death. Some STDs, such as herpes, produce obvious symptoms

in both sexes; others – syphillis, for example – may produce obvious symptoms only in men; and still others – AIDS – produce no obvious symptoms
initially. All STDs can be diagnosed by blood tests.

Testing, diagnosis and treatment is done at special clinics attached to all
main hospitals. Confidentiality is strictly maintained, but because of the
highly infectious nature of STDs, all sexual contacts of an infected person
must be traced, notified and examined for possible infection. Syphillis can
be cured if treated early enough; otherwise, it can be fatal. Herpes can be
treated to alleviate the painful symptoms; it cannot be cured but it is not
fatal. There is no cure for AIDS.

AIDS (acquired immune deficiency syndrome) is a breakdown in the
body's natural ability to fight infection. It is caused by the human im-
munodeficiency virus (HIV), of which there are several strains. AIDS can
be transmitted sexually, by infected injection needles and from an infected
pregnant women to her unborn child. The virus is not passed on through
casual social contact such as shaking hands and there is no evidence that it
can be transmitted by hugging, lavatory seats, eating from the same plate or
drinking from the same glass or cup. In the United Kingdom the danger of
infection through the transfusion of infected blood products, by artificial
insemination and by transplants of organs or tissues has now been elimin-
ated through careful screening. This is not always the case overseas and
travellers are advised to seek information about any country that they intend
to visit.

The medical community and the government are trying to contain the
spread of AIDS by educating the public about the disease and promoting
safe sex, particularly the use of condoms. To avoid being infected, everyone
is advised to know the health and life-style of his or her sexual partner
before having intercourse; to use a condom; avoid anal intercourse even
when using a condom; and avoid oral sex, mutual masturbation and 'French'
or 'wet' kissing if either partner has cuts or sores in the relevant areas.

Promiscuity

Early sexual encounters can cause acute embarrassment, distress and confusion, and promiscuity in young girls is often considered by psychiatrists to
be a cry for help. Parents worry about the dangers of their children's sexual
promiscuity not only because of the immediate and long-term emotional
damage it can cause, but also because of the danger of pregnancy and
sexually transmitted diseases, particularly AIDS.

Apart from educating their children and setting an example, there are only certain actions parents can take to prevent them from becoming sexually promiscuous, and these are mainly in making and upholding family rules. However, even when it is possible to maintain a certain amount of control over an adolescent's social life, parents should remember that sexual activity is not confined to late nights. Parents who suspect that their youngster may be 'sleeping around' would be wise to seek professional help, either from the family doctor or from an organization such as Parents Anonymous (see p. 139).

Sexual abuse

A public opinion poll conducted in 1985 found that one in ten adults – male and female – had suffered some form of sexual assault in childhood. Many such assaults occur within the family. Helen Kenwood, a social worker specializing in child sexual abuse, said:

> In the past we overlooked many cases of sexual abuse because it was obscured by physical abuse. Often where there is one, there is the other. Fathers frighten children into doing what they want or into keeping quiet about it in a number of ways. They often threaten to hurt something the child loves, such as a dog, or saying the mother will leave home or the father will be put in prison.[6]

Sexual abuse most commonly starts when children are quite young but, says Helen Kenwood:

> If a child says nothing when the abuse starts, it can go on for a very long time . . . When a child grows to 14 or 15, and starts going out more, a father who is abusing his daughter will become very repressive to try to stop her meeting other children. It is when children start comparing experiences that it comes out.[7]

Children's complaints should always be taken seriously, but if a wife suspects that her husband has been sexually abusing a child, it may take an enormous amount of courage for her to report him to the authorities. The risk of ensuing family breakup may frighten her, yet the effect of the abuse on the child could well be more catastrophic than the trauma involved in being removed from the home or the disintegration of the marriage. One source of help is the Probation Service. Although it is court-based, one senior probation officer pointed out:

> We are not a statutory body and have no power to take a child away

from the family. Therefore in cases of incest or child abuse where, for example, a mother might be aware that something is going on and doesn't know what to do, she may find it easier to come to the Probation Service for help.

In some cases professional counselling and therapy for the entire family may make it possible to preserve the marriage.

Children and young people can also be the victims of sexual abuse by someone outside the family. All such assaults should be reported to the police. Cases of rape need to be reported to the police immediately and especially before the victim bathes or changes clothes, even though this contradicts her instinctive reaction. Psychiatrists involved with rape victims and their families insist that it is most important for parents to accept the problem and be supportive, and, above all, to encourage the young victim to talk about the experience. No blame should be attached to the girl, nor should the parents take the blame for the outrage on themselves. Some form of professional counselling is usually necessary to pave the way towards communication and acceptance. The victim's future ability to establish healthy, successful relationships may depend on it.

Where to go for help and advice

The family doctor is the first source of help and advice for almost all the situations discussed in this chapter. If he is unable to be of help himself, he can refer parents to other relevant sources. Other helping agencies are listed below and are open during normal office hours unless stated otherwise. Many of them will supply lists of their own publications – factsheets, leaflets, magazines, books – on request.

Obesity

Weightwatchers
Tel: 0753–856751
   Will provide information about nearest classes.

Mental illness

(*See also* Chapter 7)

MIND (National Association for
   Mental Health)
22 Harley Street
London W1N 2ED
Tel: 01-637-0741

Advisory service open 2–4 p.m. weekdays.

Leading mental health organization in England and Wales, with comprehensive information service. Telephone advisory service is not a counselling service but guide towards finding appropriate kind of help. For details of nearest local association, contact appropriate regional office. For list of publications, send s.a.e. to MIND Mail Order (pl) at South East MIND offices.

REGIONAL OFFICES

North West MIND
21 Ribblesdale Place
Preston PR1 3NA
Tel: 0772–21734

Northern MIND
158 Durham Road
Gateshead, Tyne & Wear NE8 4EL
Tel: 091–478–4425

South East MIND
Fourth Floor
24–32 Stephenson Way
London NW1 2HD
Tel: 01–380–1253

South West MIND
Bluecoat House
Saw Close
Bath BA1 1EY
Tel: 0255–64670

Trent & Yorkshire MIND
First Floor Suite
The White Building
Fitzalan Square
Sheffield S1 2AY
Tel: 0742–21742

Wales MIND
23 St Mary Street
Cardiff CF1 2AA
Tel: 0222–395123

West Midlands MIND
Third Floor
Princess Chambers
52–54 Lichfield Street
Wolverhampton WV1 1DG
Tel: 0902–24404

OTHER AGENCIES

Depressives Anonymous
36 Chestnut Avenue
Beverley,
North Humberside HU17 9QU
Self-help organization. Co-ordinates groups throughout the country.

Mental Health Association of Ireland
14 Menion Square
Dublin 2
Tel: 0001–764310

Mental Welfare Commission for Scotland
22 Melville Street
Edinburgh EH3 7NS
Tel: 031–225–7034
Helps people who because of mental disorder may be unable to help or protect themselves.

The National Schizophrenia Fellowship
78–79 Victoria Road
Surbiton, Surrey KT6 4NS
Tel: 01–390–3651

Help and support for sufferers and their families.

National Schizophrenic Society
5 Mountain Road
Newtownards, County Down
Tel: 0247–813420

The North West Fellowship
46 Allen Street
Warrington, Cheshire WA2 7JB

Northern Ireland Association for
    Mental Health
Beacon House
84 University Street
Belfast BT7 1HE
Tel: 0232–28474/5

The Northern Schizophrenia
    Fellowship
38 Collingwood Buildings
Collingwood Street
Newcastle-upon-Tyne NE1 1JH

Richmond Fellowship
8 Addison Road
London W14 8DL
Tel: 01–603–6373
    Runs forty therapeutic communities in the London area and south and south-west of England. Many of these specialize in helping troubled adolescents, who may be referred by their GP or social worker. It is possible to self-refer, but the fees are very high and are usually found by a local authority, for whom referral must be official. *See also* p. 225.

Samaritans
    Confidential telephone support for people in distress. Almost all branches can be telephoned 24 hours a day, every day of the year, and can be visited any day or evening. The local telephone number is in the telephone directory. If no directory is available, dial 100 and ask the operator for the Samaritans.
    There is also a branch for correspondence only:

PO Box 9
Stirling

Scottish Association for Mental
    Health
67 York Place
Edinburgh EH1 3JB
Tel: 031–556–3062

Anorexia

Anorexia Aid
The Priory Centre
11 Priory Road
High Wycombe, Buckinghamshire
Tel: 0494–21431
    Lay help for anorectics and their families.

Anorexia Anonymous
24 Westmoreland Road
London SW13
Tel: 01–748–4587
    Lay advice and help for anorectics. Will advise on nearest self-help group.

Self-injury

Women Listening to Women
Bristol

Tel: 0272–354105
Self-help group for women victims of self-injury.

Suicide threats

Samaritans
See above.

Physical abuse

Childline
Tel: 0800–1111
A free, nation-wide, 24-hours-a-day telephone help and advice service for children suffering any form of physical, sexual or emotional abuse.

Childwatch
60 Beck Road
Everthorpe
Brough, North Humberside
A pressure group campaigning for more help for families.

Kidscape
82 Brook Street
London W1Y 1YT
Tel: 01–493–9845

NSPCC (The National Society for the Prevention of Cruelty to Children)
and
RSSPCC (Royal Scottish Society for the Prevention of Cruelty to Children).
Anyone who believes a child is being abused can telephone the NSPCC or RSSPCC at any time:
the local number is in the telephone directory. These agencies provide immediate help for children and then work with the entire family to help them to identify and overcome problems and difficulties. Callers are guaranteed confidentiality.

Opus
29 Newmarket Way
Hornchurch, Essex
Tel: 040–2451538
Help and advice for parents who have abused, or feel they might abuse, their children physically or mentally.

Parents Anonymous
6–9 Manor Gardens
London N7 6LA
Tel: 01–263–8918
Offers friendship and help to parents who are tempted to abuse their children.

Sexual identity

Gay Switchboard
BM Switchboard
London WC1N 3XX
Tel: 01–837–7324 Line open 24 hours a day.
Information and support service for gay men and women. Gives details of gay switchboards and groups throughout the country.

Lesbian & Gay Christian Movement
BM Box 6914
London WC1N 3XX
Tel: 01–283–5165

Offers help nation-wide for gay Christian men and women, especially those under 26.

Lesbian & Gay Youth Movement
BM GYM
London WC1N 3XX
Tel: 01–317–9690
A campaigning and co-ordinating body nation-wide. Has a pen-friend scheme and up-to-date lists of gay youth groups.

Lesbian Line
BM Box 1514
London WC1N 3XX
Tel: 01–251–6911
Information and support services for homosexual women only.

Parents Enquiry
16 Honley Road
Catford, London SE6 2HZ
Tel: 01–690–1815
A counselling service for parents of young homosexuals.

Contraception, pregnancy and adoption

Adoptive Parents Association of Ireland
17 Clyde Road
Ballsbridge
Dublin 4
Tel: 0001–682685
An adoption and fostering agency.

Birth Control Trust
27–35 Mortimer Street

London W1N 7RJ
Tel: 01–580–9360

British Pregnancy Advisory Service
Second Floor
245 North Street
Glasgow G3 7DL
Tel: 041–204–1832
Help and advice on problems arising from pregnancy.

British Agencies for Adoption and Fostering
11 Southward Street
London SE11 1RQ
Tel: 01–407–8800
Help, advice and information.

Brook Advisory Centre
233 Tottenham Court Road
London W1P 9AE
Tel: 01–580–2991
A full family planning service for anyone under 26. List of local branches available.

Family Planning Association
27–35 Mortimer Street
London W1N 7RJ
Tel: 01–636–7866
A professional training and education service on all aspects of personal relationships and sex education.

Federation of Services for Unmarried Parents and Their Children
11 Clonskeagh Road
Dublin 6
Tel: 0001–961744
Help for unmarried parents.

Irish Family Planning Association
15 Mountjoy Square
Dublin 1
Tel: 0001–729574
   Advice, help, information and a
full family planning service.

National Children's Home
   Adoption Society
85 Highbury Park
London N5 1UD
Tel: 01–226–2033
   Help, advice and information.

Parent to Parent Information on
   Adoption Services
Lower Baddington
Daventry,
Northamptonshire NN11 6UB
Tel: 0327–60295
   Information, advice and support
for families involved in adoption.

Protestant Adoption Society and
   Single Parent Counselling Service
71 Brish on Road
Rathgar, Dublin 6
Tel: 0001–972659
   Help, advice and information.

Scottish Adoption Association Ltd
69 Dublin Street
Edinburgh EH3 6NS
Tel: 031–556–2070
   Help, advice and information for
adopters and adoptees.

Ulster Pregnancy Advisory
   Association Ltd
338A Lisburn Road
Belfast
Tel: 0232–667345

   A full family planning and
counselling service.

AIDS

In addition to the agencies listed
below, help and guidance can be
obtained from Health Education
Units of local or district health (or
health and social services) boards;
from medical, dental and nursing
staff responsible for the child and
school health services; and, in Wales,
from Principal School Medical
Officers. Addresses and telephone
numbers can be found in the
telephone directory.

AIDS Detection Centre
City Hospital
51 Grenbank Drive
Edinburgh
Tel: 031–447–1011   Line open
   during office hours
031–447–0411   Line open after
   5 p.m. and at weekends

AIDS Helpline
Northern Ireland
Tel: 0232–226117   Line open 7.30–
   10 p.m. weekdays

AIDS Information Service
Department of Health and Social
   Security
Tel: 0800–535535   Line open 24
   hours a day
   A free, nation-wide telephone

service dealing with queries and providing free literature.

BBC AIDS Advisory Service
Tel: 0800–567123
   Nation-wide, free telephone helpline.

The Buddy Scheme
see The Terrence Higgins Trust

Haemophilia Society
PO Box 9
16 Trinity Street
London SE1
Tel: 01–407–1010

Health Education Council
73 New Oxford Street
London WC1
Tel: 01–637–1881

Healthline
Tel: 01–980–4848
   Plays information tapes on request.

Healthline Telephone Service
Tel: 01–981–2717, 01–980–7222
   and 0345–581151 for callers outside London, who will be charged at local rate.

Infectious Diseases Unit
Ruchill Hospital
Glasgow G20 9NB
Tel: 041–946–7120

SCODA (Standing Conference on Drug Abuse)
1–4 Hatton Place
London EC1 8ND
Tel: 01–430–2341

Scottish AIDS Monitor
PO Box 169
Edinburgh EH1 3UU
Tel: 031–558–1167
   and
HELPLINES:
Dundee Tel: 0382–25083
Line open 10 a.m.–12 noon Sun.

Edinburgh Tel: 031–558–1167
Line open 7.30–10 p.m. weekdays

Glasgow Tel: 041–221–7467
Line open 7–10 p.m. Thurs.

The Terrence Higgins Trust
BM AIDS
London WC1N 3XX
Tel: 01–833–2971   Line open 3–10 p.m.
   A registered charity that provides practical support, help, counselling and advice for anyone with, or concerned about, AIDS or HIV infection. Runs the Buddy Scheme, in which AIDS victims are offered friendship and support by individual volunteers. Up-to-date leaflets available.

Welsh AIDS Campaign
PO Box 348
Cardiff CF1 4XL
Tel: 0222–223443

Sexual abuse

Rape should be reported to the police immediately, who will provide medical and emotional help.

Incest Crisis Line
Tel: 01–422–5100 and 01–890–4732

Rape Crisis Centres: all lines open
24 hours a day
Birmingham
Tel: 021–233–2122
Exeter
Tel: 0392–30871
London
Tel: 01–837–1600

or see number in local telephone directory.

Run by women for women. Offers confidential, practical, medical and legal advice and emotional support.

See also: Physical abuse listings, p. 139.

Notes

1. MIND, *Understanding Mental Illness*, London, 1987
2. MIND, *Factsheet 7: Depression*, London, n.d.
3. Ibid.
4. MIND, *Understanding Schizophrenia*, London, 1987
5. Joint Council for Gay Teenagers, *I know What I Am*, London, 1980
6. *The Independent*, 26 June 1987, p.3
7. Ibid.

Chapter 5

Education and Employment

The teaching profession considers maintaining close links between home and school especially important during the early years of education, but recognizes that a move from primary to secondary school coincides with a young person's need for greater independence and therefore no longer fosters close parental involvement. At this stage it is easy for parents to feel they are losing touch with their children's lives. Adolescents spend more time out of the home and are less forthcoming about their everyday activities than small children and so parents may not learn about a growing problem at school until it has reached a serious stage.

It is bewildering and frightening for parents to receive a telephone call from the headteacher summoning them to the school to discuss problems of which they had, until that moment, been completely unaware. This situation probably arises most often because of disruptive behaviour by a student who has no history of behavioural difficulties at school or at home, and may coincide with a deterioration of standards of achievement in academic work. Although ideally parents should be informed immediately of a distinct change in their child's behaviour, since it is often a sign that there is a problem in the home, frequently they are not notified until that behaviour has disrupted the entire class and alienated the teachers, and the standard of schoolwork has fallen to a dangerously low level.

What kind of help can parents expect to receive from the school and how can they in turn help their children? Unfortunately there are no easy answers. Schools and teaching staff vary greatly in terms of the quality of understanding, advice and help they can offer parents. This chapter focuses on the most common problems and the ways in which parents can effectively help themselves.

Choosing a school

It is natural for parents to want the best for their children and in terms of education they may know what kind of school would be ideally suited to their needs, but realistically what choices do they have and how should they make them? In urban areas there may be some choice of comprehensive school, but in rural areas there may be only one local school and so no real choice within the state, or maintained, system. There are, of course, independent schools for those who can afford them and assisted places for some of those who cannot (see p. 157). Which school parents choose for their children may be influenced by their financial resources, but should also be determined by the nature of the school and the quality of education it provides.

Some of the best known research into secondary education has been conducted by Professor Michael Rutter and his colleagues at the Institute of Psychiatry. In one study they followed children in twelve schools through their secondary education to evaluate the effect of various factors on attendance, behaviour, academic achievement and delinquency.[1] The factors the team highlighted and the results of their study provide parents with some useful guidelines in making their choice.

SIZE

The twelve schools ranged in size from about 450 to 2,000 pupils. The research team found that the size of the school did not have any significant effect on pupils although it may have had an impact on the school's character and style.

SPACE

Spacious buildings did not seem to be necessary for producing successful pupils. In fact, much to the researchers' surprise, they found that overcrowded schools had somewhat better results.

BUILDINGS

The school buildings varied in age from about 10 to over 100 years old. Some of them were said to be 'decidedly unattractive and not well designed for contemporary approaches to secondary schooling'. Regardless of age, however, the team found that there were striking differences in the care with which the buildings were maintained:

In some, great care was taken to provide attractive decorations, pictures and plants, and to keep the building in good order by ensuring that any graffiti were rapidly removed and that damage was immediately repaired. In others, decorations were allowed to become dirty; there were delays in repairing broken windows and furniture; the walls were devoid of pictures and posters, and graffiti tended to be ignored.

Although the researchers concluded that the age of the buildings had no significant effect on the characteristics measured, variations in the care and decorations of buildings did prove to be related. They found particularly that schools that displayed a lot of the children's work on the classroom walls tended to have a better academic result.

SPLIT-SITE SCHOOLS
The team were surprised by their findings concerning split-site schools, which they initially saw as a disadvantage, especially from a teacher's point of view. However, results showed that there were no differences between single and split-site schools in attendance or academic attainment, and split-site schools had better results when it came to testing behaviour and delinquency, although the reasons for this were not clear.

THE HEADTEACHER
In a large comprehensive school with about 1,000 pupils the head will operate as part of a management team, but in a smaller school he or she will be a much more central figure. Although the head's influence is obviously considerable, the team found that the various styles of leadership were not necessarily significant in providing better results in the evaluations. Much more important was the relationship between the head and the staff. As might be expected, the schools in which obvious co-operation existed between departments, individual staff and the head, and in which teachers felt that they could rely on the head for support in dealing with specific problems, showed significantly better results.

This feeling of mutual respect was extended to the children in a number of ways, especially in terms of staff concern for their needs. Children's behaviour was better in schools where they were readily able to consult teachers about problems, and where many children were in fact seen by teachers. There was also better behaviour, better attendance and less delinquency in schools where the teachers gave children the responsibility for looking after books and papers, and where pupils were given posts of responsibility and trust.

PASTORAL CARE
The schools involved in the study adopted a variety of methods for organiz-

ing pupil welfare. Some favoured a year-based system in which one teacher was responsible for all children of a particular age. Others were based on houses with a house teacher responsible for a group of children of varied ages. The research showed that both systems could work effectively and neither appeared to have a particular advantage.

SCHOOL'S ATTITUDE TO ACADEMIC WORK

The team felt that the most obvious indication was provided by the school's use of homework. They found that the schools that set homework frequently and where there was a check on whether staff did in fact set it, tended to have better results than schools that made little use of homework. (It is noted, though, that the time spent on homework each evening was rather short – from an average of 15 minutes in one school to 35 minutes in another.) Higher standards of academic achievement also correlated with teacher expectations that a high proportion of the children would do well in national examinations.

It was also found that in the schools that were more successful in terms of good attendance and low delinquency, courses were planned by groups of teachers under the guidance of the heads of departments.

THE SIZE OF THE CLASS

The pupil-teacher ratio was not found to be significant, in spite of variations in class size from 22–30.

DISCIPLINE

Discipline seemed not to be linked with punishments in any relevant way, whereas all forms of reward, praise or appreciation yielded more positive results. Consistency was an important factor. The researchers write: 'Outcomes tended to be better when both the curriculum and approaches to discipline were agreed and supported by the staff acting together.' The particular rules set and different techniques applied were thought to be less significant in achieving successful results than the establishment of some principles and guidelines that were clearly recognizable and accepted by the whole school: 'Exam successes were more frequent and delinquency less common in schools where discipline was based on general expectations set by the school (or house or department), rather than left to individual teachers to work out for themselves.'

In conclusion, the researchers write:

> The findings as a whole suggest that children tended to make better
> progress both behaviourally and academically in schools which placed

an appropriate emphasis on academic matters. This emphasis might be reflected in a well-planned curriculum, in the kinds of expectations teachers had of the children they taught, and in the setting and marking of homework.

They also concluded that their results carried 'the strong implication that schools can do much to foster good behaviour and attainments, and that even in a disadvantaged area, schools can be a force for the good'.

OTHER CRITERIA
In addition to the factors examined by Rutter and his team, parents should consider the social environment and academic facilities in some detail. To assess the school as a social institution, some of the questions they might ask are:
1. Do children move about quietly, without pushing, shoving, running?
2. Are the specialist facilities well-used?
3. Does the school extend its facilities to the community for activities after school hours; if so, are the children welcome to join in?
4. What clubs, societies, outings and other activities are arranged out of school time?
5. Does the school arrange holiday trips abroad and exchange with pupils from schools overseas?
6. Is there room for small-group teaching, and for the drama club, school orchestra or gymnastics team to rehearse?
7. What leisure and refreshment facilities are there?
8. How safe are the lavatories?
9. Are there lockers for all pupils?
   This last factor seems to me to be an important one. In one school I visited there were no facilities for children to hang up their coats or lock up their personal equipment. (This policy – and it is not uncommon – was adopted by the school after a long period of theft and vandalism had rendered the previously existing lockers a hazard.) In consequence many children turned up in bad weather conditions underdressed and inadequately shod because there was 'nowhere to leave our boots and it's too much of a bore to carry a coat around the different classrooms all day'.
   If the school has a uniform it is important to know what proportion of pupils wear it and to what degree they are allowed to alter it. Some schools will send children home if there is a slight deviation in dress, while others will accept a certain level of individuality. Balance is an important factor in the curriculum. A wide range of subjects should be available in the early

years and there should be plenty of subjects from which to choose for more detailed study later. Parents should find out:

1. What external examinations are taken in academic and non-academic subjects?
2. Who chooses the subjects, the teachers or the pupil and parents guided by the teachers?
3. When do the choices have to be made?
4. What criteria does the school use to decide whether or not a child is capable of passing specific exams and at what level?

The public sector: comprehensive schools

Comprehensive schools account for 90 per cent of children in secondary education. In theory comprehensive education is meant to enable each and every pupil to achieve his or her full potential, and one of its prime functions is to ensure that a wide range of pupil abilities is recognized and assessed. In practice it does not always live up to these ideals. Mrs Caroline Benn is the editor of *Comprehensive Education*, a publication that campaigns for change and improvement in the system. A long-time champion of the cause, she points out that after twenty years

> . . . there is still the old 11-plus system in many areas. There is still widespread hidden selection – at 11, at 12, at 13, at 14 and 16. There is nation-wide selection at 11 through to 16 for assisted places and for private schools which receive public subsidies. There is internal comprehensive school selection through streaming and through unreformed areas of the curriculum and assessment system.[2]

Because the public examination system exerts such influence over the curriculum, there tends to be a bias towards academic subjects in the majority of comprehensive schools. Non-academic subjects are likely to be optional, offered to lower ability pupils and often not available as examination subjects even when local examination boards make them available. Thus many schools throughout the country are comprehensive in name only and still operate along traditional grammar school lines. In most comprehensives the largest departments are those concerned with traditional academic subjects and, since many were formed through merging grammar and secondary modern schools, former grammar school teachers have generally ended up in the most senior positions.

Glenn Turner, Research Fellow in the School of Education at the Open University, is personally dedicated to the ideology of the comprehensive system, but his research reflects so many problems within it that he had been, inaccurately and unfairly he feels, described as being against it. He says:

> The assumption that certain subjects are appropriate only for certain types of pupil extends of course to ability as well as to gender stereotyping. I have already commented on the low status of practical and technical subjects in many comprehensive schools. However, not only are such subjects usually relegated to option subjects with little time devoted to them, but they are also frequently perceived to be subjects which are only suitable for low ability pupils, and low ability of course means low academic ability.[3]

Turner found that 'academically inclined' pupils in some schools are prevented from taking certain practical or technical subjects. He cites in particular a large comprehensive where a course in typing was not available to those pupils who were taking more than five O levels, despite the fact that some would have liked to have had the skill. 'The implication of this restriction is obvious,' says Turner.

> The high ability pupil is an academic pupil who should not be allowed to waste his or her time gaining practical or technical skills. The evidence suggests that staff attitudes in comprehensive schools are an important factor in the differential status accorded to academic and non-academic subjects, and that it is not solely the examination boards which have been responsible for promoting academic abilities in assessment at the expense of other potentially important aspects of achievement. However, this should not be taken as an indication that for the majority of teachers in comprehensive schools academic criteria are of paramount importance in the assessment of pupils. As members of subject departments, they may well collectively emphasize the importance of their own subject, but as *individuals*, they may value pupil abilities which are not recognized in the examination-dominated school curriculum. My data suggest that what counts most to many teachers in assessing pupils is the personal–social dimension which is probably the area assessed least by public examinations. In fact, in talking to teachers about the 'ideal' pupil, there seems to be a considerable discrepancy between the criteria of public examinations and the criteria mentioned by teachers.[4]

In the comprehensive school in which Turner carried out his research, the teachers interviewed all stressed the importance of factors that are not explicitly assessed in public examinations. The headmaster looked for 'the basic attributes of a civilized human being' in his pupils, and asked that they should be 'courteous, polite, considerate of other people and respect authority', the head of social studies rated co-operation and motivation highest on his list of pupil attributes, and the head of geography considered effort and attitude important qualities.

Despite these shortcomings most senior educationalists view the first twenty years of comprehensive education with considerable optimism. Fred Jarvis, the General Secretary of the National Union of Teachers, writes:

> Comprehensive education has brought enormous benefits to the education system of England and Wales. Pupils enter comprehensive schools on equal terms with their peers, and they are able to benefit from a curriculum and system of organization designed from the outset to cater for pupils of all abilities – flexible enough to stretch the academically able and less able alike, while greatly expanding the opportunities available to all, resulting in a broader, richer and more balanced curriculum than either the grammar or the secondary modern schools could provide.[5]

Peter Newsam, who organized comprehensive schools in North Yorkshire, suggests that although the proportion of an age group leaving school with formal qualifications still remains too low, it is far higher than it had been under selective systems. He also feels that parental satisfaction has generally increased:

> Anyone dealing with admissions to secondary schools twenty years ago knows the degree of bitterness there was amongst parents when three-quarters of the children were deposited, at the age of 11, in schools from which there was very little hope of achieving access to worthwhile jobs or to further or higher education.[6]

Professor Marten Shipman of the Roehampton Institute for Higher Education, the largest teacher training establishment in the country, has pointed out that the real success story of comprehensive education can be seen in the rise in the number of students leaving school with some formal qualification – 80 per cent in the mid-1980s as opposed to around 50 per cent in the mid-1960s.

SCHOOLS INFORMATION
The Education Act (1980) requires local education authorities (LEAs) in England and Wales to make generally available the address and telephone

number of the authority's offices and the following information about each school for which it is responsible:

1. Name, address and telephone number
2. Size and age range
3. Classification (comprehensive, sixth-form college, coeducational or single-sex, etc.) and denominational affiliation
4. Number of pupils entered for public examinations
5. Arrangements for transport, school meals, clothing and other welfare grants.

This information can be found in the local public library.

Each school is also required to publish details about its organization, curriculum and policy on entering pupils for public examinations. The way in which the school handbook is presented will give some indication of the professionalism of the headteacher and staff, and their attitude towards parents.

The Education (Scotland) Act 1981 has similar requirements, but Scottish LEAs do not have to publish the number of pupils that it is proposed to admit to each school, although they have to consult school councils (equivalent to governors) and, where appropriate, church bodies about these numbers.

Copies of the reports of Her Majesty's Inspectors on individual schools in England, Wales and Scotland, which have been published since January 1983, may be obtained from the LEA or from the Department of Education and Science (see p. 180).

APPEALS

Not all children are granted their first choice of school. In that situation the primary school headteacher, who plays a vital role in the process of secondary transfer, will suggest two alternatives to parents: make a second choice – visit other schools and talk to other parents – or make an appeal. In deciding whether to appeal, it is important to be clear as to why the allocated place has been rejected, what is wanted instead and why, and how far parents are prepared to go to try to get the place they want for their child. There is a set procedure, which can be lengthy. The Advisory Centre for Education (ACE) (see p. 179) are experts at handling appeals, and set out the general principles in their handbook *School Choice Appeals*.

The private sector

Parents who choose private education for their children should be aware that the differences between the 'good', the 'mediocre' and the 'bad' schools are a great deal more marked than in the maintained sector, where the strengths and weaknesses are open to the public gaze and where LEAs are answerable for any serious defects. Yet, despite the fact that there are many private schools with very low standards, the overall image – and usually the reality – is one of achievement. Three out of four children at independent schools leave with five or more O levels, compared to less than one in four in the state sector, and more than half leave with one or more A levels. Although independent schools educate only about one child in twenty of the population, a quarter of the students at universities have been educated at private schools.

Entry to an independent school may be based on the results of the Common Entrance examination or the school's own exam and an interview or, in some cases, an interview only. There is one Common Entrance exam for boys, who take it at the age of 13, and another for girls, who take it at 11, 12 or 13. The papers are marked by the school to which the child has applied and the mark considered acceptable varies from school to school. Details of the entrance requirements are included in the school's prospectus and parents should contact the head of the school if they require more information.

It is quite easy for parents to find out how schools choose their students, but how do parents choose a school? Many parents turning to the independent sector have not been privately educated themselves, and therefore it can be difficult for them to know what to look for and what to expect. Until 1978 independent schools could apply to the Department of Education and Science (DES) to be 'recognized as efficient' by the same criteria applied to LEA schools. Independent schools still have to be open to DES inspection and registration, but in reality this means little more than ensuring that the premises meet the minimum safety and hygiene requirements and that none of the staff is on List 99, the DES list of proscribed teachers. To compensate for this lack of regulation, the Independent Schools Joint Council and the Incorporated Association of Preparatory Schools set up their own accreditation system in 1978, and there are two agencies that specialize in giving parents advice about independent education.

The Independent Schools Information Service (ISIS) is a national organization committed to furthering the interests of the private sector and to preserving 'the fundamental freedom of parents and children to have a choice of education'. It is sponsored by the Governing Bodies Association (which includes the Headmaster's Conference and the Society of Headmasters of Independent Schools), the Governing Bodies of Girls' Schools

Association (associated with the Girls' Schools Association), the Incorporated Association of Preparatory Schools and the Independent Schools Association Incorporated. It has its national headquarters in London, six regional offices in England and Wales, one in Scotland and one in Ireland, with representatives in the north and the south. ISIS also operates an advisory service for parents whose children have special educational needs, and ISIS International advises parents who live abroad on suitable schools in the United Kingdom.

Although ISIS aims to 'answer parents' questions about independent schools and help them with their educational problems', they are careful to point out that 'it is not our function to recommend individual schools, rather to list schools which have joined our voluntary service'. Before they are allowed to join the service, schools are vetted and continue to be vetted thereafter. The schools are listed, with all the relevant information, in the ISIS book *Choosing Your Independent School*. The regional organization means that ISIS is a particularly good source of advice on local independent day schools. Each region publishes a handbook that lists all the member schools in the area and gives brief information about their fees, numbers and age range of pupils, entrance requirements, and scholarships and bursaries. ISIS advisors are unlikely to condemn a particular school, but may indicate that it is not on their list.

Gabbitas-Truman-Thring Educational Trust is a charity that exists to give free educational advice. In response to inquiries, it sends parents details of relevant schools on its lists; by the terms of its charter, Gabbitas must be totally objective and recommend a suitable school even if it is not on its list. Like ISIS, Gabbitas is unlikely to condemn a school, but might suggest that parents make further inquiries of their own among parents of current pupils. Gabbitas-Truman-Thring also advises parents living abroad of suitable schools for their children in the United Kingdom.

Gabbitas' real expertise lies in knowing about boarding schools and boarding and day tutorial colleges, most of which have been visited and all of which are constantly checked for changes. It receives about 40,000 inquiries a year, its phones being especially busy after exam results are known and parents are in a last-minute scramble to find places for their children to study for resitting them. A spokesman for the organization told me that since the 1960s there has been a marked swing away from boarding schools towards independent day schools. Consequently, it is no longer necessary to register children for a particular boarding school at birth – the one exception being Eton. In fact, most secondary boarding schools do not accept registration until children are 7 or 8 years old, and few are completely full in any given year.

For further advice on how to select a boarding school I talked to Roger W. Ellis, retired headmaster of Marlborough College. The two main influences in a child's life, Mr Ellis stressed, are

> the expectations of the parents and the expectations of the school. The most important thing is to ensure that the expectations of both are realistic – neither too high nor too low for the ability and talents of the child. The 'right' school will enhance a child's self-esteem; in the wrong hands this vital quality will become so low as to affect both behaviour and achievement. There is nothing more devastating to a youngster's self-esteem than to be floundering helplessly at the bottom of the ladder without the ability to gain some kind of success.

He added that parents should beware of choosing a school on the grounds that they went there themselves.

> It might have suited them well enough, but it might now be the worst possible place for their child . . . Parents should never choose schools for snobbish reasons. However famous the name of the school, however well established, . . . it does not necessarily mean that it will suit all children.

Mr Ellis recommends that parents choose two secondary schools, preferably with different characteristics – a large and a small school, for example. It is difficult, he says,

> with any degree of accuracy to prejudge most children's potential, particularly when it comes to slow learners or those with specific learning difficulties. They are apt to 'take off' at varying stages and it helps to have a school in mind which will accommodate their needs by the time they reach Common Entrance.

Having decided upon whether their child should board or attend day school, it is best, he says, that parents visit the schools twice before making up their minds: the first time to gain an overall impression and the second, with the child, to look more closely at the day-to-day running of the school. He advises parents to

> look in on classrooms while teaching is in progress, ask questions about the size of classes, the O and A level results in the context of the ability spread of the school's entry, and if their child is especially interested in sport, ask questions about the facilities available and the amount of time allotted to games. On the other hand, if a child pales

at the very mention of the games field and generally detests sport, find out if there are alternatives and how much sport is mandatory.

Roger Ellis also advises parents to make sure that on this second visit they meet two housemasters.

> Obviously the way a house is run depends to a great extent on the particular style of the housemaster. Some will lead from the front with clear instructions; others will prompt from the background. A child will tend to respond more favourably to one style or the other, depending on his nature.

Although parents should listen to their children's views with the greatest care ('their opinions and impressions can often be very astute'), Ellis felt that many youngsters will be impressed by superficialities. He quoted his own experiences:

> While my son was being charmed by a potential housemaster, who convinced the boy that the house was right for him, my wife and I could smell the cigarette smoke wafting from various corners of the building. When we vetoed our son's choice on this occasion, he was obviously disappointed, but later on, when he was installed in the house of our choosing, he told us how glad he was to have been overruled! In making our selection we relied on the judgement of a number of those who had sons in this particular house. But parents should beware of choosing a school or house on the experience of only one or two. Gossip about schools is often second or third hand and, what is more, out of date. Always go and look for yourself.

FINANCIAL HELP

School fees can be very expensive, but financial help is available in the form of scholarships, bursaries, grants and loans. In the first instance parents should inquire about scholarships and bursaries at the schools themselves. Many award scholarships to children of high academic ability, assessed by a competitive examination, or, in some cases, outstanding ability in music or art.

Bursaries are awarded on the basis of financial need and are completely discretionary. Some schools may give preference to children whose parents are former pupils or are in certain occupations, such as the clergy, members of the armed forces or teachers.

LEAs have very limited funds for this purpose, but may give grants to children to allow them to continue in private education after the death of a parent, or to especially able children if it is shown that the maintained sector is unable to fulfil their needs. They may make grants for children to attend private boarding schools if the children are over the age of 11, in need of boarding education and that need cannot be met by one of the authority's own boarding schools. Any one of the following circumstances is commonly accepted as making boarding education necessary.

1. Both parents are abroad.
2. Parents may have to move frequently because of their occupations.
3. Home circumstances are prejudicial to the normal development of the child.
4. The child has a special aptitude – for example, for music, singing or dancing – requiring training that can be given only in a boarding school.
5. The child suffers from a handicap that makes boarding education desirable.
6. The child lives in a remote part of the country and cannot reach a day school.

Through the Assisted Places Scheme, the Department of Education and Science may pay part or all of children's tuition fees, depending on the parents' income. The scheme is open to all children aged 11 or older who have been resident in the United Kingdom, Channel Islands or the Isle of Man for three years before the start of the calendar year in which the award would take effect, and whose parents could not otherwise afford the tuition fees. Parents who wish their children to be considered for an assisted place should first approach the school of their choice. Candidates are usually asked to sit an exam in January or February for entry to the school in September. The award is for tuition fees only, but an assisted place may be given to children to attend boarding schools if their boarding fees are being paid by other sources.

Children whose fathers are serving overseas in the diplomatic service or are members of the armed forces serving at home or abroad are eligible for grants from the appropriate government department to help pay for boarding education.

There are a number of grant-giving trusts that will provide assistance with school fees for children in certain categories, such as orphans, children from broken homes and children of the clergy, missionaries and teachers. Some will consider applications from anyone in genuine need of help. Applicants to such trusts have to show that the child *needs* to go to the school proposed, that there is no less expensive alternative and that no LEA school is suitable; that the family or guardians cannot manage from their own resources, for example, because of the severe illness of one of the parents or because the child has a special need for which they cannot provide; and that the child does not qualify for an assisted place or a grant from the LEA or any other source. Parents who think they might qualify for help from a grant-giving trust should first choose a school that can cater for their children's needs – preferably one that can offer some help with the fees – and discuss the application for a grant with the head of the school.

Some professional associations also give grants for school fees to needy members, and some international companies and organizations provide grants, scholarship schemes or low-interest loans for school fees to their employees, particularly those who have to work abroad.

There are a number of banks and insurance companies that offer special financial planning for school fees, from covenants to loan schemes, and there is such a variety of schemes available that parents should shop around for the one that suits them. There are tax advantages for divorced couples if the father is paying maintenance under a court order.

Special educational needs

Learning difficulties

According to the Education Act 1981 a child has special educational needs if he or she has a specific learning difficulty that requires special education. Children in this category are usually those with physical disabilities – blindness, deafness or impaired mobility, for example – mental handicaps or severe emotional problems.

The Act promised 'a joint endeavour to discover and understand' the special educational needs of individual children. Parents can ask for an assessment of their child from birth to the age of 19 and if a child is aged 2 years or older, the LEA cannot refuse 'unreasonably'. In the case of a child of school age, the headteacher may decide to make the assessment himself. If he or the parents feel this is inappropriate, it is the responsibility of the LEA's chief education officer to ask for reports from a group of appropriate professionals, which may include doctors, an educational psychologist and a teacher – usually the headteacher or, if a child is not attending school, someone who has had teaching experience – social workers or other welfare officials.

If the LEA decides that a child has special educational needs that require it to provide special education, it must issue a Statement of Special Educational Needs, in which it gives its opinion and states the special provision it thinks is suitable together with the type of school it considers appropriate, naming it if possible. The overall aim of the Act was to encourage the integration of all children, whatever their disabilities and special needs, into the ordinary school.

However, ACE suggests that the reality falls far short of the promises and intentions. Its information sheet states:

> ACE's contacts with parents of children with special educational needs have produced few signs of the 'partnership between teachers and other professionals, and parents' and their 'joint endeavour to discover and understand the nature of the difficulties and needs of individual children' . . . Many parents have naïvely initiated 1981 Act procedures in order to get a clearer commitment from the LEA to meet their children's special needs in present ordinary schools, only to find themselves fighting what they believe to be wholly inappropriate special school placements.[7]

If the LEAs are failing to fulfil the intentions of the Act, perhaps the most significant advantage that parents have is the right to question the LEA's decision and ask for information concerning other suitable schools. If parents do not agree with the LEA's assessment or placement proposal, they must appeal against the decision within fifteen days of receiving it. The LEA must then arrange a meeting with the parents to review the decision. If the parents are still not satisfied, they can appeal to the local appeals committee and, ultimately, to the Secretary of State for Education and Science. It is important that parents use the appeals procedure if they are in any doubt about the LEA's decision, because once a child has *entered* a special school, he or she cannot be removed during compulsory school age without the permission of the LEA, which usually requires further assessment. ACE can give help and advice concerning the assessment procedure, representations and appeals. It is particularly helpful in advising the correct format for correspondence from parents to their LEA.

While many parents of disabled or handicapped children want them to attend ordinary schools, there are others who feel that a special school is more appropriate to their children's particular disability. The 1981 Act provides a continuing role for special schools, which cater for a wide range of disabilities and learning difficulties. These fall into four main categories.
1. Maintained schools: most LEAs have special day and boarding schools. Some authorities may use schools run by another LEA in another area for less common disabilities.

2. Non-maintained schools: these are often run by voluntary organizations and charities, but places are usually paid for by LEAs.
3. Independent schools: LEAs sometimes pay for a child to attend a private school catering for special needs (see also pp. 156–7).
4. Hospital schools: these may be maintained or non-maintained, and are attached to a hospital so that constant medical attention is available.

DYSLEXIA

Dyslexia has been the subject of much controversy and misunderstanding. The dictionary defines it as 'word blindness' and the British Dyslexia Association explains that it describes 'the disorder whereby children and adults, for no apparent reason, experience problems in learning to read and write'. Some educationalists and psychologists do not think the condition is confined to reading and writing, which can include spelling and the written expression of ideas, but can also affect speech and number skills. Thus they see it as a 'blind spot' in development. On the other hand, there are some teachers, psychologists and LEAs whose vocabulary does not include the word dyslexia at all.

Call the condition what you will, those who, like myself, have a child whose learning difficulties were professionally diagnosed at an early stage as being dyslexic and who have over the years witnessed the problems being gradually overcome with great success by specialist teaching are grateful that the symptoms were recognized and treated accordingly.

E. Stirling has more than fifteen years experience of teaching dyslexic adolescents at the Dyslexia Unit at University College of North Wales in Bangor and at St David's College in Llandudno. In the introduction to her book *Help for the Dyslexic Adolescent* she points out the special problems faced by teenagers with this condition:

> Helping a dyslexic of this age is very different to teaching a young dyslexic. The young child is not usually aware of the nature and extent of his handicap and he has no long history of failure. The older dyslexic has had a daily confrontation with failure for perhaps eight or ten years. He may be good at art or singing, he may play cricket well – but none of these skills is valued as highly in the world around him, even amongst his peers, as literacy . . . Literacy is equated in his mind with high intelligence, so to be dyslexic is to be thick.[8]

Although dyslexia is not specified in the Education Act 1981 (which repealed the sections of the Chronically Sick and Disabled Persons Act 1970 that included it in defining the local authorities' duties towards specific handicaps), the British Dyslexia Association advises parents who want to apply for special help to describe the condition as 'the specific learning difficulty of dyslexia'. Every parent has the right to ask for an assessment to be made free of charge by an educational psychologist attached to their LEA. If there is a long waiting list over a period crucial to a child's academic future, parents may decide to refer to a psychologist in private practice. However, a spokesman at the British Dyslexia Association warned that as LEAs are not obliged to accept private assessments, parents should write to the LEA first, stating their reason for seeking one.

If the LEA cannot provide the special help required, parents may have to fight hard to persuade it to send their child to a private school, but they can succeed. Caroline Smith's case is a good example. The LEA agreed that her son, Darren, was severely dyslexic and needed special education. However, there was no place available at the special school to which the LEA usually sent such pupils. The officials became 'aggressive and angry', Mrs Smith said, when she pointed out to them that she knew of an appropriate private school that would accept her son.

> I had a real battle with them. Eventually all the fees were paid, but it needed a great deal of persistence. In retrospect, I feel that had I not been confident enough to approach the LEA in the firm belief that it was my son's right to have this form of special education, I might well have lost the fight.

SPECIAL NEEDS AT 16 +

The Warnock Report, which provided much of the inspiration for the 1981 Education Act, stated that 'unless opportunities are available to young people to continue their education in special or ordinary schools, in colleges of further education or in other establishments, all the earlier efforts made on their behalf may come to nothing'. All young people are entitled to receive full-time education up to the age of 19, but many LEAs do not make adequate educational provision for 16- to 19-year-old handicapped students. If a formal request to the LEA for further education is not successful, parents can complain to the Secretary of State for Education, demanding that the LEA be made to fulfil its legal obligations. Courses available vary from area to area, but in general, they include:

1. Link courses. Pupils spend up to two days a week with a local further education college while still at school. Most courses are for pupils with moderate learning difficulties, but some are for those with physical, sensory, mental and emotional disabilities.

2. Bridging courses. These aim to fill any gaps in basic education, increase independence and encourage confidence, with emphasis on job training and work experience.

3. Special courses. These are focused less towards future employment and more towards independent living, and include reading, writing and maths in relation to daily life.

4. Mainstream courses. The range of mainstream further education courses is enormous and entry will depend on the student's needs and abilities. A minimum educational standard may be required. Details are available from the LEA or individual colleges of further education.

Gifted children

All parents feel that their own children are special, but some parents are convinced that their children are outstandingly clever or talented. There is, however, a great difference between children who are 'above average' and those who are recognized as 'gifted'. The National Association for Gifted Children uses four criteria to identify gifted children.

1. High intelligence – IQ 140+
2. High performance in anything, from playing snooker to playing the cello
3. High powers of logical thought
4. High powers of imagination or creativity

To these four categories, the director of the association adds a fifth, a quality he calls 'docibilitas' and describes as 'a ready willingness to be taught'.

Gifted children can develop behavioural problems as a result of not receiving the level of stimulation and the outlets for expression that they need. One educational psychologist explained:

> The most common danger . . . is that they tend to become bored with the normal content and pace of a school curriculum, and great care must be taken to see that this does not happen, for if it does and continues for any length of time, then the situation may become hard to remedy. They will be best suited by a school where there are not only other pupils but also teachers with a similar level of intelligence, for it is only in these surroundings that they will be adequately stimulated and stretched.

Parents need to have their children's exceptional abilities confirmed professionally and be advised on what the most suitable academic and social environment would be and how to gain access to it. An educational psychologist can test children's intelligence, assess their abilities and recommend an appropriate course of action. There are schools that cater for gifted children, and financial aid to pay the fees may be available (see pp. 156–8). The National Association for Gifted Children is an invaluable source of help and advice.

Intelligence testing

There are a number of different tests used by psychologists to evaluate an individual's intelligence. The results are usually given as a number, known as the intelligence quotient, or IQ. However, intelligence testing is not an exact science and some people place too much importance on this number alone, without fully understanding its implications. One psychologist told me of her simple way of overcoming this problem:

> I don't give people their IQ in terms of numbers because, first of all, they don't know how to interpret them. An IQ of 134, for example, actually could mean anything from 130 to 138. Numbers in this context are very imprecise and somewhat meaningless. I prefer to use the terms 'average' and 'above average'. I use a range of ability tests which generally give a better indication of individual strengths and weaknesses.

While there is considerable disagreement as to the accuracy and even usefulness of intelligence testing, most psychologists and teachers would agree that it can act as a general guide to a person's ability and an indicator of possible learning problems. Parents have the right to have their child assessed by the LEA (see p. 161), but if there is a long waiting list may choose to see an educational psychologist privately. This can be expensive, and parents should inquire about the costs as well as about the tests that will be given and what they can reveal.

Alternative education

It shall be the duty of the parent of every child of compulsory school age to cause him to receive efficient full time education suitable to his age, ability and aptitude, and to any special educational needs he may have, either by regular attendance at school or otherwise.'

Thus the law clearly states that education is compulsory but that school itself is not. It should, therefore, be a straightforward matter to opt out of the school system, but it isn't. The Education Act does not in any way define what constitutes a 'suitable' education, so it is left to individual LEAs to make that decision.

Parents must notify the LEA if they want to educate their children at home, and the onus is on them to prove that they are providing a satisfactory education. An LEA adviser, who usually is a former teacher, will visit the home to assess the physical environment and the proposed curriculum. The adviser will also want evidence that the child or children will not be isolated socially, but will have ample opportunities for mixing with other children.

If the LEA adviser is satisfied that the alternative education arrangements are 'appropriate', the LEA will give its approval and the adviser will review the situation regularly. If the adviser is not satisfied with the arrangements, the LEA can issue a School Attendance Order, which requires parents to ensure their children's regular attendance at school. If the parents fail to comply with the order, they can be brought before the magistrates and fined. After two offences, the magistrates have the power to impose a gaol sentence.

Mrs Brown came before the magistrates eight times before she won her case to educate her daughter, who suffered from school phobia (see p. 167), at home. She employed a tutor to teach maths and English, and taught other subjects, including domestic science, herself. For the most part, Mrs Brown fought the authorities on her own and stood a real chance of having her daughter taken into care. Then, after she read an article about Education Otherwise (see p. 182), she contacted the local co-ordinator, from whom she received real help and guidance.

Although parents can win the approval of the LEA to take their children out of the school system, ACE advises them that: 'Home tuition may be beneficial if your child has a particularly unhappy time at school but it should not be regarded as a long-term solution.'

Choosing home tutors

In some circumstances LEAs can provide education out of school. ACE points out that if your child is temporarily out of school while waiting for placement arrangements to be made, and 'there is a delay in placing your child in another school, which you consider to be justified, you should ask the LEA to provide home tuition to prevent your child falling behind while arrangements are completed'.

If parents have to choose the tutors themselves, either because they want to have their children educated completely at home or have additional coaching in certain subjects, they must be very careful. Almost anyone can start a home tuition agency. No educational qualifications are required, nor is it necessary to be recognized by the DES or to have LEA approval. All that is needed is a licence issued by the Employment Agency Licencing Office for a small fee. Many such agencies interview their tutors on the telephone and rarely check their qualifications and references.

If a child needs coaching in one or more subjects, parents can approach the school staff, whom they know to be qualified. In this case, however, they need to make sure that their child agrees to this proposal, as nothing can be gained without his or her co-operation. Whether the tutor is contacted through a friend (often the best source), local agency or advertisement, it is important for parents to check his qualifications and references and, even if he comes from the school or LEA, to conduct a careful interview wherever the coaching is to take place. It is also a good idea to suggest a trial period of, say, one month to see how pupil and teacher work together.

Further and higher education

According to statistics published by the Manpower Services Commission, only 50 per cent of the nation's 16-year-olds continue their education, and within one year the proportion has fallen to less than 33 per cent.

Educational provision for those aged 16 and older ranges from opportunities to repeat pre-16 work and general pre-vocational studies to specialized academic and vocational teaching. The work is undertaken in a variety of institutions – school sixth-forms, sixth-form colleges and further education (FE) colleges – that are governed by different regulations. The provision available will depend largely on the individual LEA. The choice between remaining at school or moving on to an FE college is still a matter of interpretation. The view of the DES is that LEAs have to secure provision either in school or a further education college for the 16–19 age group, but not necessarily in order of preference. Another view interprets Section 8 of the Education Act to mean that an LEA is obliged to secure sufficient provision in schools for those who want to continue their education. By offering a place in an FE college, it would not therefore be discharging its duty.

For students continuing their education in school, there are no fees. LEAs are legally entitled to charge fees for courses in FE colleges, which are broadly similar to those in schools, and because of government cutbacks, some do.

Outside the London area, LEAs are not obliged to accept an FE student resident in another authority's area; if they decide to do so, the home authority is not obliged to pay any fees unless it has agreed that the education should be provided. It is possible to gain a place in another LEA's college but it may be necessary to pay for tuition oneself.

Young people have a right to full-time education in school or college up to the age of 19, and some LEAs may be breaking the law by turning away would-be students and offering places only on a selective basis. If a 16–19 year old is refused a place by their LEA, they or their parents should immediately contact ACE for help and advice.

Problems at school

Truancy and school phobia

In February 1986 a circular from the Department of Education and Science declared:

> Unjustified absence from school is a matter for local and national concern, whatever the reasons for it and whether or not the parents condone it. In some schools attendance rates are worryingly low, particularly among pupils in the 14–16 age range. Parents, schools and local education authorities, sharing as they do the duties and responsibilities arising from legislation relating to compulsory education, each have a part to play in reducing the incidence of unjustified absence from school.

There are several reasons why young people absent themselves from school, not the least of which is that in the fourth and fifth years many see little point in continuing in a system that they consider has little relevance to their lives. For many young people in the 14–16 age range, truancy is a symptom of disillusionment and despair. In children of any age it can also be a sign of anxiety or distress as a result of personal problems. Obesity or clumsiness, for example, may prompt a child to truant to avoid physical education; a family crisis, such as divorce, parental separation or the formation of a new relationship by a parent may result in behaviour problems and academic decline.

Some parents condone or actively conspire in their children's truancy. They know their children are absent from school and do nothing to prevent it either because they cannot or, if the children are working, because they consider the earnings more important than education (see pp. 177–9).

School phobia, also referred to as school refusal, is distinct from a child's truancy from school in order to work or amuse himself elsewhere. It is not typical of that adolescent behaviour by which a child tries to express his independence, but rather the reverse. One consultant psychiatrist described it to me as

> ... frequently less the fear of school but more the fear of leaving home. It is not uncommon for a young person to become school phobic at the moment of transfer from primary to secondary education. At this stage, which coincides with the onset of puberty, there is a natural inclination for the adolescent to withdraw. School phobia is an abnormal extension of that withdrawal, which may point to certain unresolved issues in the home.

It is part of a teacher's job to monitor pupils' attendance and to inform the local education welfare department of truants. Although all local authorities have an education welfare department, it is not a statutory service, does not have the same powers to enforce the law as the police, and can differ considerably from place to place in how it performs its job. Some authorities are swift to prosecute truants; other will prosecute if a child does not return to school after a specified period, possibly four weeks; still others adopt a more gradual, less authoritarian approach.

A senior education welfare officer (EWO) told me that 'the prime concern of the education welfare service is to ensure that children and young persons of school age are adequately cared for and receive maximum benefit from the educational opportunities available.' The EWO endeavours to discover the causes of truancy, usually by visits to the home and discussions with the child. He also tries to encourage parents to take an active interest in their children's education, and helps to forge links between the home and the school. In the cases of financial hardship, where lack of proper clothing or money for school meals or special trips forms part of the problem, the EWO can make certain allowances available. If a child is encountering academic or personal problems, the EWO can ask the school to make special arrangements to suit the child's needs or refer the child to other professional bodies, such as the school psychological service or a child guidance clinic, for help and advice.

Such professional help can be especially important in cases of school phobia. One consultant psychiatrist told me that he was 'marginally optimistic' that, with the co-operation of the family, school refusers can be helped. A more positive attitude was expressed by Robin Skynner, pioneer of group and family therapies and co-author of *Families and How to Survive Them*. He told me that in his experience the right method of family therapy is almost always rapidly successful in returning school phobics to the classroom. He found that common to all families whose children refused to go to school was the fact that fathers tended to play an outside role – or in the case of single-parent families, no role at all.

> Psychiatrists are trained to have a very nurturing, caring, gentle attitude towards young people and they find it easier to relate to a mother and child. Many find it extremely difficult to work with fathers. Nevertheless, the father plays a vital part in helping the child make the emotional break away from the 'cosiness' of mother to the harshness of the school environment. Without the father's active involvement in the progress of a young person's natural move towards a more independent status, the leap from home to school is often just too great for a child to make.

In work first reported by Dr Skynner in 1974 it was shown that out of a total of twenty children treated for school phobia, one returned to school almost immediately and fifteen returned after a month and stayed. One boy returned to school and remained for a year, after which the team lost touch with him because he moved from the area. Only three children failed to attend regularly after the family therapy sessions, but they were considered to have exceptional problems in addition to their school phobia and needed special care.[10] Although earlier researchers had found that they were able to treat school phobics under the age of 11 more successfully than children of 11 and over, Dr Skynner and his team found that the age of the pupil made no difference to the outcome.

Dr Skynner's method is to encourage the father to play a key role as a bridge between home and school, supporting both child and mother while using his authority to help them towards more healthy separation and independence. In the case of single-parent families, the father-figure may be a relative or friend. Alternatively, Dr Skynner explained,

> the psychiatrist has to play the role himself or even herself. The most important thing is to achieve a triangular effect in the relationship. Above all, families should be given the utmost support, warmth and sympathy by the therapist. There is a positive way of saying almost everything.

Where truancy or school phobia is concerned, the worst thing parents can do is to do nothing.

Exams

Examinations inevitably place young people under strain, and for some the burden is intolerable. Most parents are well aware of the dangers of pushing children too hard to succeed, but because they feel so strongly the impact failure can have on their children's future, they often cannot keep their own anxiety at bay as exams approach. Kathryn Redway, who teaches study skills and has written extensively about exam stress, explains the difficulties and offers some advice:

> Examinations and stress involve two kinds of actors: the children and their parents. The stress is experienced by each set of actors differently, but both suffer from the interaction. Parents project on their children their own success. That could be positive; but they also project their failures. Their offspring – they hope – will not be exposed to the same disgrace. Thus their expectation is very high, and they do not believe that their own children will let them down. Parents view exams as the door to a decent job or the opening to university, which will ensure their children good qualifications for the job market. They know from experience that a prospective employer will first look at academic achievements before he gives the adolescent or young graduate his first chance to prove himself or herself using his own intelligence, knowledge and other skills.
>
> Parents, like their children, refuse to consider the question of failure in advance in order to prepare adequately for such an event should it occur. If it does, it then becomes 'My child has failed – failed the exams, failed me.' Emotions run high and decisions are coloured by the psychological effect. Parents and children should consider the possibility of failure well in advance in order to establish a plan, or strategy, so that if it happens, the news does not come out of the blue, leaving everybody dumbfounded. It restores children's sense of worth if they know that an alternative has been prepared for them.
>
> Children generally do not see the relevance of what they learn when they try to link it to everyday life. This in itself makes learning an abstract process which does not motivate them. Exams are viewed as tests to check whether they have absorbed and understood this abstract learning. Most children are not taught how to take exams and they

fear that they will be asked about a subject they do not know anything about. In their minds, the prospect of an exam is far away – several months maybe – and they waste invaluable time by not revising as they go along. Consequently, they cram in at the end – a week or so before the exam – as much as they can. It may work for one subject, but it will not work for several others. Stress is greatest at the time, when, shortly before the exam, they do not know how to handle the vast quantity of material in front of them. In the end, they give up and hope that the questions on the exam papers will deal with what they know and that they will be lucky.

Children feel stress in the examination rooms, too. They are working against the clock, dealing with subjects they know inadequately and, above all, they have not practised this ordeal often enough, so that they treat it as routine work. They dread failure – not because they know fully what it means, but because their parents' attitude towards it indicates that they will be rejected if they do not succeed. Most children know their own limitations but are loath to tell reluctant parents until it's too late. They would feel less stressed if they knew better what the future entailed; that is, if they had had the chance to discuss with parents and teachers the opportunites which lay open to them in the light of both success and failure.

APPEALS AGAINST EXAMINATION RESULTS

Examination boards are willing to receive pleas on behalf of candidates who were unwell at the time they took a paper. However, once the grades have been awarded, nothing can be done until they have been officially received by the candidate. If the result, in the opinion of the pupil or the school, seems wrong, the school can appeal. A parent may also appeal but since boards do not like dealing with individual parents, it is advisable to appeal through the school.

There are generally three kinds of appeals, all of which are subject to a fee. The least expensive is a simple check that the candidate's marks have been added up correctly. The second is more widely used by schools that find that numbers of their pupils otherwise expected to perform well in the examinations have unexpectedly poor sets of marks. In this case a school may ask for a report on a group in order to ascertain what went wrong. The third and most expensive kind of appeal is for a re-mark and a written report on a child's papers in a particular subject. The chances of a board changing a grade are very remote. On the other hand, the report is helpful if a candidate has to resit a subject.

Disruptive behaviour

Some of the symptoms of the behavioural problems of adolescents described in the preceding chapters will be noticed at home, of course, but others will confine their appearance to the classroom and school playground. This emphasizes the need for parents to maintain contact with the school, especially if the normal family routine has been disrupted in any way and they are concerned about their child's behaviour at home. It is equally important for the school to contact the parents at the first indication of behavioural problems.

If a child seems to be under stress or is exhibiting behavioural problems in the classroom, a teacher may suggest he goes to see the school counsellor, but may have difficulty in persuading him to do so. Even if ordered to attend regular counselling sessions, there is little that can be done to force a child to communicate. None the less, because school counsellors have an intimate knowledge of their schools, they should be able to obtain a closely observed picture of the child in the school context and thus can still be a useful source of advice and help for parents.

While schools, with their limited sanctions, offer little incentive for pupils to modify their behaviour, at home parents hold the key to a number of highly prized privileges, including the family exchequer and the television. Recognizing this powerful influence at home, a school in Kings Lynn, Norfolk, began trying to work in partnership with parents to keep troublesome pupils in the classroom while trying to modify their disruptive behaviour rather than sending them to a special unit (see p. 173) or residential school. The parents agreed to provide rewards or sanctions at home according to daily reports on their children's performance at school. When the first twenty cases were evaluated, educational psychologists Keith Melton and Martin Long found that school staff reported behavioural improvement in eighteen, or 90 per cent; very few pupils who are removed to special units improve enough to rejoin the mainstream school. According to Melton and Long:

> The overall level of commitment from parents has been high, even in cases where home/school relationships have been previously poor. In exceptional cases some parents may not develop the coping skills, or may not choose to use them, and the rewards and sanctions agreed at the start are not consistently applied. These cases may lead to long-term home tuition, court action or residential placement. In effect, children in this category are beyond the control of their parents.[11]

It seems clear that, at best, parents and teachers can act together to alleviate a teenager's stress and help him towards a solution of his problems; or, at worst, by their action or inaction exacerbate those problems.

SUSPENSION

I know how frightening and bewildering it can be to have a child suspended from school. I am not one of those strong-minded people who 'know my rights' and I was totally unprepared for the event, which at the time seemed to me to be quite catastrophic. My ignorance also made me over-anxious and vulnerable, and when it came to facing the headteacher and the staff to discuss my child's behaviour, weakness and defencelessness served to prolong my agony and my child's sentence. I had received no indication of any previous trouble when my teenager daughter walked into the house one morning during school hours and said: 'Hi, Ma, I've been sent home and they won't tell me when I can go back.' I telephoned the school immediately and was told that she had indeed been officially suspended, but that it would be three days before I could meet the head and discuss the problem 'because he is too busy', and 'until a meeting had taken place, there is no possibility of knowing when your child will be allowed back'.

It is very difficult for parents to know whether a school has acted fairly in suspending their child, and they may be confused about the rules governing suspension. The fact is that there are no hard and fast rules. Suspension is entirely at the discretion of the governors of the school in the case of voluntary schools, and the governors and the LEA in the case of county schools – and there are enormous local variations. What is certain is that suspension should never be the first indication received by parents of persistent difficulties in school – but frequently is. The Advisory Centre for Education (ACE) is extremely concerned about what it describes as 'clear signs that schools are abusing their power to suspend non-conforming school students. Procedures vary enormously from LEA to LEA but few show a concern for the educational rights of students and parents.' ACE publishes an information sheet, 'Suspension', which is recommended for parents facing this crisis.

THE SPECIAL UNIT

Suspension is often used as a step towards moving children into special education and most LEAs now have units for children with behavioural problems, either within the school or in a separate establishment. Pupils in these special units, often referred to unofficially as 'sin bins' may be offered a limited curriculum, in some cases only part-time education, and they may miss examination courses. Although the avowed intention of most units is to return students to the mainstream school, statistics show that if a student is aged 13 or over on referral, the chances of getting him or her back are slight. Children in special units remain on the register of the parent school; referral is, therefore, a 'within institution' change requiring no special procedure, and parents and children do not have any *formal* right to oppose it.

However, A CE points out that if your child has been suspended and the school has suggested transfer to a special unit, 'you do not have to accept any alternatives without a fight, and you can always appeal to the Secretary of State under Section 68 of the 1944 Education Act, on the grounds that the governors or the L E A is acting "unreasonably".'

Secret school records

All schools and L E As keep a record on every pupil. Although the ways in which information is recorded varies from one L E A to another, the content is similar – information about educational attainment, some medical details and, often comments about the child's social and family background, behaviour, personality and predictions about potential. The records start as soon as children enter nursery school and accompany them throughout their school life, transferring with them from one school to another. They are used to prepare references for jobs and further and higher education, and are particularly relied upon in large schools where the person writing the reference may have had little personal contact with the pupil. Records are kept at the school and also frequently at the L E A offices. They may be passed to, and contain comments from, welfare officers, social workers, psychologists, careers advisers and, in some cases, the police. Parents and students, however, have no legal right to see these records, nor any control over who else has access to them.

Teachers have the power to record judgements that can be immensely damaging long after they have been committed to paper. It is possible that the picture of a particular child that emerges from a record will be a reflection that is at best sketchy, and at worst downright inaccurate: and such a record will be presented to the head of the school (who may not even be able to put a face to the child) from which to gain information to pass to the head of department at a college of further education or to a prospective employer.

For young people whose school career has not been smooth, the recorded information can present a very real problem, which the secrecy itself exacerbates. They may never be given a chance to explain themselves, and in the crucial interview that will determine their path in life after leaving school, they cannot say, 'I realize that the school found this or that behaviour or action especially reprehensible, but it will not recur in the future.' The rougher the passage through school, the greater the handicap will be when the time comes that references are needed for college or job applications. Because a child has a reputation for unpunctuality at, or even truancy from, school, it does not necessarily follow that the pattern will continue at college or work. The change in behaviour in the mid to older teens can be dramatic, but may come too late to be reflected in the references. Parents who are concerned about the effect the school records might have on their child should contact A CE for further information (see p. 179).

Sex discrimination

That sex discrimination is practised in schools and colleges is not in dispute. Perhaps the practice of overtly excluding individuals from a particular course of study because of their gender is on the wane, but there is plenty of evidence that the same policy is more subtly pursued and the attitudes on which it is based continue to exist.

Judging from senior education lecturer Pat Mahoney's research findings in *Schools for the Boys? Coeducation Reassessed*, girls are the undoubted losers. In *Girls and Mathematics* researchers Rosie Walden and Valerie Walkerdine found that although there was no great discrepancy between the performance of boys and girls through to the fourth year of secondary school, they were profoundly affected by teachers' attitudes towards their mathematical 'flair'. They noted that 'girls can be successful in terms of mathematical attainment, gaining by taking responsibility in the classroom, but remain relatively powerless in terms of teachers' judgements of their performance', and that there was a clear tendency of teachers to enter fewer girls than boys for O levels.[12]

However, a report published by the Schools Council in 1983 pointed out that boys suffer as much as girls from the lack of equal opportunities at school. Anne Sofer felt that the facts and figures that came before her while serving on her local authority's Equal Opportunities Committee showed adolescent boys to be both deprived and misunderstood, while research has shown that boys receive poorer sex education than girls.

The Sex Discrimination Act 1975 applies to discrimination against both sexes. The specific practices in school that may be deemed to be discriminatory are outlined in a pamphlet published by ACE:

1. Exclusion from particular courses of study solely on the grounds of sex
2. The operation of a quota system to maintain balance in the number of boys and girls
3. The use of separate tests for boys and girls
4. The use of sex norms in test scores
5. Sex discrimination in careers guidance
6. Exclusion from courses due to single-sex schooling
7. Exclusion from extracurricular activities, visits, community/social service projects on grounds of sex
8. Exclusion of pupils from other benefits, facilities or services provided by a school solely on the grounds of sex
9. Sex discrimination in the appointment and promotion of staff
10. Transition from single-sex to coeducational schools: a transitional exemption order must be obtained in order to limit the admission of one sex during the period of transition from a single-sex to coeducational intake.[13]

Parents or pupils who think that their school is guilty of discriminatory practices should first write to the head of the school. If that is not successful, they should protest to the governors, and then to the LEA. If unlawful discrimination is suspected, the Equal Opportunities Commission should be informed. ACE is also an excellent source of help and advice.

Racial discrimination

In 1985 the Swann Committee published its findings on race discrimination in education. In a controversial chapter on achievement, which was heavily revised by Lord Swann amid rows and resignations, the report stated:

There is no doubt that West Indian children as a group and on average are underachieving both by comparison with their school fellows in the white majority as well as in terms of their potential, notwithstanding that some of them are doing well.[14]

A school-leaver survey showed that, apart from Bangladeshis, Asian children tend to do as well as white pupils except in English language studies, but seem to be the most frequent object of animosity. Another study focusing on 16-year-old pupils of Asian and Afro-Caribbean descent found that they were subjected to racially-biased comments from teachers as well as other pupils.

The Race Relations Act has been in force since 1976. It distinguishes two types of discrimination. Direct discrimination refers to treating one person differently than another because of his or her racial or ethnic origin. For example, it is unlawful for an educational establishment to refuse to admit or to have different entry requirements for students of different racial or ethnic groups. Indirect discrimination can be shown most easily by example. It is not discriminatory to rule that all pupils who want to pursue an exam course in English literature must be able to read and write English, but it is indirect discrimination to rule that only pupils whose *native* language is English will be accepted.

Although the Act allows individuals who believe they are being, or have been, discriminated against to bring proceedings in a county court, the most insidious aspects of racism and discrimination in education do not fall within the legal definitions. Parents who think that their children are the victims of racial discrimination should contact their local Community Relations Council for advice.

Careers guidance

Brian Heap, a careers teacher in a large comprehensive school in Preston, Lancashire, has been advising on the subject for more than twenty years. He described the careers advice in schools as being generally 'pretty awful'. Careers officers 'tend to leave young people in the lurch'. Although advising on careers begins well before young people sit their exams, Mr Heap points out, 'at the time they most need guidance and advice, when exam results come through in August, careers officers are away on holiday!' However, although the school's advisor might be best able to help young people at this time because he knows them and their background, it is only fair to point out that there are other careers advisors within the local authority who would be available at this critical time.

Of course, it is best not to leave careers planning to the last minute. It can be very useful for parents to begin going with their children to the annual careers exhibitions before the children have to decide which GCSE courses they will take. For youngsters who have no idea what kind of job or career they would like eventually, it shows them what some of the possibilities are; for those who have already focused on a few areas of interest, it tells them what qualifications they will need. There are also numerous careers advice books in the library.

There are also other careers counselling services (see pp. 182–3). Before going to any fee-charging agency, parents should ask for a prospectus and study it carefully to find out how the service operates, what it charges and what kind of qualifications the counsellors have. Brian Heap warns of the 'immense danger' of the type of service where clients simply fill out a questionnaire and the answers are fed into a computer, which then produces a list of supposedly suitable jobs or careers. The great disadvantage of this kind of 'advice', Mr Heap told me, is that the client is just a piece of paper. 'Without prolonged personal contact, how can one possibly offer the right kind of careers advice?' he said. Not all the contact has to be face to face, he pointed out: after the initial interview, the telephone is an excellent means of quick and easy contact.

Unemployed school-leavers and working pupils

The frustration of teenagers who leave school and are unable to find a job can exacerbate the violent mood swings that are a natural part of adolescence. Parents concerned to keep their children motivated and prevent or alleviate their depression can perhaps do no more than encourage them to go to the job centre regularly, investigate training schemes, visit the local centre for the unemployed and join a local self-help group.

It is ironic that while many school-leavers cannot find jobs, a great many young people still at school have part-time jobs during school terms. Research carried out by the Low Pay Unit and the Open University on 1,700 children between the ages of 11 and 16 in London, Luton and rural Bedfordshire found that 40 per cent were working part-time during school terms. The jobs ranged from shop work and newspaper rounds to farmwork, cleaning and construction. Of those who were working, 83 per cent were doing so illegally, less than 20 per cent received any kind of protective clothing, 30 per cent had had an accident at work, and 33 per cent said they suffered from fatigue.

The Employment of Children Act 1973 has never been implemented because of lack of resources, so the main national law on child employment is the Children and Young Persons Act 1933. It forbids anyone to employ children under 13 in any job, and those under 17 in street trading. Children may not work on Sunday, for more than two hours on a school day, before 7 a.m., during school hours or after 7 p.m. Local authorities can make their own by-laws. In County Durham, for example, the by-laws state:

1. No child under the age of 14 shall be employed.
2. No child shall be employed on school days except between the hours of 5 and 7 p.m.
3. No child shall be employed on any Saturday or other school holiday for more than four hours or before 9 a.m. or after 7 p.m. . . . [and] the child shall be free for rest and recreation for a continuous period of not less than five hours.
4. No child shall be employed for more than twenty-four hours in any week in which the school is not open.

Although the by-laws vary throughout the country, those of County Durham are fairly representative, but it hardly matters since all these laws are largely ignored. It may be argued that without the part-time employment of schoolchildren, many shops and small businesses would close, families on low incomes would be seriously affected by the loss of the children's weekly contribution, and children would be denied a rich source of independence and a vital boost to their spending power. Parents, however, should be aware that, whatever the benefits, there are also serious drawbacks: children do less well at school, are at high risk of accident and injury, and are generally extremely poorly paid.

Teachers are well aware that 'all work and no play makes Jack a dull boy'. Children who work long hours during term time tend to arrive late, without having done their homework and sometimes so tired that they fall asleep during lessons. They also tend to rush away at the end of the day without taking part in any extra-curricular activities or attending detention.

If education is considered a priority, parents will want to make sure that their children can cope with a particular job in addition to the demands of school. If parents do not consider education a priority, they will still want to ensure that their children are safe at work, well looked after and paid fairly.

Where to go for help and advice

The organizations listed below are open during normal office hours unless stated otherwise. Many of then will supply lists of their own publications – factsheets, leaflets, magazines, books – on request.

Public sector

Information about schools in the LEA can be found in the public library.

Advisory Centre for Education
  (ACE) Ltd
18 Victoria Park Square
London E2 9PB
Tel: 01–980–4596 Line open 2–5.30
  p.m.
  The only independent advice service for parents of children in state-maintained schools. The services are free. ACE answers every conceivable kind of question relating to education. It also refers callers to other relevant organizations concerned with every aspect of the education service, and to relevant books, journals, pamphlets and reports.
  In the case of parents who are in dispute with their children's school or LEA, ACE will advise them on their legal position and effective ways they can make their own representations; help them prepare letters and write on their behalf to schools, governors and LEAs;

and help them take action beyond their LEA.
  ACE does not give comparative information about schools or LEAs, does not provide information about schools in the private sector, and acts only as a referral agency on questions about grants, careers and courses in further, higher and adult education.

Private sector

Gabbitas-Truman-Thring
  Education Trust Ltd
6–8 Sackville Street
London W1X 2BR
Tel: 01–734–0161
  See p. 154.

Independent Schools Information
  Service (ISIS)
56 Buckingham Gate
London SW1E 6AG
Tel: 01–639–8793/4
  See pp. 153–4.

  and
Educational Grants Advice
ISIS
Brockhill Lodge

West Malvern Road
The Wyche
Malvern, Worcestershire WR14 4EJ

Assisted places

Department of Education and
   Science
Room 3/65
Elizabeth House
York Road
London SE1 7PH
Tel: 01–934–9211

ISIS
   See above.

Scottish ISIS
22 Hanover Street
Edinburgh EH2 2EP
Tel: 031–225–7202

Service Children's Education
   Authority
Institute of Army Education
Court Road
Eltham, London SE9 5NR

Welsh Office Education Department
Cathays Park
Cardiff CF1 3NQ
Tel: 0222–823347

Special educational needs
There are numerous societies
catering for specific handicaps. The
most up-to-date list of individual
helping organizations is kept by the:

Voluntary Council for Handicapped
   Children

8 Wakley Street
London EC1V 7QE
Tel: 01–278–9441

OTHER AGENCIES
ACE
   See above.

Centre for Studies on Integration in
   Education (CSIE)
   and
1981 Action
16 Fitzroy Square
London W1P 5HQ
Tel: 01–387–9571
   1981 Action is an umbrella
organization for parents' groups and
individuals promoting the
integration of children with special
educational needs. Offers
information and advice on the
workings of the 1981 Education Act.

Children's Legal Centre
20 Compton Terrace
London N1 2UN
Tel: 01–359–9392

Disability Alliance
25 Denmark Street
London WC2 8NJ
Tel: 01–240–0806

Independent Panel of Special
   Education Experts
20 Compton Terrace
London N1 2UN
   Write only.

Invalid Children's Aid Association
   (ICAA)
126 Buckingham Palace Road
London SW1W 9SB
Tel: 01–730–9891

MIND (National Association for
   Mental Health)
22 Harley Street
London W1N 2ED
Tel: 01–637–0741
   See pp. 136–7.

National Council for Special
   Education
1 Wood Street
Stratford upon Avon CV37 6JE
Tel: 0789–205332

Northern Ireland Council for the
   Handicapped
2 Annadale Avenue
Belfast
Tel: 0232–64001/2/3

Physically Handicapped and Able-
   Bodied (PHAB)
42 Devonshire Street
London W1N 1LN
Tel: 01–637–7475

Royal Association for Disability and
   Rehabilitation (RADAR)
25 Mortimer Street
London W1N 8AB
Tel: 01–637–5400
   Stocks own and other
publications, including access and
holiday guides, DHSS handbooks
and legal documents. Send large
s.a.e. for list.

Royal Society for Mentally
   Handicapped Children and
   Adults (MENCAP)
117–123 Golden Lane
London EC1Y 0RT
Tel: 01–253–9433

Scottish Information Service for the
   Disabled
18 Claremont Crescent
Edinburgh EH7 4QD
Tel: 031–556–3882

Dyslexia

British Dyslexia Association
Church Lane
Peppard, Oxfordshire RG9 5JN
Tel: 04917–699
   Represents autonomous local
Dyslexia Association Charities and
co-ordinates their activities, which
include counselling parents and
others, giving advice on obtaining
remedial help, and vocational
guidance and help for students who
wish to apply for special
consideration in examinations.

Gifted children

The National Association for Gifted
   Children
1 South Audley Street
London W1Y 5DQ
Tel: 01–499–1188
   A charitable organization
concerned to increase public
awareness of the problems facing
such children, and to provide
information and advice for parents,
teachers and others in contact with
gifted children. Parents of gifted
children can meet through the
association and its local branch
groups.

Alternative education

Association of British
 Correspondence Colleges
53 Great Sutton Street
London EC1V 0DQ

Council for Accreditation of
 Correspondence Colleges
27 Marylebone Road
London NW1 5JS

Education Otherwise
25 Common Lane
Hemmingford Abbots
Cambridge PE18 9AN
 Information, advice and support
for parents educating, or seeking to
educate, their children out of
school.

National Extension College
18 Brooklands Avenue
Cambridge CB2 2HN

TUC Postal Courses Office
Tillicoultry
Clackmannanshire FK13 6BX

Sexual discrimination

ACE
 See p. 179.

Equal Opportunities Commission
1 Bedford Street
London WC2
Tel: 01–379–6323

Racial discrimination

ACE
 See p. 179.

Catholic Commission for Racial
 Justice
1 Amwell Street
London EC1

Commission for Racial Equality
 (CRE)
Eliot House
10–12 Allington Street
London SW1E 5EH
Tel: 01–828–7022

Institute of Race Relations
2 Leeke Street
London WC1
Tel: 01–837–0041

National Association for Multiracial
 Education (NAME)
23 Doles Lane
Findern, Derby DE6 6AX

Careers

Careers and Occupational
 Information Centre
Pennine Centre
20 Hawley Street
Sheffield S1 3GA

Careers Research and Advisory
 Centre (CRAC)
Bateman Street
Cambridge CB2 1LZ

Youth Information Resource Unit
Scottish Community Education
 Council
Atholl House
2 Canning Street
Edinburgh EH3 8EG
Tel: 031–229–2433

Notes

1. Michael Rutter *et al.*, *Fifteen Thousand Hours: Secondary Schools and Their Effects on Children*, Shepton Mallet, Open Books, 1979
2. Caroline Benn, 'Editorial', *Comprehensive Education*, no. 50, 1985, p. 1
3. Glenn Turner, 'Assessment in the Comprehensive School: What Criteria Count' in Patricia Broadfoot (ed.), *Selection, Certification and Control*, London, Falmer Press, 1984
4. Ibid.
5. Fred Jarvis, 'Practice and Principles', *Comprehensive Education*, no. 50, 1985, p. 7
6. Peter Newsam, 'What Wise Parents Wish', *Comprehensive Education*, no. 50, 1985, pp. 9–10
7. ACE, *Children with Special Needs*, London, n.d.
8. E. G. Stirling, *Help for the Dyslexic Adolescent*, Llandudno, St David's College, 1987
9. Section 36, Education Act (1944) as amended by the Education Act 1981
10. A. C. Robin Skynner, 'School Phobia: A Reappraisal', *British Journal of Medical Psychology*, vol. 74, no. 1, 1974, pp. 47–62
11. Keith Melton and Martin Long, 'Alias Smith and Jones', *Times Educational Supplement*, 11 April 1986, p. 23
12. Rosie Walden and Valerie Walkerdine, *Girls and Mathematics: From Primary to Secondary Schooling*, Bedford Way Papers 24, London, Institute of Education, London University, 1985
13. ACE, *Sex Discrimination in Education*, London, n.d.
14. Baron Swann, *Education for all: the Report of the Committee of Inquiry into the Education of Children from Ethnic Minority Groups*, London, Department of Education and Science, 1985

Chapter 6

Young People and the Law

Juvenile crime

The Children and Young Person's Act 1969 describes juvenile crime as illegal offences carried out by young people between the ages of 10 and 17. After their seventeenth birthday, people are regarded as adults in terms of criminal law. According to a report published by the National Association for the Care and Resettlement of Offenders (NACRO) in May 1985, based on Home Office statistics, the rate of juvenile crime is falling. The number of known juvenile offenders rose steeply in the 1950s and 1960s, fluctuated during the 1970s and in 1983 was 10 per cent lower than in 1974. On the other hand, the number of offenders aged 17 to 20 rose 40 per cent in the same period and the British Crime Survey in 1983 estimated that the number of criminal acts committed by juveniles was roughly four times greater than that recorded by the police.

The most likely age for offending is between 14 and 17, and the peak age for criminal activity is 15 for boys and 14 for girls. Throughout the world crime is a disproportionately male pursuit. Although the proportion of female juveniles involved in offending is rising in Britain, a juvenile who is cautioned for an indictable offence is about three times more likely to be male than female, and a juvenile who is sentenced is roughly nine times more likely to be male. Female juvenile offenders are, in fact, cautioned far more often than prosecuted. For the small minority of young offenders who receive custodial sentences, the reconviction rate is very high – and the younger the individual, the greater the likelihood of reconviction. On the other hand it is estimated that approximately 70 per cent of young offenders who are cautioned by the police do not offend again.

This last figure tends to support the opinion that juvenile delinquency is often just a passing phase. In their book *Crime and Human Nature* Professors Richard Herrnstein and James Wilson, both of Harvard University, echo the conclusion of most researchers about the developmental forces that make adolescence and young adulthood a time of risk for criminal and other unconventional behaviour: 'This is when powerful new drives awaken, leading to frustrations that foster behaviour unchecked by the internalized prohibitions of adulthood. The result is just youthful rowdiness, but in a minority of cases it passes over the line into crime.'[1]

The police forces throughout the country work within the same organizational framework and the same tight legal system, but have a considerable amount of flexibility in how they operate. The Juvenile Bureau in Feltham, Middlesex, is fairly representative of the country as a whole, although not all police forces have a separate section for dealing with juvenile crime. Its Referrals section receives reports of all crimes, public order offences and traffic offences involving juveniles, each case being assigned to an individual police officer. The type of offences committed by the 1,664 10- to 16-year-olds referred to the bureau in 1985 are shown in the table below; as the figures indicate, many of the individuals had committed more than one offence.

Juvenile crimes reported

TYPE OF CRIME	NUMBER OF OFFENCES
Assaults on police	7
Indecent assault	8
Grievous bodily harm	11
Misuse of drugs (usually glue and other soft drugs)	33
Drunkenness	65
Actual bodily harm	85
Criminal damage (vandalism)	215
Auto crime	222
Burglaries	274
Theft: dishonesty offences (e.g. stealing bicycles)	435
Traffic offences (often associated with motor bikes)	518
Theft (e.g. shoplifting)	573

Police action

The first indication to parents that their child is in trouble with the law is likely to be the shock of a telephone call or a visit from the police to ask them to attend a police station where the child is being held. Many police officers who deal with juvenile crime prefer not to detain young offenders at the station but to interview them and their parents at home. In this way families are made to feel more at ease, the police have a clearer picture of the parents' attitude towards the offence and the offender and, with their help, usually have a better chance of learning the truth. The police attitude towards the young offender, initially at least, is authoritarian. One officer told me:

> At first we go in fairly hard. Even if we decide not to take any action, we must at least have a deterrent effect. Sometimes strong words are all that's needed. Parents often phone us for help, particularly single mothers who want a male figure to come and talk to their sons, although we are not an agency that can really offer very much except advice and support.

If a juvenile admits an offence, the officer may decide that a home visit and informal caution will be sufficient. If he thinks stronger action is necessary, he may decide the juvenile should receive a formal caution. There is no statutory provision for cautioning, but a procedure generally known as the 'instant caution' was adopted in 1984 because of the number of minor offences committed by juveniles. Usually the young offender is taken to the police station, his parents are asked to attend and an oral reprimand is formally delivered by a senior officer.

If the victim and/or the police feel that the juvenile should receive a stiffer punishment than a formal caution, they can bring the case to court. Before making this decision, the police will take into account any information received from anyone who may be involved with the child or the family, such as a social worker, teacher or doctor. Parents will be told what action is planned after the arrest. If there is to be a court hearing and they plan to consult a solicitor, they should do so as soon as possible. If they cannot afford to pay for legal advice, they may apply for legal aid for their child (see pp. 199–200).

If the juvenile denies committing the offence, he may not be cautioned and the case must go to court. If he is convicted – whether he pleads guilty or not guilty – it will be officially recorded. Although it is usual practice for the police to destroy this record when a juvenile reaches the age of 17 – 'in order to allow him to enter adulthood with a clean slate', as one police officer put it – convictions in the juvenile court can be quoted in the adult court if they form part of a series of offences. A conviction can also be a bar to many jobs and professions. For these reasons parents should not allow a child to be persuaded to plead guilty to an offence he denies just to reach a speedy conclusion.

COMPLAINTS AGAINST THE POLICE

If a young person has been charged with an offence and wishes to make a complaint against the police arising out of the same incident, it is very important to discuss it with the defending solicitor before making the complaint. A complaint may be made orally at the police station, but it is better to send a letter stating fully the grounds giving rise to the complaint to the chief of police for the police force concerned. The two main areas of complaint are:

1. Discreditable conduct: where a member of a police force acts in a disorderly manner or in any manner likely to bring discredit on the reputation of the force or of the police service.
2. Abuse of authority: where a member of a police force makes an arrest without good or sufficient cause, or uses unnecessary violence towards any prisoner or other person with whom he may be brought into contact in the execution of his duty, or is uncivil to any member of the public.[2]

In the London area complaints are dealt with by the District Complaints Unit or, in the case of serious allegations, by Scotland Yard's Complaints Investigation Bureau. Elsewhere, an investigating officer will be appointed – in the case of a serious allegation, from a different division, branch or force. The investigating officer will see the complainant, take a statement and interview any witnesses. Statements are then shown to the officer against whom the complaint has been made for comments. The statements, comments and the recommendation of the investigating officer are then given to the chief officer or deputy, who decides what action should be taken.

The police officer against whom the complaint has been made may be summonsed for a hearing before the chief officer. If there is a possibility of a criminal offence having been committed, for example, assault, the papers are sent to the Director of Public Prosecutions to decide whether there should be a criminal prosecution.

The Police Complaints Board, which is composed of lay people, has the duty of supervising the complaints system except where a criminal offence is alleged to have been committed or the complaint involves a police officer of the rank of superintendent or above. The board receives the papers on a complaint where no disciplinary action is to be taken or the charge is denied by the police officer. It may insist that proceedings can be taken in cases where the chief officer has decided not to and that the proceedings should be heard not only by the chief officer or deputy but also by two members of the board. Disciplinary tribunals are rare, but where they do occur and the complainants are young people, they are allowed to be accompanied by a friend, relation or other person who is not to be called as a witness.

Criminal court proceedings [3]

If the child or young person admits an offence and his case is sent to court, any positive action he and his parents take before the hearing may have a considerable effect on the attitude of the magistrates. For example, in deciding his punishment the magistrates may take into account the fact that the offender has written a letter of apology to his victim, helped to repair the damage he may have caused or tried to earn and save money towards paying a fine or any compensation that may be ordered, and that his parents have imposed a curfew or some other form of punishment.

If there is to be a court hearing, there may be a delay of several weeks or even months. It is important for the child or young person to remember what happened, so it is a good idea to write down the events as he recalls them as soon as possible after the arrest. If he denies the offence, any witnesses to support his story should be contacted immediately.

A person under the age of 17 is sent to a juvenile court, where he appears, before not more than three magistrates, one of whom is the chairperson and speaks for the others. There is no jury and the general public is not admitted. Members of the press may attend and publish reports about the case, but are not allowed to publish any information that will lead to the identification of a defendant unless given special permission, which is very rare. The court is run as simply as possible so that the people who appear there can understand what is happening. Both parents should attend if possible, but one parent or guardian must attend or the hearing may be postponed.

In court, the child will be asked to stand in front of the magistrates; seats are provided nearby for the parents. After the child's name, address and age have been stated, the charge is read out. The court will want to make sure that the charge is thoroughly understood by the child, who will be asked if he admits or denies it. If he pleads guilty, the magistrates are told the circumstances of the offence, and the child and his parents are given an opportunity to speak before the magistrates decide what action is taken.

If the child denies the offence, the prosecutor will call witnesses in support of his case. When each one has finished giving his evidence, the child, aided by his parents or his solicitor, can question him. If the child does not have a solicitor, the court, through its clerk, will help. When the prosecutor has finished, the child can take one of the following actions.

1. He can promise to tell the truth and then relate his side of the story. He may then be questioned.

2. He can give his story without promising to tell the truth. Because he made no promise, he will not be questioned and the court may find it difficult to believe everything he says.

3. He can say nothing. He will not be questioned, but if there is no evidence in his favour, the magistrates may find him guilty.

Whether or not he speaks himself, the child has the right to call any witnesses he wishes to speak for him. They must promise to tell the truth and may be questioned. The magistrates will then decide whether the child is innocent or guilty.

If the child has admitted the offence or been found guilty, the magistrates will be told if he has been the subject of any previous court order or cautioned for an offence. They will then consider the best way of dealing with him. In reaching this decision the magistrates must, among other things, have regard to the child's welfare, and various reports may be available to help them. There will usually be a report from the child's school and there may be a social inquiry report on his health, conduct and home surroundings, prepared by a probation officer or a local authority social worker. If reports are not available at the hearing, the magistrates may postpone a decision until they have been prepared. In the interim they may allow the child to return home with the parents, place him in the care of the local authority or, in certain circumstances, remand him in custody.

Parents are expected to attend the resumed hearing with their child – the child's solicitor may also attend – to hear the court's decision.

Court orders

There is a wide range of actions the court can take, depending on the offence and the child's age. Parents can help their children by seeing that the terms of any court order are kept, fines are paid and the child keeps out of trouble.

ABSOLUTE DISCHARGE
No further action is taken. Although no penalty is imposed, if the defendant is found guilty, the outcome will be recorded and may be used in evidence on another occasion.

CONDITIONAL DISCHARGE
If the child does not commit another offence during a stated period, there is no further action; if he does commit another offence, a penalty could be imposed for the present offence.

FINE
Parents or guardians are responsible for paying fines for offenders under 17 unless there are exceptional circumstances. They may ask for time to pay. Maximum fines by magistrates for 10-to 13-year-olds are £100, and for 14-to 16-year-olds, £400.

COMPENSATION
In addition to a fine, monetary compensation to the victim for injury, loss or damage perpetrated at the time of the offence may be ordered up to £1000, and takes precedence over fines if both cannot be paid. The offender's means must be taken into account.

COSTS
If parents are ordered to pay costs the amount is unlimited; if the order is against the young person, the costs must not exceed the amount of the fine.

DEFERRED SENTENCE
All courts may defer sentencing young offenders (with their consent) if satisfied that this is in the interests of justice. The final sentence will take into account the offender's 'conduct after conviction (including where appropriate the making by him of reparation for his offences) or to any change in his circumstances'. The sentence must not be deferred longer than six months.

ATTENDANCE CENTRE
The child will have to attend at a named place and time on a number of occasions. Parents are usually encouraged to attend on the first such occasion. The aim of attendance centres is to impose loss of leisure as well as to teach offenders the constructive use of leisure. They are regulated by the government, and are usually run by police, who organize physical exercise and other instruction.

SUPERVISION (PROBATION)

The child is placed under the supervision of a social worker or probation officer for a stated period. The supervision order may contain a condition that the child receive 'intermediate treatment', which will require him to be involved in activities with a group and may include some residential periods away from home. The order may include a requirement to attend school regularly.

CARE

The child is placed in the care of the local authority for an unstated period. If the child is already the subject of a care order for offending, the court can order that, for a period of up to six months, he shall not be allowed to be under the charge and control of a parent, guardian, relative or friend, or that he shall be under the charge or control only of a specified parent, guardian, relative or friend. If the child already in care has a history of absconding, the court may order that he be kept in secure accommodation.

YOUTH CUSTODY

Juveniles over 15 may be kept in custody for up to six months for one serious offence or up to twelve months if more than one serious offence is involved. If the court thinks that more than twelve months custody is appropriate, the offender can be sent to the Crown Court to be sentenced by a judge. The government has made it clear that custody is to be seen as a last resort and should be imposed only if the young person seems 'unwilling or unable to respond to the non-custodial penalties', custody is 'necessary for the protection of the public' or the offence is so serious that a non-custodial sentence is unjustifiable.

Young people sentenced to youth custody will usually first go to an 'allocating establishment' (which may be an adult prison) for between four and fourteen days. Unless they have received a very short sentence, they will then be sent to one of the centres situated in various parts of the country. Which one is chosen will depend on the individual's needs (for example, educational, medical or psychiatric), where his or her home is and whether a closed centre is deemed necessary (for example, because of an offence of violence, sex or drug trafficking, or a history of absconding).

DETENTION CENTRE

Only male offenders aged between 14 and 20 can be sent to a detention centre. The sentence is short, normally between twenty-one days and four

months. Detention centre regimes are based on a basic two-week programme

> founded on unskilled work, basic education, physical education,
> parade and inspections of a kind to which newly-sentenced young
> offenders can be introduced quickly so that they spend the greater
> part of a fortnight on a full regime. For those due to spend more than
> two weeks in custody, each individual will undergo a programme
> building on the initial two weeks and involving a range of occupations
> appropriate to the length of sentence, including work with a greater
> element of skill, a broader education programme, and short basic
> training courses when these can be provided.

COMMUNITY SERVICE ORDER

Young people over 16 can be ordered to do unpaid service for the community
for between 40 and 120 hours during a period of twelve months under the
supervision of the Probation Service. The young person must agree and the
court must hear a report from probation or social workers that he or she is
suitable and that viable arrangements for community service exist in the
area.

HOSPITAL

If it is considered appropriate, the court can make an order committing a
child to hospital.

BINDING OVER

The court can order parents of a young offender between 14 and 16 (or 10–
13 guilty of homicide) to be bound over, making them responsible for their
child. The sum of money included in the binding over may be forfeited if the
parents fail in their responsibility, which may be to ensure that the child
attends school or keeps out of trouble. The order may be in effect for not
more than three years or until the young person is 18, and the recognisance
must not exceed £1000. Young offenders can themselves be bound over for
up to a year to keep the peace and be of good behaviour if the offence
conditions of a care order are met. The amount must not exceed £50.

APPEALS

The parents or the child may appeal against the way in which the court has
dealt with the child, whether the plea was guilty or not, and against a
finding of guilt if the child denied the offence. Appeals are heard by a higher

court, and action on an appeal must be started within twenty-one days of the date of the magistrates' decision. The appellant should consult a solicitor or the office of the Clerk to the Justices. Legal aid is available for appeals.

The Probation Service

The Probation Service encompasses a very wide range of duties. Its main duties are advising the courts, supervising offenders who are on probation or subject to supervision and community service orders (see pp. 191, 192), and providing welfare services to offenders in custody and those released from custody. It also works in the community to limit the distress involved in the breakup of families and participates in victim support, housing, education and employment schemes.

The age at which young people can be placed under the supervision of the Probation Service (as opposed to a branch of the social services) differs throughout the country, but the minimum is likely to be 14.

Civil court proceedings [4]

Not all children who appear before a juvenile court are charged with a criminal offence. They may be the victims of cruelty or neglect, or be beyond the control of their parents, for example, by repeatedly truanting from school. Parents will be informed of the reason for court action being taken and, except in applications for a place of safety order, there will be a court hearing before magistrates as in criminal proceedings. Both sides may produce evidence, call and question witnesses and have legal representation. Legal aid is available.

Court orders

PLACE OF SAFETY ORDER

A place of safety order can be made when it is necessary to remove a young person from the family home in an emergency – for example, if it is believed that he will suffer some physical harm. The law states that any person can apply to a magistrate for a place of safety order, but in practice it is almost always a social worker, a police officer or an officer of the National Society for the Prevention of Cruelty to Children (NSPCC). The application may be made relatively informally and at any time of day or night. The magistrate must be satisfied that there is reasonable cause to believe that the young person is being neglected or ill-treated or that the grounds for care proceedings (see Compulsory Care, below) warrant it.

Parents and the young person must be told the reasons for the order as soon as practicable, but do not have the right of appeal against it. A young person detained in a place of safety is not actually in care and his treatment is not covered by the normal care regulations. It is uncertain who, if anyone, has the power to take decisions about his life during the period of the order, but in that time the local authority must decide whether to allow him home or start care proceedings.

A place of safety is defined as 'a community home provided by a local authority or a controlled community home, any police station or any hospital, surgery or other suitable place, the occupier of which is willing to receive a child or young person'.

COMPULSORY CARE
If the social services consider it is in a young person's interests to be in care, but the child and/or the parents do not agree, the local authority can apply to the court for a compulsory care order. The authority has to prove that the child is 'in need of care or control which he is unlikely to receive unless the court makes an order'. The grounds for such an action are specified in the Child Care Act 1980, details of which can be obtained from the Children's Legal Centre (see p. 201). Most care orders are made in respect of young people under the age of 17, but the court can make an order on a 17-year-old, which will have effect until he or she is 19.

The child care officer

The role of the child care officer is to monitor the welfare of children under the age of 18 who come to the notice of the police other than for reasons of crime. The officer can be a great source of help and advice to families who feel that they have lost control and are afraid that their children may be in some kind of danger because they no longer have the ability to protect them. 'Very often a talk with the child, either individually or with his parents, has a salutary effect,' a care officer told me.

If not, and things reach crisis point, at which time a parent may phone and say 'I've taken your advice; it doesn't seem to have made any difference. I can't control the child', in law, the parent has a right to have that child taken into the care of the local authority. If, on the other hand, the social services refuse to take the child into care, they can apply to the Magistrates' Court and put the case before them. At this stage it helps to have police involvement.

Voluntary care

If parents ask for their child to be taken into care, they can remove him at any time in the first six months; after that, they must give twenty-eight days' notice. According to the Child Care Act 1980, local authorities must try to ensure that care is taken over by a parent or other relative, guardian or friend if that is consistent with the welfare of the young person. If that is not possible, the child may be placed in the care of foster parents or in a residential home – a children's home, adolescent unit or hostel. In some authorities the majority of residential homes are within the area; in others, they may be some distance away.

When a young person has been placed in voluntary care, the local authority may take the day-to-day decisions about his or her life, but this should not remove the parents' right to control major decisions regarding, for example, education, medical treatment, religion and, it can be argued, access and placement. Unfortunately, this position is not often made clear to parents and they can encounter problems if they try to exert control in such matters.

Sometimes young people themselves see going into care as better than being at home or the only solution to problems there. The law makes no stipulation about children who ask to be taken into care. Some local authorities accept self-referrals, some will do so only if the parents have consented and others will do so only if the person has reached the age of 16. It is important that young people who want to go into care are told and fully understand what might happen to them, that they will not necessarily be able to dictate where they are placed or be able to leave care before they are 18; these will be matters for the local authority to decide.

Assessment centres

Assessment centres are fundamentally short-term residential reception units to which children and young people are sent initially after a care or place of safety order has been made. A full assessment should take about eight weeks, at the end of which time, young people are generally ready for placement in a residential home, a foster home or any other place of care which is thought best suited to their individual needs. However, if there is no appropriate vacancy available, children can remain in an assessment centre for many months.

Assessment centres vary a good deal in terms of resources, style of leadership and the use to which they are put by the local authority. One senior social worker described the centre for which he was responsible as

> a dumping ground. After kids have been in here for a while – and the average stay is three to four months – they are often worse off than when they arrived. They are always in an extremely vulnerable condition and can be adversely influenced by the hard-core element.

A centre that wants

> to provide an emotionally secure, caring environment which will initially help a child to cope with and contain his/her emotional distress; to build relationships and to provide nurturing care, while at the same time, continuously assessing the young person's needs

can all but fail because of problems that arise from the inadequate training and lack of experienced staff. At one unit, for example, out of the fifteen members of staff required for the maximum of sixteen children accommodated, only two were qualified. While the strength of caring and sympathy for the children was not in doubt, it was evidently no easier for the staff to exert proper control over them than it had been for the parents or guardians.

Drugs

Controlled drugs

Some dangerous or otherwise harmful drugs are classified as controlled drugs under the Misuse of Drugs Act (1971). They are divided into three categories:

Class A includes heroin, morphine, cocaine, opium, methadone and other narcotics, LSD and other hallucinogens, cannabinol and derivatives, and injectable amphetamines.

Class B includes amphetamines, barbiturates, drinamyl (purple hearts), cannabis and cannabis resin, benzedrine, dexedrine, and methaqualone.

Class C includes various amphetamine-type substances, dextropropoxyphene and diethylpropion.

It is an offence under Section 8 of the Act for an occupier or person concerned with the management of any premises to knowingly allow the premises to be used for the smoking of cannabis or opium, the preparation of opium or the production and supply of controlled drugs. It is also an offence to knowingly give false information if questioned in relation to offences under the Act. In both cases, the prosecution must prove the defendant knew what was going on. Police may search premises for drugs with a warrant obtained from a magistrates' court.

Alcohol

Between the ages of 5 and 16 a child may drink alcohol but only on private premises. Children under 14 are not allowed in bars during licensing hours; though a pub may provide special facilities for them. Young people between 14 and 16 are allowed into a bar but are not allowed to buy or drink alcohol there. They do not have a legal right to be there, so a licensee can exclude them. If young people are over 16, they may have beer, cider or perry with a meal in a bar. Only when they reach 18 and are legally adults can they buy alcohol.

Cigarettes

It is not illegal to smoke in private at any age, but it is an offence under the Children and Young Persons Act 1963 to sell tobacco, cigarettes or cigarette papers to someone who is or appears to be under 16 when it is for that person's use. Following a complaint, a court can order the owner of premises where an automatic cigarette machine is being used by young people under 16 to take precautions to ensure they do not use it or to remove it altogether.

If a young person under 16 is found smoking in a public place – for example, a park, garden or railway station – a uniformed police officer or park keeper can seize all tobacco and cigarette papers (but not a pipe or tobacco pouch!).

Solvent abuse

It is not illegal to sniff glue or other solvents and it is unlikely to become so since a ban on sales would be difficult to enforce. However, in dealing with young glue sniffers the police can and do use their power to detain them in 'a place of safety' (see pp. 193–4) for up to eight days.

Health and sexual activity

The age of majority

In 1969 the Family Law Reform Act (England and Wales) and the Age of Majority (Northern Ireland) Act set the age of majority – the age at which people can first vote and marry without parental consent – at 18. These Acts define people as medically adult from the age of 16, which means they have the right to consent to their own surgical, dental and medical treatment, including contraception and abortion, and have the right to decide what information, if any, may be passed on to their parents.

In Scotland the Age of Majority Act 1969 sets the voting age at 18 but does not refer to marriage since people there have always been able to marry at 16 without parental consent. The act is also silent on the matter of medical consent, but in practice 16 is the accepted age.

The age of consent

Section 5 of the Sexual Offences Act (England and Wales) 1956 makes it an absolute offence for a man to have sexual intercourse with a girl under 13. Section 6 makes it an offence for a man to have sexual intercourse with a girl between 13 and 16, but he may enter a defence if he believes himself validly married to the girl or if he is under 24, has not previously been charged with the same offence, and believes the girl to be over 16. The maximum penalty for unlawful sex with a girl between 13 and 16 is two years' imprisonment.

The Sexual Offences (Scotland) Act 1976 Section 3 prohibits intercourse with a girl under 13 years old. The maximum penalty is life imprisonment. Section 4 makes it an offence to have sexual intercourse with a girl between 13 and 16. The maximum penalty is two years' imprisonment or three months on summary procedure.

The Criminal Law Amendment Act (Northern Ireland) 1885 fixes a maximum penalty of two years' imprisonment for unlawful carnal knowledge of a girl between 14 and 17 years. The age of sexual consent is thus 17, a year older than in the rest of the United Kingdom, although the minimum marriage age is 16 with parental consent. Sexual intercourse with a girl under 14 carries a maximum penalty of life imprisonment. There is no defence that the man believed the girl to be over 17.

Legal aid

Young people are often hesitant about getting legal advice or representation because of the costs involved. However, the state-subsidized legal aid scheme enables those on low incomes to obtain these services free or relatively inexpensively. Young people over 16 may apply for legal aid for themselves and only their own disposable capital and income will be assessed in deciding whether or not they are eligible. Except in criminal cases, young people under 16 must apply through an adult intermediary (a parent, guardian or other adult in whose care they are), in which case the financial resources of any adult who is liable in law to maintain them – including one or both parents and fathers of illegitimate children, but excluding foster parents – will be assessed.

There are three kinds of legal aid.

1. Legal advice and assistance on any legal problem under the green form scheme (so called because of the colour of the application form). This includes cases in which a young person is indirectly involved in a civil case, for example in a divorce case where the child wants to tell the court where or with whom he wants to live.

2. Legal aid for direct involvement in civil court proceedings; for example, if a young person is suing for damages to compensate for injuries received in an accident, or is the subject of care proceedings.

3. Legal aid for criminal court proceedings. Young people who have been charged with or are being prosecuted for a criminal offence do not need to act through an adult intermediary. They can instruct solicitors directly and apply for legal aid at any point during the case. Legal aid is not available to bring a private criminal prosecution.

The Lord Chancellor's Office is directly responsible for criminal legal aid; civil and green form legal aid are administered by the Law Society under the Lord Chancellor's general guidance. The Law Society divides the country into legal aid areas, each with a legal aid office and general and area committees composed of local solicitors and barristers. The general committee considers whether an application is reasonable, and has the power to refuse legal aid if it is not; and the area committee deals with appeals against refusal.

Emergency legal aid can be granted – over the telephone if necessary – when it is considered to be in the interests of justice. But if the applicant is later found not to be financially eligible for legal aid, the certificate will be revoked and he or she may have to repay the Law Society for any costs already incurred by the solicitor.

How to find a solicitor

Each year the Law Society produces the Legal Aid Solicitors List for each area, which gives the names and addresses of solicitors and the categories of work in which they are prepared to assist under the legal aid scheme. The list, which is available at most libraries and advice centres, makes no recommendations and is not a guarantee of ability. Youth clubs, citizens' advice bureaux, social services, law centres and friends and relatives are probably the most useful source of recommendations.

It is important to remember that lawyers, although they may give professional diagnoses and advice, can take action only on their client's instructions, and that any service they give under legal aid must be as good as it would be if the client were paying privately.

Where to go for help and advice

The organizations listed below are open during normal office hours unless stated otherwise. Many of them will supply lists of their own publications – factsheets, leaflets, magazines, books – on request.

Barnardo's
Tanners Lane
Barkingside
Ilford, Essex IG6 1QG
Tel: 01–550–8822

Operates a variety of family support and child care services throughout the country, including youth training schemes and preventive work among adolescents.

Children's Legal Centre
20 Compton Terrace
London N1 2UN
Tel: 01–359–6251
Line open 2–5 p.m. weekdays
   An independent, national
organization offering free and
confidential advice to young people,
parents and professionals on all
aspects of law and policy affecting
children and young people in
England and Wales. Publishes a
detailed information sheet on legal
aid for young people, a monthly
bulletin and other leaflets,
handbooks and reports.

Church of England Children's
   Society
Old Town Hall
Kennington Road
London SE11 4QD
Tel: 01–735–2441
   A Christian charity operating
throughout England and Wales.
Offers children and young people,
regardless of religious belief, help
with problems of truancy and
delinquency. Runs several
alternative-to-custody schemes,
which aim to help persistent
offenders. *See also* p. 75.

Crisis Concern for the Alleged
   Shop-lifter
National Consumer Protection
   Council
18 Woodward Avenue
London NW4 8NY
Tel: 01–202–5787/6303
   Offers help and advice to those who

have been wrongly accused of shoplifting.

Justice for Children
35 Wellington Street
London WC2E 7BN
Tel: 01–836–3917
   Legal help and pressure group for
children in care or in trouble with
the law.

Law Centre
14 University Street
Belfast
Tel: 0232–46984
   Help, advice and information.

Law Centres Federation
164 North Gower Street
London NW1
Tel: 01–387–8570
   Head office for all Law Centres.

Law Society
113 Chancery Lane
London WC2A 1PL
Tel: 01–242–1222
   Help, advice and information; civil
legal aid.

Law, the Scottish Council for Civil
   Liberties
146 Holland Street
Glasgow G2 4NG
Tel: 041–332–5960
   Legal help and advice.

The Lord Chancellor's Department
Nevill House
Page Street
London SW1
Tel: 01–211–3000
   Criminal legal aid.

Magistrates Association
28 Fitzroy Square
London W1P 6DD
Tel: 01–387–2302
  Help, advice and information.

MIND (National Association for
  Mental Health)
22 Harley Street
London W1N 2ED
Tel: 01–637–0741
  Advice, referral and
representation on social, legal and
other mental health issues. *See also*
p. 136.

National Association for the Care
  and Resettlement of Offenders
  (NACRO)
169 Clapham Road
London SW9 0PU
Tel: 01–580–6500
  A registered charity that promotes
the care and resettlement of
offenders in the community, helps
victims of crime and involves the
community in the prevention of
crime. It provides a range of hostels
and shared housing schemes for
offenders and other single homeless
people; up to one year's training and
employment in community
programme schemes and help in
finding permanent jobs; and a two-
year programme of training and
planned work experience for 16- to
18-year-olds who have been in trouble
with the law or are at risk of getting
into trouble. Also works with
prisons and community-based

agencies to set up systems that allow
prisoners access to the advice and
services they need when coming out
of prison.

National Association of Citizens'
  Advice Bureaux
110 Drury Lane
London WC2
Tel: 01–836–9231

National Association of Young
  People in Care
Second Floor
Maranar House
28–30 Mosley Street
Newcastle-upon-Tyne NE1 1DF
Tel: 0912–612178
  Help and advice for young
people.

National Council for Civil Liberties
21 Tabard Street
London SE1 4LA
Tel: 01–403–3888
  Exists to defend and extend civil
liberties within the United
Kingdom.

Northern Ireland Women's Aid
  Federation
143A University Road
Belfast 7
  Offers help and legal advice.

Nottingham Youth Action (NYA)
The Resource Centre
28 Handel Street
Nottingham NG3 1JE
Tel: 0602–585111
  Project set up to develop ways of
working with groups of young

people who may be at risk or in trouble. Because the team is small, it can work only in a limited number of areas at one time, but may be able to put groups in touch with sympathetic workers in their neighbourhoods. It publishes *Get It Right*, a simple, direct information booklet on the rights of young people in trouble with the law.

The Rainier Foundation
89A Blackheath Hill
London SE10 8TJ
Tel: 01–691–3124/3654

Provides services for adolescents in need, including young offenders and young people in care.

Scottish Women's Aid
Ainlie House

11 St Colme
Edinburgh
Tel: 031–225–8011

Co-ordinating body for local women's aid groups throughout Scotland; offers legal help and advice.

UKIAS (United Kingdom Immigrants Advisory Service)
Seventh floor
Brettenham House
Savoy Street
Strand
London WC2
Tel: 01–240–5176

Has offices in various parts of the country, and gives legal help and advice on immigration problems of all kinds.

Notes

1. Richard Herrnstein and James Wilson, *Crime and Human Nature*, New York, Simon & Schuster, 1985
2. Chris Davey, *Working with Young People: Legal Responsibility and Liability*, London, Children's Legal Centre, 1984
3. This section adapted from Veronica Gillespie and Barbara Bullivant, *Children and Young People in Trouble*, Sheffield, Home and School Council Publications, 1984
4. Ibid.

Chapter 7

Whose Help? Whose Advice?

It is often very difficult to ask for help. We may find it difficult to accept that we really do need help, and even when we are desperate for it, we may be embarrassed or humiliated at having to discuss our problems with strangers. Asking for help with family problems, one psychiatrist told me,

> is more difficult than anything else. If you thought you might have cancer, you would probably be sick with worry, but actually going to the doctor and saying 'I can't manage my children' or 'my marriage isn't good' is just as hard to cope with, if not harder. The major obstacle is actually making that phone call or having that first interview, and it's a tremendous reflection on the family that they have put their standard of parenting so high that they will sacrifice their pride in order to refer themselves.

The more anxious we are, the more we tend to stand in awe of the expert whose advice we seek. This overwhelming diffidence that covers us with confusion in the presence of a professional, to whom we may even be paying a great deal of money for a consultation, seemed to me such a universal phenomenon that I asked Dr Anton Obholzer, a psychiatrist and chairman of the Tavistock Clinic, what it is in these circumstances that renders people ordinarily quite capable of speaking up for themselves almost inarticulate. He says:

> The problem with professionals is that they are perceived as having specialized knowledge to which we need access. We feel that we have no choice but to put ourselves in their hands and to trust them. What makes the ordinary relationship with a doctor so particularly affecting is that in our fantasy he stands between us and death, of which we are all afraid.

Thinking about it calmly and objectively, we know that the doctors and other professionals we are consulting are people like ourselves, who differ only in their training and experience. It is precisely because of that training and experience that we go to them for help, but we should remember that they need to share *our* experiences in order to employ their skills. That fact alone provides a more equal footing. We should also bear in mind that we don't necessarily have to accept any advice that is given if we think it's not really relevant or helpful; we can 'shop around'. As one doctor pointed out, 'The helping professions cover a very wide field and they offer a very mixed level of service, but so do dentists and so do surveyors. There are obviously people around who are very indifferent; there are people around who are excellent.'

There are three ways of asking for help: by telephone, by letter or in person. In all cases the golden rule is to ask, not demand. Strident demands can antagonize the very people we need to help us whereas a request is more likely to be met with sympathy and understanding, kindness and a willingness to do the best that can be done.

Using a variety of examples, this chapter examines in greater detail some of the help available in dealing with adolescent problems.

The professionals

General practitioner

For all problems related to our physical health and that of our children, we do not hesitate to turn to our GP, but it is not always so simple when it comes to problems that place an abnormally heavy load on the mind or emotions. We may worry that the doctor will not give us sufficient time to explain the problem, or we may ring the surgery to find that our own doctor is away and we can't get an appointment with another doctor for two days – which might be too late if the situation is desperate. In some cases – drug addiction, for example – some doctors are not too anxious to help. None the less, the family doctor is still an excellent first source of help. If our own doctor is away or the appointment book is full, making it clear that we are desperate and are willing to wait can result in being fitted in between or after other patients. If the doctor is unable to provide adequate help himself, he has access to a number of other agencies that may be able to. This is particularly true in urban areas, but may be less so in more isolated parts of the country.

Social workers

Social workers have a wide range of responsibilities for the entire population in the fields of housing, education, physical and mental health and welfare, adoption and fostering, child guidance and court work. They have a great deal of power and considerable expertise, and so are one of the most positive and practical sources of help for a number of problems. Even if they are unable to provide the necessary answers or help themselves, they will at least be able to offer advice on alternative sources of assistance.

Psychiatrists, psychologists and counsellors

To some extent the professionals who deal with emotional and mental problems are viewed with scepticism and even suspicion by the general public. Perhaps this is partly because we cannot understand how they can diagnose and treat problems that are not necessarily physically apparent and partly because they speak more often of change than cure. In fact, there are many different kinds of professionals in the field of mental health care and although they are distinct from each other in certain respects, there is considerable overlap in others. In choosing any form of psychological help it is essential to check the credentials of the individuals involved.

Psychiatrists are fully trained medical doctors who, following their basic qualification, have specialized in the study and treatment of mental disease and have themselves undergone psychoanalysis. They can determine if a person's problems have an organic or emotional basis and provide medical treatment or psychological therapy. As doctors, they are listed on the medical register.

Psychologists are trained in the science of behaviour, the underlying physiological and mental steps that govern human actions. Psychologists who are called 'doctor' have a doctorate – a PhD; they are scientists, not medical doctors. There are many different kinds of psychologist, each specializing in a different aspect of behaviour. Educational psychologists, for example, work with children who have learning or behaviour problems at school, and social psychologists are concerned with people who have problems relating to and interacting with others.

Counselling is fundamentally about helping people to help themselves and concentrates on the day-to-day issues in their lives. However, anyone can call himself a counsellor; it simply means someone who gives advice and does not necessarily indicate any specialist training or recognized qualifications. Similarly, anyone may call himself a therapist, but only someone who has a recognized degree in psychology or psychiatry can call himself a psychotherapist. The British Association for Counselling (BAC) has developed a code of ethics and an accreditation scheme. It also publishes a book that lists helping agencies and counselling training courses throughout the country. The BAC is especially helpful if you are having difficulty in finding suitable help or are unsure of the credentials of a particular counselling service.

Types of therapy

For many people, suggests Dr Obholzer, going into a therapeutic programme is like crossing a bridge. Approaching the bridge, he says, a person may be afraid and worried by such questions as:

> Am I going to be helped? What are they going to think of me? What am I going to say? Will I be late? What will happen if I am late? It is how one copes with the anticipation that is important. At this stage it is not uncommon for people to turn back, although they may make another attempt to cross it again some time in the future. Finally, on leaving the bridge, what do you do with the experience gained along the way? Do you denigrate it; do you 'appreciate' it but ignore it; or do you weigh up the results and consider which to retain and which to throw out?

There are also certain risks attached to getting this help. There is a risk of dependency – foregoing one's own adult judgement; a risk of idealization – expecting too much; and in the event of feeling disappointed, there is a risk of reacting with undue denigration. Dr Obholzer's advice to those seeking help is: 'Don't expect everything to turn out perfectly, but do give things a chance. Help is a relative condition, which can only be enhanced by mutual co-operation.'

Individual

As the name indicates, the person needing help is seen on his or her own by the therapist. There are many types of individual therapy, of which psychoanalysis is just one. It is important to find out what a particular therapist plans to achieve and how he plans to approach the problem before agreeing to the therapy. I asked one therapist if she felt that establishing a sympathetic relationship between herself and a patient was an important factor in successful therapy. 'No, I don't,' she replied.

> If I were to go to someone for help, I would want to make sure that the person was adequately trained for a start, but I wouldn't expect to have a major friendship with my therapist. Therapy is about change; change is a very uncomfortable procedure and it may come best through an uncomfortable therapy which people may, in fact, feel quite angry about at a later stage. But if it has actually introduced some kind of difference into the way they've done things, then it's actually been successful. Being a therapist isn't about being liked. You may be, and for some people that's very important, and maybe that's how they achieve success, but it's not necessarily a criterion.

On the other hand, Jane Malcolmson, a psychotherapist who works as a counsellor in a school for maladjusted girls, and runs a private counselling service, finds that in working with youngsters it is essential to establish a personal relationship.

> Whereas I would never allow an adult to see what I felt, with kids, you have to be real. One day when I turned up at school and none of the girls wanted to see me, I let them see my disappointment, saying something like, 'What a pity! Oh, well, that's me out of a job this morning then.' By midday I had my usual string of girls clamouring at the door. With adults, however, I think it is important to keep a distance in order that they should have their own space in which to make decisions and accept responsibility.

Dr Susan Isaacs Elmhirst, a consultant psychiatrist with great experience in the psychoanalysis of children and adolescents, suggests that the most essential ingredient in the relationship between patient and therapist is trust.

> It doesn't matter whether one is liked or disliked – and during the prolonged sessions required by psychoanalysis, one is probably both loathed and loved at various times – trust is the vital element. I also happen to believe that the attitude of a psychiatrist towards a patient is more important than the setting. Patients come to you for help for what they consider to be a serious problem. They deserve respect and they need your fullest attention.

Group

In this type of therapy various numbers of people meet with one or two therapists. Some groups deal with specific areas – drug abuse, for instance – others with a mixture of problems. Some have a constant membership for a fixed lifetime while in others, members of the group can drop in or out of the sessions whenever they wish. The advantages of group therapy are that people needing help may be more receptive when they realize that they are not the only ones with problems and they benefit from each other's experiences.

Family

Family therapy is based on the principle that the problems that exist are not concentrated in and confined to the individual but lie in the interaction between individuals. Therefore it makes the family aware, without apportioning blame, that it owns the problem and that the difficulties of an adolescent currently on the mat for causing mayhem and disaster cannot be dissociated from the rest of the unit, who may feel that his behaviour has nothing to do with them.

Its prime function is to act as an agent for change. As Gill Gorell Barnes, senior social worker at the Institute of Family Therapy, writes in her book *Working with Families*: 'The therapist aims to help people, not by trying to change them, but by making a family look at their problems in a different light in order that they themselves can see where change might be made.'[1]

In *Family Therapies: Full Length Case Studies*, Dr Marion Walters explains how she does this:

> I think change requires that families be presented with concrete alternatives to the impasse or dilemma which brings them into therapy and that they try them on in the interview. I try to give the family a new perspective of the situation they are in. The business of giving the picture a new frame is as important for the therapist as for the family ... I need to create a workable reality; to select and reframe a piece of the action where some change can be initiated.[2]

During family therapy all relevant members of the group are brought together in one room. Later it may be thought appropriate to see one or two members independently, but initially the therapists look carefully at the whole family to see how the unit is structured and how the individuals interact. While attempting to discover the circumstances that might be made in order to secure a way forward. The number of sessions varies depending on the needs of the particular family.

Family therapists usually operate as a team. One member of the team may remain with the family while the others sit in an adjacent room and watch the session through a two-way mirror. The session might also be recorded on video, enabling the team to review it and consider more closely the dynamics of the family relationships. Most families to whom I spoke agreed that they soon forgot about the camera and felt comforted by the fact that they were supported by a team, however invisible it might be. By its nature, of course, a team has more expertise and experience than an individual and serves to dilute any extreme position that might be held by one person.

Not all parents to whom I spoke who had undergone family therapy felt that the experience had been helpful and some were vehement that it 'did more harm than good'. Of course, for a family in crisis – perhaps finding themselves together for the first time after a period of separation, each member on display to one another and to the therapist – the situation is almost bound to be fraught with anxiety and pain. There may be difficulties in ensuring that all the family members are present on a number of occasions and additional tension if children have to be absented from school or the parents need to take time off from work. It is also difficult not to feel hostility towards a process that challenges the status quo and leaves it open to question and change.

At a time of crisis following my divorce and remarriage, when my daughter became seriously disturbed and unhappy, I found myself having to test the results of my own research. For me family therapy was indeed painful, but invaluable. In a split family it is well nigh impossible for parents to obtain an accurate picture of life 'on the other side'. At a time when his loyalties are perhaps distressingly divided, a child's-eye view is especially unreliable and the only indication to parents that all may not be well is an alarming alteration in the pattern of their youngster's behaviour. Without the two sides coming together to get a clear picture of what is happening, even with the sincere desire to do what is best for a child, there can be serious mistakes in decision-making, which can have disastrous consequences. During our therapy it became evident that a fairly radical change was needed to help my daughter over a period of crisis. Together the family decided that a new school and a new structure to her home life were required. Once secure in the altered routine, she became more stable, more communicative and a great deal happier.

Although the success of family therapy is hard to evaluate empirically because there tends to be very little feedback from families, Dr Christopher Dare of the Child and Adolescent Unit at the Institute of Psychiatry at the Maudsley Hospital in London, and one of the country's most experienced practitioners in the field, argues that the evidence available suggests it is very effective 'in about 98 per cent of cases. In the remaining 2 per cent, things might actually be made worse.' He maintains a preference for helping families 'who don't think they have a problem, only a problem child. When families see the difficulties as lying within themselves, they are half-way cured.'

He points out that adolescence tends to occur at the same time as parents are entering mid-life, and the changes and adaptation that this transition requires may be painful and even frightening. The fact that their children are growing up and will move away from home forces them to examine their own relationship – and they may not like what they see. 'Can I live with this man or this woman, alone, without the children, until death do us part?' A future together might look decidedly bleak for some parents. Children are a main source of parental unity and in cases where a family does have a 'problem' teenager, parents often bury their own anxieties within the concern they feel for the child whose problem lends stability and generally organizes the family unit. Dr Dare sees family therapy as an attempt to forestall a situation in which a child wants to become a psychiatric patient – wants to live an illness (as with anorexia, for example) as a lifestyle. 'It can be a full life-task being a psychiatric patient,' he said, 'and parents who find it impossible to adapt to a post-parenting phase are rewarded by having a young adult on their hands who is as dependent upon them as an 8-year-old.'

Settings

Most therapists regard the setting in which therapy takes place as crucial – not necessarily to the outcome of the treatment, but as to how the clients view themselves in relation to their surroundings, the experts involved and the kind of therapy they are experiencing. Setting has a good deal to do with the expectations of both the client and the therapist. For example, Dr Dare points out that the Maudsley, being a large psychiatric hospital, is regarded by local residents as 'the bin'. Its image – however unfair and inaccurate – still retains shades of the Victorian madhouse, and children and adolescents referred there are generally sent by their school or family doctor or by other therapists who are unable to make progress in a case. Families seldom self-refer at the Maudsley, although they may certainly do so. Because of the nature of the setting, Dr Dare tends to view the family as a pathological unit that requires treatment. Although therapists in different settings may adopt a less clinical, more pragmatic approach, the methods used to promote the spirit of change remain broadly similar.

Child guidance clinics

Nation-wide, psychiatric help for young people is rather scarce – the London area is exceptional in the wealth and variety it has to offer – so it is particularly unfortunate that child guidance clinics, which are one source of help freely available throughout the country, have such a tarnished image. This may be a result, at least in part, of the fact that these clinics are jointly funded by the local health and education authorities and the local social services department. As the members of staff – psychiatrists, psychologists, psychotherapists, social workers and remedial teachers – are responsible to different departments, there are inevitably conflicts of interest.

When parents seek help from, or are referred to, a child guidance clinic, they have no guarantee as to which professional is placed in charge of their case, although if they insist on seeing a psychiatrist, there is a good chance that they will be able to do so. It is important for families to be aware of the general background of the professional into whose hands they are about to commit themselves, as it will affect the approach he takes and the treatment he considers appropriate.

Since the policy on confidentiality varies from clinic to clinic, it is also a good idea to establish at the beginning what information, if any, is to be seen by anyone other than the individual handling the case. A senior social worker told me:

> It is an issue that parents should check out when they go to clinics. I think it is a matter which should be taken seriously. I can only tell you of the pattern which exists in the places where I have worked, but I would guess it is fairly common; and that is, if the referral comes from someone other than the family themselves, you would communicate with that referrer – for example, the general practitioner, the educational psychologist or the health visitor. Initially, they would be given some information in outline terms. This would perhaps be followed by an interim report, but probably in the majority of cases

the family would be informed as to whom I was writing and what I would be mentioning. If a family have referred themselves, then anybody one communicates with is by negotiation.

If a family is referred through the school, their child's record will indicate that a referral has been made and the reasons for it, but in cases of self-referral, parents can insist on privacy. In such a case, the social worker said,

it would be up to me or the therapist to decide whether or not we felt you were putting yourself at a disadvantage by not discussing the problem with another. I can think of an instance, for example, where it would have been of great advantage to the family if we had been able to contact their child's school, but they did not give their permission for us to do so. But that's their choice.

Despite these difficulties child guidance clinics can provide real help, particularly in rural areas, when resources are often limited.

Adolescent units

Most families in search of some form of psychotherapy are likely to be referred to a unit attached to their local hospital. The organization and professional involvement is roughly similar throughout the country, as the following examples show, although the age range treated may vary from hospital to hospital.

The Department of Child and Family Psychiatry at the Charing Cross Hospital in London is a typical out-patient psychiatric unit. It accepts children and adolescents up to the age of 16, at which time the older teenager moves into the province of adult care. Young people can refer themselves to the clinic but seldom do so. Most are sent there by their parents, family doctor, the court (for psychiatric reports), the police, the educational welfare officer or other therapists.

Dr Peter Reder, who heads the team of psychiatrists, psychologists, psychotherapists and social workers at the unit, explains how it works:

If parents telephone us and say 'Can you help?', an appointment is made for them with a particular member of the team, either because he or she has interests or skills especially suited to the case or because they may be less bogged down with casework at that time. Each patient, however, must be seen by a psychiatrist. We have the advantage of being the only part of the health service for which there is no formal waiting list. Often, prompt intervention makes therapy unnecessary.

If Dr Reder or a member of his team consider it beneficial, an adolescent can be referred to a residential unit.

The Hill End Adolescent Unit in St Albans, Hertfordshire, provides residential care for people under the age of 16, although the main emphasis is on pre-admission work. 'Admission to hospital is always seen as the last of all possible choices', a doctor at Hill End stated. Because psychiatric disturbance in younger adolescents can often be seen as rooted in questions of authority and family ties, the unit aims to work closely with whoever may be legally in charge. Although referral must be by the family doctor or other professional, it is the parents or legal guardians who must finally decide whether their youngster should be admitted. Family members are invited to all meetings with teams comprising psychiatrists, nurses and social workers. At Hill End schooling continues during term time and is provided in an adjacent building, where day pupils are also accepted.

The Lothian Health Board in Scotland is unusually fortunate in that it supports two adolescent units – the Young People's Unit attached to the Royal Edinburgh Hospital and the Adolescent Unit at Bangour Village Hospital in Broxburn. The latter, the first such unit to be established in Scotland is situated in an area of small towns and villages. The unit accepts requests for help from any source, but families seldom self-refer. There are facilities for residential care and an out-patient service, where individuals are counselled separately and families can be seen as a group. Like most adolescent units throughout the country, the young people who come to Bangour Village Hospital are those described by a consultant psychiatrist as having 'problems negotiating adolescence', including stealing, truancy, and behavioural and sexual difficulties.

Therapeutic communities

Dr Don Batten, of the Young People's Unit at the Whitchurch Hospital in Cardiff, describes a therapeutic community as 'an organization built around a community of people who live and work together to solve psychological problems'. In his unit, Dr Batten emphasizes, considerable effort went into attempting to reduce the hierarchical pyramid,

> although in the end the inevitable image of 'me patient – you therapist' remains, especially in an adolescent unit, where there is the adult versus adolescent relationship and the added problem of control. Here, we use individual therapy to help people to cope with their internal problems – their worries, if you like – and we use family therapy to

help them overcome problems at home. Youngsters are also asked to participate in the community and to relate to non-family members.

A particularly good description of a therapeutic community comes from the Northgate Clinic's information sheet for patients. A regional unit in Hendon, it operates a catchment area within the North-West Thames Regional Health Authority, where referrals derive mainly from consultant psychiatrists, social workers, probation officers, family doctors and education departments.

The clinic offers help to young people between the ages of 16 and 21 years with severe emotional and social difficulties. It aims to create an environment in which patients can explore their difficulties and find alternative ways of dealing appropriately with them. A lot of emphasis is placed on patients living together in the community, sharing difficulties and anxieties, and being able to offer each other support. Patients spend a lot of time talking to staff and each other about their experiences and problems, trying to understand what has happened to them, and why they feel as they do. The length of stay at the clinic is variable: how long patients stay and what they do when they leave is a constant topic of discussion with staff and other patients. Patients are encouraged to maintain contact with their homes, and the patient's family may be invited to the clinic to meet with staff, sometimes together with the patient.

Patients are expected to stay at the clinic during the week and attend programme activities. Whenever possible, they will spend weekends at home . . . The formal treatment programme lasts from 9.00 a.m. to 5.00 p.m. Monday to Friday, and is described in detail below. The informal contact with patients and staff during free time in the evening is also considered to be an essential part of the overall therapeutic experience.

The Clinic's Therapeutic Programme
All groups involve both patients and staff, and the young people taking part can always feel reassured that the staff members present will be aware that new people may feel nervous of joining in, and support is always available.

The programme begins each day with the community meeting at 9.00 a.m. This is a large group involving all the patients, and usually focuses on 'everyday' issues affecting the young people in their day to day living in the clinic, such as the difficulties involved in living together.

On three afternoons a week patients meet together in a small psychotherapy group. The discussion here is of a more personal nature than in the community meetings, but less so than in individual therapy. An important task is for the group to share and support each other with mutual problems.

Once a week patients attend boys and girls groups. These are single-sex groups where the young people present may feel less inhibited about discussing relevant issues which concern them without the opposite sex present.

Social skills group takes place one morning a week and is designed to help patients identify and work on any practical problems they may have. It deals with such diverse difficulties as poor abilities in looking after yourself, washing and cooking, problems of communication such as in using the telephone or travelling on public transport and, towards the end of your stay, in coping with interviews and looking for jobs.

On Thursday afternoons the psychodrama group meets. This group makes more use of non-verbal forms of communication than any other group in the programme, using a wide variety of techniques to explore the individual's problems and relationships. It provides the opportunity for exploring bodily tension, for playing and for people to feel more comfortable with themselves and with others.

Each patient also has individual psychotherapy for two sessions of fifty minutes each week. Here the deeper and more sensitive parts of your difficulties can be discussed.

On Mondays at 5.00 p.m. a patients' meeting takes place, which staff do not attend. This is an opportunity for patients to discuss and recognize any activities they would like to carry out themselves.

Art therapy is once a week, to explore difficulties and develop creativity through the medium of paint.

The Occupational Therapy Department is open every day and provides a range of activities, such as painting, pottery, carpentry, discussion groups, keep fit/relaxation, to help you develop your creative and practical skills.

Each patient meets with their Management Team once a week on average. The team consists of two nurses, your individual therapist and a member of the Occupational Therapy Department. Together they will work closely with you in the management and supervision of any problems that arise, in supporting you in times of stress and in reviewing your progress at the clinic.

In certain circumstances patients may be prescribed medication. In such instances, it is important that the patient follows the directions of the doctor at all times. Medication is always supervised by nursing staff.

CONCEPT HOUSES

These therapeutic communities, which specialize in helping people with drug and drug-related problems (see Chapter 3), are based on a hierarchical structure. In working through the programme, residents work their way up the hierarchy until many of them become members of staff themselves. Phoenix House in London describes its style of operation in the following way:

> There are compulsory group activities, including encounter, gestalt, psychodrama and bioenergetics. There are task groups and social skills groups which residents are expected to participate in. Individual counselling is provided as and when necessary by the staff. The resident is interviewed by the psychiatrist on admission and thereafter on an *ad hoc* basis.

ST CHRISTOPHER'S FELLOWSHIP

The Fellowship provides residential care for young people between 16 and 20. It does not classify its homes as therapeutic communities – they are less structured and more informal – and they can perhaps be seen as an intermediate stage between such places and self-help groups. Although based in and around the London area, its doors are open to youngsters from anywhere in the country. Young people may refer themselves, although most come through the social services.

Residents are counselled individually and any formal therapy that is needed takes place outside the unit. Liz Bailey, who runs St Christopher's residential unit in Chiswick, London, trained as a social worker and specialized in residential care. Like other specialists working with adolescents, she feels that although group work and family therapy have their place, it is important, especially with the older teenagers, to help them establish their identity on a personal, one-to-one basis. 'Very often,' she explained, 'young people are desperate to get away from "the group", which can mean the family or an institution. They have very little confidence in themselves and need to see themselves as individuals, not just as one of a crowd.'

There are nine members of staff at Chiswick House to care for twelve young adults, who may remain in the unit for a minimum of one and a maximum of two years. Prior to admission and for the first six months a care plan is drawn up for each newcomer, which identifies their needs and plots out a personal programme, which is constantly reviewed. A 'link worker' is assigned to each resident on arrival and has special responsibility for him throughout his stay. Liz Bailey told me:

> Young people who come to us troubled and depressed, tend to have a very limited view of their future. It is as much as they can do to live with their anxieties from day to day. It is our job to help them towards a recognition that, first, they have a future and, secondly, that the kind of future in store for them will be as a result of their own efforts and forward planning. Here, we are looking at their future all the time. It may sound odd, but the moment they arrive, I begin to think of their departure! Being here is not easy. It's challenging because young people are required to make choices and take responsibility for their own lives.

To this end, residents are encouraged to do their own laundry, learn to look after themselves, to buy their own food within a given budget and to prepare all their own meals. All residents have their own bedrooms, which they are at liberty to decorate in any way they like – although the line is drawn at black walls and graffiti. Newcomers are encouraged to find jobs as soon as possible, and a member of staff will accompany them to Job Centres and wait while they attend interviews.

The move away from the Fellowship residence can be difficult, so the leave-taking is carefully planned with a series of rituals, which include present-giving and a special dinner of the leaver's choosing. The link worker helps the young person to settle into new housing and there is a six-week period when contact with the unit continues to exist on a formal basis. During that time the individual's bed is kept empty in case of illness or a rare emergency. 'It wouldn't be right to expect them to look after themselves in new surroundings with a bout of flu,' Liz Bailey says, 'but people usually manage pretty well and, as yet, no one has actually returned to take up the vacancy.'

Self-help groups

Groups such as Alcoholics Anonymous (AA), Gamblers Anonymous (GA) and Families Anonymous (FA) rely on the experience of their members rather than professional advice to help people overcome their problems. Emotions Anonymous (EA) is a self-help group that developed out of AA. The kind of help it offers appears to be invaluable in particular situations.

Frank and Penny were at their wits' end. Both had been to the doctor for depression and stress-related illnesses when the actions of one of their three sons threatened to bring about the collapse of the family. The boy, Steve, left school at 16. He refused to attend the college that had offered him a place and he would not look for a job. His behaviour at home was often abusive and sometimes violent and when, finally, he refused to leave the house, confining himself to his bedroom for most of the day, his parents took him to see a psychiatrist. Steve was admitted to a hospital adolescent unit, but promptly discharged himself and returned home to his parents. Frank and Penny were left with the knowledge that for another two years at least their problem would remain unsolved and unrelieved. They turned to EA in desperation and attend the weekly meetings. They feel that with the support of other members of the group, they are 'beginning to get the whole thing in perspective. We spend less time at home agonizing over Steve and our attention is directed more towards the other two children, who we feel have been somewhat neglected during the crisis period.' Frank and Penny agreed that the stress that was beginning to threaten their own relationship had been lessened by the regular visits to EA and that they felt closer as a result.

Support groups

Support groups are like self-help groups, but are led by professionals, who act as advisers rather than therapists. Especially anxious to transform the popular them-and-us concept into a partnership in which parents and professionals share their experiences, are Ruth Schmidt, a child psychotherapist, and Carolyn Douglas, a family therapist, the founders of Exploring Parenthood. They began their careers in child guidance clinics, but found that although the clinics generally offered an excellent service, the setting was not attractive to many parents. It also seemed to them that the acute problems that families were experiencing at the time of their attendance might well have been prevented by professional intervention at an earlier stage: 'You don't have to wait for a crisis to happen before seeking help,' they say. They see Exploring Parenthood as a community project, begun in response to a growing need for help and advice in bringing up families in the stressful conditions of modern life. Schmidt and Douglas head a team that includes psychiatrists, psychologists, psychoanalysts, teachers and art therapists, all of whom have special interests in children and adolescents, and are expert at working within a group. They also have a peripatetic team who are prepared to travel throughout the country in response to requests from groups of parents experiencing difficulties in particular areas of family life. 'Exploring

Parenthood is constantly changing to fit in with the needs and wishes of parents, and we are able to tailor-make our programmes to suit them,' Ruth Schmidt told me. 'The membership is £5.00 a year, but no one is ever turned away from the workshops on the grounds that they are unable to afford the fees.'

The Andover Crisis and Support Centre offers a refuge to adults and youngsters in critical circumstances. Operating twenty-four hours a day, seven days a week, it provides counselling, information and short-term accommodation service for people in need. Accommodation is usually restricted to people from the age of 16; mothers with younger children will be accepted in times of crisis. Individuals are referred through a variety of agencies and organizations, and may also refer themselves; many simply walk in from the street. Since the centre does not operate a catchment area, its doors are open to all-comers. It offers a sanctuary to those who have suffered from violence and abuse at home, a chance for a new start for those who have been in trouble with the law and a place to 'cool off' after a row with parents.

The centre's work is based on the idea of crisis intervention. It aims to provide a framework within which clients can work towards resolving their own problems and difficulties. It describes its philosophy thus:

> The crisis and support centre does not purport to 'solve' problems, but rather attempts to provide an informal friendly atmosphere where people have immediate access to time, space, quiet, a sympathetic ear, companionship if wanted, advice if asked for, food and a bed when needed. Our approach is non-professional, non-directive and hopefully offering warmth, accurate empathy, non-judgemental listening and encouragement towards the mobilization of one's own resources. The centre attempts to respond to any person with any problems, offering anonymity and respecting confidentiality and the uniqueness of each individual.

For those needing accommodation, there is a three-week maximum stay. 'We could fill the house with youngsters every day,' a spokeswoman told me. 'It is not always in their best interests to stay here for a longer period. They must move on eventually, and we do our best to set them up for the future by assessing what their problems are, deciding whether we can help them and then whether we can help them to help themselves.'

Telephone counselling

It is often as difficult for adolescents to talk to their parents as it is for parents to 'reach' their children. A friendly and sympathetic voice at the end of a telephone can be a great source of help and comfort in times of crisis or distress and, for many, this form of counselling has the advantage of being anonymous. It can be especially useful to those who live in an area of the country where appropriate helping organizations are few and far between.

Many telephone counselling services, like Gay Switchboard (see p. 140) and Gamblers Anonymous, specialize in particular problem areas, while others offer advice and help on any difficulty a caller happens to present. One of the best known – and the oldest – is the Samaritans. They are a round-the-clock crisis telephone counselling service with branches throughout the country. The telephone number can be found in the local directory or the operator will put you through. If a caller does not have the money to pay for a prolonged session, the Samaritans will telephone back at their own expense (although they are quick to distinguish cases of genuine hardship from those who can afford the cost of a call). If there is a branch nearby, callers are urged to come to the centre in person, where they can talk to a Samaritan worker in private. The workers are volunteers who have been carefully trained to be sympathetic listeners.

In many people's minds the Samaritans are associated primarily with the support they give to potential suicide cases, but that ultimate cry for help is just one aspect of desperation that they deal with. They say:

All sorts of people use the Samaritans, more and more of them young. People find life difficult for many reasons and call the Samaritans with many different problems. Since it is an emergency service, many people call when things are suddenly too much, particularly if they are feeling so bad they are thinking about suicide. They ring because they want to tell someone how they feel. Some people want to be advised but find that when they have talked about it, they know themselves what they want to do. Often they do not have to do anything, they just need someone to listen. Callers are befriended. A volunteer acts like a sympathetic friend. Sometimes there will be only one visit or call, other times a caller may want to keep in contact until things are going better. If decisions have to be taken, the Samaritan volunteer helps the caller think about the different results of different actions. Above all the volunteer tries to make it easy for the caller to talk about how he feels, about why everything is so awful. No information is passed on to anybody; not parents, not friends, not police, not school, unless the caller wants it. A caller does not have to give a name.

In 1979 the National Children's Home responded to the International Year of the Child by setting up a phone-in service around the country. Called Family Network, its aims are to support families and individuals under stress and to generally promote family life. In some areas the Family Network service has been linked to a local radio station that broadcasts programmes featuring aspects and concerns of family life. Piccadilly Radio Family Careline in Manchester is just such a project, offering confidential, non-judgemental help and support to callers who they identify as people 'who would fight shy of going to a statutory agency, or perhaps feel that their problem is too small or maybe too embarrassing to take to a professional'. The volunteers at the end of the line are trained in telephone counselling skills and can, if necessary, call for further specialist advice from a team of experts working alongside them. For the majority of callers, being able to talk over their troubles with a sympathetic and informed listener is help enough, but about 40 per cent of the calls are concerned with more serious problems and are referred elsewhere for further help and advice.

The Family Network counselling service is regionally based and reflects the needs and concerns of families in specific areas. The volunteers in the regions also tend to differ in terms of their age and experience. For example, in Manchester the group are mostly aged between 20 and 30 and may often be post-graduates, whereas at the Redrose Careline headquarters in Preston, the volunteers are between 33 and 50, and are, in the main, mothers whose children are school-aged or who have left home. Tina Samuels, Redrose Careline co-ordinator, pointed out the differences involved in running the same project in a predominantly rural area where, she explained,

> families live in close-knit communities, which are generally supportive and caring. They also have a tradition of thinking that the best place to solve a problem is within the family. Although we cover the whole of Lancashire, we receive fewer calls than our colleagues in Manchester, where the population is transient and cosmopolitan. There are very few self-help groups in the surrounding area of Preston. We work closely with the N S P C C in cases of incest and sexual abuse, and of the 4,000 annual phone calls, many come from adolescents who feel unable to talk to their parents, even though they would like to do so. In such cases we often suggest that they imagine we are a parent and get them to express their difficulties to us in the hopes that the practice will help them to communicate at home.

Parents Anonymous (London) runs a helpline telephone service manned by volunteers, which was designed originally to offer help to parents who have abused, or felt that they might abuse, their children. Now the brief extends to all problems associated with family life. Although help is given initially over the telephone, a befriender scheme exists to provide further support. The volunteers who answer calls have taken a short training course, supervised by a qualified social worker. In addition to information concerning specialized agencies, they have direct contact with a team of experienced professionals.

Where to go for help and advice

The organizations listed below are open during normal office hours unless stated otherwise. Many of them will supply lists of their own publications – factsheets, leaflets, magazines, books – on request.

General

MIND (National Association for Mental Health)
22 Harley Street
London W1N 2ED
Tel: 01–637–0741 Advisory service open 2–4 p.m. weekdays
Leading mental health organization in England and Wales, with comprehensive information service. Telephone advisory service is not a counselling service but a guide towards finding appropriate kind of help. For details of nearest local association, contact appropriate regional office. For list of publications, send s.a.e. to MIND Mail Order (pl) at South East MIND offices.

REGIONAL OFFICES

North West MIND
21 Ribblesdale Place
Preston PR1 3NA
Tel: 0772–21734

Northern MIND
158 Durham Road
Gateshead, Tyne & Wear NE8 4EL
Tel: 091–478–4425

South East MIND
Fourth Floor
24–32 Stephenson Way
London NW1 2HD
Tel: 01–380–1253

South West MIND
Bluecoat House
Saw Close

Bath BA1 1EY
Tel: 0255–64670

Trent & Yorkshire MIND
First Floor Suite
The White Building
Fitzalan Square
Sheffield S1 2AY
Tel: 0742–21742

Wales MIND
23 St Mary Street
Cardiff CF1 2AA
Tel: 0222–395123

West Midlands MIND
Third Floor
Princess Chambers
52–54 Lichfield Street
Wolverhampton WV1 1DG
Tel: 0902–24404

OTHER AGENCIES

Mental Health Association of
  Ireland
14 Menion Square
Dublin 2
Tel: 0001–764310

Mental Welfare Commission for
  Scotland
22 Melville Street
Edinburgh EH3 7NS
Tel: 031–225–7034
  Helps people who because of
mental disorder may be unable to
help or protect themselves.

Northern Ireland Association for
  Mental Health
Beacon House
84 University Street

Belfast BT7 1HE
Tel: 0232–28474/5

OPUS (Organizations for Parents
  Under Stress)
26 Manor Drive
Pickering, Yorkshire
Tel: 0751–73235
  Umbrella organization for various
groups that help parents under
stress. Will advise on help available
locally.

Parents Anonymous
6–9 Manor Gardens
London N7
Tel: 01–263–5672 (office)
Lifeline: 01–263–8918

Scottish Association for Mental
  Health
67 York Place
Edinburgh EH1 3JB
Tel: 031–556–3062

Adolescent Psychiatric Units

The Association for the Psychiatric
  Study of Adolescents
13 Bonaly Drive
Edinburgh EH13 0EJ
Tel: 031–225–3108
  Maintains a register of adolescent
psychiatric units operating within
the National Health Service.

Independent Centres

The Association for Family Therapy
6 Heol Seddon
Danescourt
Llandaff, Cardiff CF5 2QX

British Paediatric Association
5 St Andrews Place
London NW1 4LB
Tel: 01–486–6151

Institute of Psychoanalysis
63 New Cavendish Street
London W1
Tel: 01–580–4952/3/4
Gives help, advice and
information about psychoanalysis,
and operates Child and Adolescent
Clinic. Charitable organization,
which charges income-related fees.

Northgate Clinic
Goldsmith Avenue
London NW9 7HR
Tel: 01–205–8012
See p. 215.

The Richmond Fellowship
8 Addison Road
London W14 8DL
Tel: 01–603–6373
Runs forty therapeutic
communities in the London area and
south and south-west of England.
Many of these specialize in helping
troubled adolescents, who may be
referred by their GP or social
worker. It is possible to self-refer,
but the fees are very high and are
usually found by a local authority,
for whom referral must be official.
The Fellowship has one house
devoted to the care of less severely
mentally handicapped adolescents
and young adults.

St Christopher's Fellowship
53 Warwick Road

London SW5 9HD
Tel: 01–370–1083/2522
Provides hostels for young people
in care, community homes with
education, bedsits for young people
preparing to leave care and bedsits
for young single homeless people in
the London area. *See* pp. 217–8.

Self-help groups

Alcoholics Anonymous
11 Redcliffe Gardens
London SW10
Tel: 01–352–3001/2/3   Lines open
    10 a.m.– 10 p.m. and 24-hour-a-
    day answerphone.
There are about 870 A A self-help
groups throughout the country.
Contact this main office for details
of nearest group. *See* p. 106.

Emotions Anonymous
Unitarian Church
Hoop Lane
London NW11
Tel: 01–722–6307, 01–458–5508

Families Anonymous
5 Parsons Green
London SW6
Tel: 01–731–8060
    and
Charing Cross Clinic
8 Woodside Crescent
Glasgow G3
Tel: 041–332–5463
A chain of self-help groups; if
there isn't one in your area, Families
Anonymous will explain how to
start one. *See also* p. 75.

Gamblers Anonymous
National Service Office
17–23 Blantyre Street
Cheyne Walk
London SW10 0DT
Tel: 01–352–3060 Line open 24
  hours a day.
  Contact national office for details
of local self-help groups for
gamblers of all ages and Gam-Anon
support groups for families and
friends of those with gambling
problems.

REGIONAL OFFICES:
Eire
Tel: 010–353–21–502398

Glasgow
Tel: 041–445–1115

Manchester
Tel: 061–273–3574

Support groups

Andover Crisis and Support Centre
17 New Street
Andover, Hampshire
Tel: 0264–66122
  See p. 220.

Exploring Parenthood Trust
Omnibus Workspace
39–41 North Road
London N7 9DP
Tel: 01–607–9647 and 01–700–4822
  See pp. 219–20.

Counselling

Acorn Youth Information

Acorn Youth Centre
55 High Street
Ealing, London W3
Tel: 01–992–5566
  National organization, providing
advice and information.

Alone in London
West Lodge
190 Euston Road
London NW1
Tel: 01–387–3010
  Help, advice and information.

Association for Jewish Youth
AJY House
50 Lindley Street
London E1 3AX
Tel: 01–790–6407

British Association for Counselling
37A Sheep Street
Rugby, Warwickshire CV21 3BX
Tel: 0788–78328/9
  and
58 Palmerston Place
Edinburgh EH12 5A2
  and
6 Hillside Park, Belfast BT9 5EC
Tel: 0232–660992
  Help, advice and information
about local counsellors and
counselling.

Catholic Marriage Advisory
  Council
15 Lansdowne Road
London W11 3AJ
Tel: 01–727–0141
  Help, advice and information
about local branches.

226

Centre for the Analytical Study of
   Student Problems
86 Harley Street
London W1
Tel: 01–580–5676
   Offers help, advice and
information.

Family Service Units
207 Old Marylebone Road
London NW1 5QP
Tel: 01–402–5175
   National organization providing
services to prevent the breakdown
of family and community life.

Family Welfare Association
501–505 Kingsland Road
London E8
Tel: 01–245–6251
   Help, advice and information.

London Youth Advisory Centre
   (LYAC)
26 Prince of Wales Road
London NW5
Tel: 01–267–4792/3

National Association of Young
   People's Counselling and
   Advisory Services (NAYPCAS)

REGIONAL OFFICES:

102 Harper Road
London SE1
Tel: 01–403–2444

17–23 Albion Street
Leicester LE1 6GD
Tel: 0533–554775 ext. 22/36

Wheels Youth
14 Justice Street

Aberdeen
Tel: 0224–21956

2A Ribble Street
Belfast
Tel: 0232– 658708

45 Hardwick Street
Dublin 1
Tel: 0001–745–398

National Marriage Guidance
   Council
Herbert Gray College
Little Church Street
Rubgy, Warwickshire CV21 3AP
Tel: 0788–73241
   Help, advice and information
about local offices.

Oasis Counselling and Teaching Ltd
72 Great North Road
London N2 0NL
Tel: 01–340–3924

Salvation Army Counselling Service
177 Whitechapel Road
London E1 1DD
Tel: 01–247–0669
   and
Salvation Army Social Service and
   Tracing Missing Relatives Branch
110–112 Middlesex Street
London E1 7HZ
Tel: 01–2427–6831

Samaritans
   Almost all branches can be
telephoned 24 hours a day, every day
of the year, and can be visited any
day or evening. The local telephone
number is in the telephone directory.
If no directory is available, dial 100

and ask the operator for the Samaritans.

There also is a branch for correspondence only:
P O Box 9
Stirling

The Westminster Pastoral
  Foundation
23 Kensington Square
London W8 5HN
Tel: 01–937–6956
A national counselling agency, which provides a confidential setting for people to receive help regardless of their financial circumstances. All counselling is under professional supervision and adapted to suit the needs of particular individuals and families. Telephone this head office for information about nearest local centre.

Young People's Counselling Service
The Tavistock Clinic
Tavistock Centre
Belsize Lane
London NW3
Tel: 01–435–7111
Free and confidential counselling to anyone 16–23 who has a personal or emotional problem.

Young Person's Advisory Service
Liverpool Personal Service Society
34 Stanley Street
Liverpool L1 6AN
Tel: 051–236–5255
Free confidential counselling and information for young people, parents and others concerned.

Telephone counselling

Family Network
  See p. 222.
Birmingham 021–440–5970
Cardiff   0222–29461
Glasgow   041–221–6722
Glenrothes   0592–759651
Ilford   01–514–1177
Leeds   0532–456456
Luton   0582–422751
Maidstone   0622–56677
Manchester   061–236–9873
Norwich   0603–660679
Preston   0772–24006
Swansea   0792–297798

Samaritans
  See above.

Notes

1. Gill Gorell Barnes, *Working with Families*, London, Macmillan, 1984
2. Dr Marion Walters, *Family Therapies: Full Length Case Studies*

Select Bibliography

Alcoholics Anonymous World Service Inc., *As Bill Sees It: The A.A. Way of life*, New York, 1967

Ausubel, D. *et al.*, *Theory and Problems of Adolescent Development*, Orlando, Florida, Grune & Sons, 1978

Baldwin, Dorothy, *All About Health*, Oxford, Oxford University Press, 1985

Barnes, Gill Gorell, *Working with Families*, London, Macmillan, 1984

Bayard, Jean and Robert, *Help! I've Got A Teenager! A Survival Guide for Desperate Parents*, Watford, Exley, 1984

Bethune, Helen, *Off the Hook: Coping with Addiction*, London, Methuen, 1985

Cohen, Steve *et al.*, *The Law and Sexuality*, Manchester, Grass Roots Books, 1978

Cole, Luella and Hall, Irma, *Psychology of Adolescence*, Eastbourne, Holt, Rinehart & Winston, 1970

Coleman, Vernon, *Addicts and Addictions*, London, Piatkus Books, 1986

Conger, John Janeway, *Adolescence and Youth: Psychological Development in a Changing World*, London, Harper & Row, 1977

— *Adolescence: Generation under Pressure*, London, Harper & Row, 1979

Dunn, Judy, *Sisters and Brothers*, London, Fontana, 1984

Erikson, Erik H., *Identity: Youth and Crisis*, London, Faber & Faber, 1968

Freud, Anna, *Psycholanalyic Study of the Child*, New York, International University Press, 1958

Frude, Neil and Gault, Hugh (eds), *Disruptive Behaviour in Schools*, Chichester, John Wiley & Sons, 1984

Gallagher, J. R. and Harris, H. I., *Emotional Problems of Adolescence*, New York, Oxford University Press, 1976

Gillespie, Veronica and Bullivant, Barbara, *Children and Young People in Trouble*, Sheffield, Home and School Council Publications, 1984

Glatt, Max, *Alcoholism*, London, Hodder & Stoughton, 1982

Greenfield, Patricia Marks, *Mind and Media*, London, Fontana, 1984

Hemming, James, *You and Your Adolescent*, London, Ebury, 1975

— *The Betrayal of Youth: Secondary Education Must Be Changed*, London, Marion Boyars, 1980

Hodder, Elizabeth, *The Step-parents' Handbook*, London, Sphere, 1985

Howard, Joanna, *Here's Health*, Oxford, Oxford University Press, 1985

Itzen, Catherine, *How to Choose a School*, London, Methuen, 1985

Kovel, Joel, *A Complete Guide to Therapy*, London, Penguin, 1983

Lawrence, Jean, *How to Help Your Child Succeed at School*, Shepton Mallet, Open Books, 1984

Mahoney, Pat, *Schools for the Boys: Coeducation Reassessed*, London, Hutchinson, 1985

The Mental Health Foundation, *Someone to Talk to Directory 1985*, London, 1985

Milner, Patricia, *Counselling in Education*, London, J. M. Dent, 1974

Morrison, John, *A Positive Future: A Careers Guide for Parents*, London, Hutchinson, 1985

Mothner, Ira and Weitz, Alan, *How to Get Off Drugs*, London, Penguin, 1986

O'Connor, Maureen, *A Parents' Guide to Education*, London, Fontana, 1986

Open University Press, *Child Abuse: A Reader and Sourcebook*, Milton Keynes, 1978

Petrie, Cairine and Conochie, Douglas, *Child Guidance*, London, Macmillan, 1975

Pringle, Mia Kellmer, *The Needs of Children*, London, Hutchinson, 1980

Rayner, Claire, *Growing Pains and How to Avoid Them*, London, Heinemann, 1984

Rofes, Eric E. and Students at the Fayerweather Street School, *The Kids' Book About Parents*, New York, Houghton Mifflin, 1984

Rowe, Jane, *Yours By Choice: A Guide for Adoptive Parents*, London, Routledge & Kegan Paul, 1959

Rutter, Michael, *Changing Youth in a Changing Society: Patterns of Adolescent Development and Disorder*, London, Nuffield Provincial Hospital Trust, 1979

— *Maternal Deprivation Reassessed*, London, Penguin, 1981

— *Helping Troubled Children*, London, Penguin, 1985

Rutter, Michael and Giller, Henri, *Juvenile Delinquency, Trends and Perspectives*, London, Penguin, 1983

Rutter, Michael *et al.*, *Fifteen Thousand Hours: Secondary Schools and Their Effects on Children*, Shepton Mallet, Open Books, 1979

Schostak, John F., *Maladjusted Schooling: Deviance, Social Control and Individuality in Secondary Schooling*, London, Falmer Press, 1983

Shipman, Marten, *Education as a Public Service*, London, Harper & Row, 1984

Spicer, Faith, *Adolescence and Stress*, Saugus, California, Forbes, 1977

Stone, Lawrence J. and Church, Joseph, *Childhood and Adolescence: A Psychology of the Growing Person*, New York, Random House, 1957

Taylor, Barry, *A Parent's Guide to Education*, London, Consumer Association and Hodder & Stoughton, 1983

Toynbee, Polly, *Lost Children*, London, Hutchinson, 1985

Trenchard, Lorraine and Warren, Hugh, *Something to Tell You*, London, London Gay Teenage Group, 1984

Turner, Glenn, *The Social World of the Comprehensive School*, Beckenham, Croom Helm, 1983

Walrond-Skinner, Sue (ed.), *Developments in Family Therapy: Theories and Applications Since 1948*, London, Routledge & Kegan Paul, 1981

Weiner, Irving B., *Psychological Disturbance in Adolescence*, Chichester, John Wiley & Sons, 1970

West, D. J., *Delinquency: Its Roots, Careers and Prospects*, London, Heinemann, 1982

Winder, Alvin E. (ed.), *Adolescence: Contemporary Studies*, New York, Van Nostrand Reinhold, 1968

Index

Figures in *italics* refer to lists of addresses

FOR THE BEST IN PAPERBACKS, LOOK FOR THE

In every corner of the world, on every subject under the sun, Penguin represents quality and variety – the very best in publishing today.

For complete information about books available from Penguin – including Pelicans, Puffins, Peregrines and Penguin Classics – and how to order them, write to us at the appropriate address below. Please note that for copyright reasons the selection of books varies from country to country.

In the United Kingdom: Please write to *Dept E.P., Penguin Books Ltd, Harmondsworth, Middlesex, UB7 0DA*

In the United States: Please write to *Dept BA, Penguin, 299 Murray Hill Parkway, East Rutherford, New Jersey 07073*

In Canada: Please write to *Penguin Books Canada Ltd, 2801 John Street, Markham, Ontario L3R 1B4*

In Australia: Please write to the *Marketing Department, Penguin Books Australia Ltd, P.O. Box 257, Ringwood, Victoria 3134*

In New Zealand: Please write to the *Marketing Department, Penguin Books (NZ) Ltd, Private Bag, Takapuna, Auckland 9*

In India: Please write to *Penguin Overseas Ltd, 706 Eros Apartments, 56 Nehru Place, New Delhi, 110019*

In Holland: Please write to *Penguin Books Nederland B.V., Postbus 195, NL–1380AD Weesp, Netherlands*

In Germany: Please write to *Penguin Books Ltd, Friedrichstrasse 10–12, D–6000 Frankfurt Main 1, Federal Republic of Germany*

In Spain: Please write to *Longman Penguin España, Calle San Nicolas 15, E–28013 Madrid, Spain*

In France: Please write to *Penguin Books Ltd, 39 Rue de Montmorency, F-75003, Paris, France*

In Japan: Please write to *Longman Penguin Japan Co Ltd, Yamaguchi Building, 2–12–9 Kanda Jimbocho, Chiyoda-Ku, Tokyo 101, Japan*

FOR THE BEST IN PAPERBACKS, LOOK FOR THE 🐧

PENGUIN HEALTH

Audrey Eyton's F-Plus Audrey Eyton

'Your short cut to the most sensational diet of the century' – *Daily Express*

Baby and Child Penelope Leach

A beautifully illustrated and comprehensive handbook on the first five years of life. 'It stands head and shoulders above anything else available at the moment' – Mary Kenny in the *Spectator*

Woman's Experience of Sex Sheila Kitzinger

Fully illustrated with photographs and line drawings, this book explores the riches of women's sexuality at every stage of life. 'A book which any mother could confidently pass on to her daughter – and her partner too' – *Sunday Times*

Food Additives Erik Millstone

Eat, drink and be worried? Erik Millstone's hard-hitting book contains powerful evidence about the massive risks being taken with the health of the consumer. It takes the lid off the food we have and the food industry.

Living with Allergies Dr John McKenzie

At least 20% of the population suffer from an allergic disorder at some point in their lives and this invaluable book provides accurate and up-to-date information about the condition, where to go for help, diagnosis and cure – and what we can do to help ourselves.

Living with Stress Cary L. Cooper, Rachel D. Cooper and Lynn H. Eaker

Stress leads to more stress, and the authors of this helpful book show why low levels of stress are desirable and how best we can achieve them in today's world. Looking at those most vulnerable, they demonstrate ways of breaking the vicious circle that can ruin lives.

PENGUIN HEALTH

Medicines: A Guide for Everybody Peter Parish

This sixth edition of a comprehensive survey of all the medicines available over the counter or on prescription offers clear guidance for the ordinary reader as well as invaluable information for those involved in health care.

Pregnancy and Childbirth Sheila Kitzinger

A complete and up-to-date guide to physical and emotional preparation for pregnancy – a must for all prospective parents.

The Penguin Encyclopaedia of Nutrition John Yudkin

This book cuts through all the myths about food and diets to present the real facts clearly and simply. 'Everyone should buy one' – *Nutrition News and Notes*

The Parents' A to Z Penelope Leach

For anyone with a child of 6 months, 6 years or 16 years, this guide to all the little problems involved in their health, growth and happiness will prove reassuring and helpful.

Jane Fonda's Workout Book

Help yourself to better looks, superb fitness and a whole new approach to health and beauty with this world-famous and fully illustrated programme of diet and exercise advice.

Alternative Medicine Andrew Stanway

Dr Stanway provides an objective and practical guide to thirty-two alternative forms of therapy – from Acupuncture and the Alexander Technique to Macrobiotics and Yoga.

PENGUIN HEALTH

Acupuncture for Everyone   Dr Ruth Lever

An examination of one of the world's oldest known therapies used by the Chinese for over two thousand years.

Aromatherapy for Everyone   Robert Tisserand

The use of aromatic oils in massage can relieve many ailments and alleviate stress and related symptoms.

Chiropractic for Everyone   Anthea Courtenay

Back pain is both extremely common and notoriously difficult to treat. Chiropractic offers a holistic solution to many of the causes through manipulation of the spine.

Herbal Medicine for Everyone   Michael McIntyre

An account of the way in which the modern herbalist works and a discussion of the wide-ranging uses of herbal medicine.

Homoeopathy for Everyone   Drs Sheila and Robin Gibson

The authors discuss the ways in which this system of administering drugs – by exciting similar symptoms in the patient – can help a range of disorders from allergies to rheumatism.

Hypnotherapy for Everyone   Dr Ruth Lever

This book demonstrates that hypnotherapy is a real alternative to conventional healing methods in many ailments.

Osteopathy for Everyone   Paul Masters

By helping to restore structural integrity and function, the osteopath gives the whole body an opportunity to achieve health and harmony and eliminate ailments from migraines to stomach troubles.

Spiritual and Lay Healing   Philippa Pullar

An invaluable new survey of the history of healing that sets out to separate the myths from the realities.